New Approaches
to
Organizational
Communication

SUNY Series, Human Communication Processes
Donald P. Cushman and Ted Smith, III,editors

New Approaches
to
Organizational
Communication

edited by
Branislav Kovačić

STATE UNIVERSITY OF NEW YORK PRESS

Published by
State University of New York Press, Albany

©1994   State University of New York

For information, address the State University of New York Press,
State University Plaza, Albany, NY 12246

Production by Bernadine Dawes
Marketing by Dana Yanulavich

Library of Congress Cataloging-in-Publication Data

New approaches to organizational communication / [edited by] Branislav
Kovačić
    p. cm.—(Suny series, human communication processes)
  Includes index.
    ISBN 0–7914–1917–7. — ISBN 0–7914–1918–5 (pbk.)
    1. Communication in orginizations.   2. Communication in
management.   I. Kovačič, Branislav, 1957–   .   II. Series: SUNY
series in human communication processes.
  HD30.3.N39   1994
  658.4'5—dc20   93–39275
  1 2 3 4 5 6 7 8 9 10   CIP

CONTENTS

Acknowledgments

ACKNOWLEDGMENTS

This project would be impossible without the eager and punctual co-operation of all contributors. It is probably not necessary to remind the reader that a collective author has supplanted, in many instances, an "omniscient" individual Author. Such a development illustrates a new wave of collective endeavors in all spheres of social life, in all types of organizations.

Another creative, "collective" contribution was provided by three anonymous reviewers of the manuscript.

My colleagues and students at the University of Hartford have discussed and criticized and, consequently, improved the ideas presented in the first chapter. My thanks go to all of them.

Special thanks go to Sharon Scorso from the Department of Communication at the University of Hartford who helped me immensely with correspondence, and who always preserved a good sense of humor while reminding me of impending deadlines.

Without my wife, Gordana Rabrenović, this project would have not come to a fruition.

BRANISLAV KOVAČIĆ

1 New Perspectives on Organizational Communication

New approaches to organizational communication—the topic of this book—pursue two interrelated interests. First, they are trying to understand from the communication point of view *intersections* between *the local organizational communication structures, processes, and practices,* and *large social structures and processes in the form of globalization* (for conceptualization see Mills 1959; Antonio 1991; Lemert 1991). Second, the new approaches are *practical* in that they are *taking seriously theorizing about communication in existing organizations in current conditions.* The same cannot be said for the "old" approaches to organizational communication which found inspiration only in the intellectual mines of various related disciplines. The "old" approaches to organizational communication—presented in five handbooks—were in the form of either philosophy and conceptual analysis as substitutes for theory, or the "conceptual grafts" generated by cross-tabulating perspectives on human communication with perspectives on organizations (Putnam and Pacanowsky 1983; McPhee and Tompkins 1985; Thayer 1985; Jablin, Putnam, Roberts, and Porter 1987; Goldhaber and Barnett 1988).

In order to contrast the "old" to the "new" approaches to organizational communication, I will (1) briefly adumbrate recent intellectual currents, (2) outline globalization processes, (3) elucidate intersections between the two developments and their implications for new approaches to organizational communication, and (4) present a

1

critical review of the new approaches articulated by the contributors to this book.

The book offers a three-pronged vision of new approaches to organizational communication: (1) it probes into the relationships between new information/communication technologies and organizational structural configurations and processes, (2) it subjects organizational communicative practices to radical/critical inquiry, and (3) it articulates organizational communication from a postmodernist point of view. Although issuing from different philosophical and theoretical wells, these new approaches are "united" in their departures from old perspectives on organizational communication, and in their interest in current conditions. Boundaries between the new approaches are fuzzy. The new approaches to organizational communication, although forming relatively distinct clusters, share some philosophical assumptions, conceptual articulations, methodological preferences, and practical consequences. For example, the contributors do not discuss intrinsic properties of new information/communication technologies. Rather, they argue that attitudes toward technology and its use, and its real use, depend upon dominant interest groups and cultural and interactional patterns of particular organizations. Such conceptualizations of technologies meander between technological determinism and voluntarism: they explicitly reject both conceptualizations of technologies as "autonomous agents" in the form of "causes/independent variables" and as "observable manifestations of deeper social forces" in the form of "effects/dependent variables" (see Kinsella 1993). Critical/radical theorists—both radical humanists blaming oppressive and privileged discourses/languages, and radical structuralists accusing monopolies of power as well as all other structural configurations characterized by inequality—throw into sharp relief the limitations of current organizational arrangements (Putnam 1982; Mumby 1987, 1988; Daniels and Spiker 1991; Deetz 1992). Not unlike their critical/radical brethren, postmodern theorists focus on the hidden rather than the overt power of inherently political meanings of the micro practices of organizational daily life. However, postmodern theorists approach ideology/culture, hegemony, and domination in terms of nihilism, skepticism, ambiguity, and multiple meanings (see Eisenberg and Goodall 1993). What all three clusters of new approaches to organizational communication have in common, then, is alternative conceptualizations of organizational communicative practices as links between human/organizational agency and social/organizational structure.

In addition to new philosophical and theoretical articulations in general, the contributors to the volume proffer three new, and important, conceptualizations of organizational communication in particular. *First,* they reformulate standards used to evaluate organizational communicative practices. At least three clusters of criteria are used to evaluate relationships between: (1) organizational communication practices and/or organizational survival, (2) new information/communication technologies and organizational structural arrangements, and (3) organizational communicative practices defined as configurations and organizational networks of power. *Second,* the contributors sketch new vital mechanisms of organizational communication. And, *finally,* the contributors more or less explicitly spell out practical consequences of the evaluative criteria and new mechanisms of organizational communication.

The manuscript, however, is silent on "interpretive," "cultural," or "process" theories, and on important advances in traditional topics such as network analysis, managerial leadership, organizational innovation, communication climate, and so forth. Because the contributors intended to sail new theoretical waters, they used work by ethnographers, semioticians, and conversational analysts as points of departure rather than navigational maps.

Intellectual/theoretical developments

The first source of new approaches to organizational communication is current intellectual/theoretical developments in social disciplines. Contemporary intellectual streams have shifted from the modernist "dream of reason" revealed as faith in science, evolution, optimism, and progress, to poststructuralism/postmodernism, to the extreme antimodernist "nightmare of reason" embodied in irrationalist conceptions of antiscience, directionless processes, pessimism, and impossibility of betterment (see Alexander 1990).

Contemporary intellectual shifts

Major intellectual shifts have occurred in philosophy, art, psychology, and social engineering (see Alexander 1990, 1991; Antonio 1991; Lemert 1991; Richardson 1991; Seidman 1991a,b). I will briefly summarize intellectual development in each domain.

In *philosophy* there was a shift from logical positivism to self-referential poststructuralist/postmodern orientations. Logical positivism assumes transcendental reason in charge of the universal, rational, objective, impersonal, and detached knowledge in the form of rational mathematical models of the external reality. It privileges the logico-empirical epistemic code. At the other end of the intellectual continuum, poststructuralist/postmodern positions postulate an arbitrary relation between words and objects, epistemic suspicion of "external" realities outside theoretical discourse, the annihilation of referents, and particular, interpretive, subjective, personally "constructed" knowledge. They privilege the narrative code favoring connections between particular events.

In *art* aesthetic orientations have shifted from functionally coherent form to one rooted in ambiguity, complexity and inconsistency. Form and representation were the first cut loose. This required the disintegration of object/image by the Impressionists and Postimpressionists, the deconstruction of space by the Cubists, and the creation of the objectless abstraction by the Suprematists and Formalists (see Gambrell 1993). A few decades later, however, postmodernism rehabilitated a "free play of images" (see Jencks 1987).

In *psychology* conceptualizations of individuals have shifted from the rational to the irrational. The rational actor is defined as an objective, impersonal, detached, unified, fixed, and unchanging self across all times and places. The irrational actor is characterized by the fragmented self—a mosaic of multiple, unstable, fluid, and ever-changing gender, racial, ethnic, class, sexual, and ability-based identities circumscribed by temporal and spatial boundaries/settings.

In *social engineering* positions have shifted from models of the world which is amenable to rational planning and control—based on knowledge undistorted by power, on pure social science which, uncontaminated by ideology, prevents power from being corrupted—to models of the fragmented world which resist planning and control in terms of abstract criteria and transcendental principles.

New approaches to organizational communication have been influenced more directly by an interplay of major intellectual shifts in organization studies and communication theory.

In *organization studies* conceptions of organizations as systems with a single, coherent rationality have been replaced by conceptions of organizations as systems with composite, contradictory rationalities. Organizations are conceived as shifting alliances of different stakeholders such as stockholders, managers, workers, consumers, suppliers, "partners," and representatives of the wider society. Not only that stakeholders have conflicting interests and various degrees of different types of power, but also alliances of stockholders, managers, and suppliers seem to be more stable and more powerful than alliances of workers, consumers, and representatives of the wider society. Leadership in such conditions is a political and symbolic struggle over the definitions of organizational reality. In circumstances of rapid change leadership is impossible without a specific, temporary, future vision that relies on—as the necessary but not sufficient conditions—flat organizational hierarchy, flexible structures, and people empowered through multiple types of teamwork. Organizational teams made of both "internal" (i.e., managers and workers) and "external" (i.e., stockholders, suppliers, customers, partners, and representatives of communities) stakeholders cannot be controlled by top-down mechanisms of coordination and integration. Rather, it is necessary that stakeholders negotiate and then mutually enforce performance standards. Such new organizations are produced, maintained or changed through new communication technologies, strategies, systems, and processes (see Clegg 1990; Blunt 1989; Cooper and Burrell 1988; Jacques 1989; Scott 1992).

In *communication* there was a proliferation of conceptions of the "interaction order" as the mediating link between the cultural and social/structural (economy and politics) realms. The "interaction order" is viewed as (1) a problematic "mix" of the routine everyday verbal and nonverbal communication practices which *reproduce* economic, political, and cultural dimensions of social order (see Goffman 1981, 1983; Chriss 1992), and communicative practices which *produce* new, emergent/unexpected consequences; (2) the micro level lifeworld where both strategic/instrumental and communicative (noncoerced, nonconformist, voluntaristic) action take place (see Habermas 1984, 1987; Burns 1992; Chriss 1992; Sciulli 1989); (3) the "order without rules"—local, contextually situated language games/practices based on heterogeneous systems of rules which form discrete, incommensurable, and/or incoherently linked social spheres/realms (Wittgenstein 1958); and (4) a continuous "discourse shifting"—a movement from one language game to another (Rorty 1982).

New conceptions of theory

In addition to foundational/empiricist and "institutional" conceptions of theory, there has been developed a new poststructuralist/ postmodernist view of (anti)theory (see Seidman 1991a,b; Agger 1991; Alexander 1991; Antonio 1991; D'Andrade 1986; Lemert 1991; Richardson 1991).

Foundational/empiricist conceptions demand from theory in the natural scientific mode to formulate the master categories/concepts and universally valid regularities—explanations. Reflection theory provides universal truth conditions in which transcendental reason—

scientists who strictly follow "objective" and "impersonal" methodological rules and procedures—establishes a representational truth
based on unproblematic and direct observations of "external" realities.
Social scientific community and managerial elites are the intended audience for this type of theory.

"*Institutional*" *conceptions* of theory stress that the traditions and
institutions of social scientific community—created and reproduced by
the personal and interpersonal actions and experiences of scientists—
are the root of reason itself. Based on the institutionally established criterion of truth, social scientists rhetorically redeem—in the form of
explanation and interpretation—both the validity of observations and
postulated regularities. In addition to social scientific community and
managerial elites, the primary intended audience also includes work-
ers/employees and the learned general public.

A new poststructuralist/postmodernist view of (anti)theory consists of two conceptual clusters. *First*, its radical, extreme, and thoroughly anitscientific cluster substitutes storytelling for interpretation
and explanation. Since all knowledge is self-referential or reflexive—
"referents" are either systematically "constructed" ideological knowledge distorted by power or simple "simulacra"/illusions—ranking of
knowledge is all but impossible. *Second*, although driven by epistemic
suspicion, its less radical cluster views theory as a "narrative with a
moral intent." It emphasizes the subjective, personal, nature of knowledge of the particular regularities within temporal and spatial settings/
boundaries or contexts. Since theory takes the form of literary and political narratives, its internal standards and external/social effects are
"rationally" evaluated by the set of social and linguistic conventions of
a given community. The intended audience includes social scientific
community, the learned public, and individuals and groups with high
stakes in particular social agendas.

Processes of globalization

The second source of new approaches to organizational communication is global transformations—multidimensional processes
of social change which, through definite, patterned temporal and
spatial sequences, make the entire world a single place. Global transformations—unfolding through novel, emergent stages, and involving
economic, political, and cultural dimensions which often display
divergent, disjointed logics—can be evaluated only by complex
evaluative standards. Global transformations in the form of the con-

tinuous and ever faster redrawing of economic, political, and cultural boundaries and their intersections are molding the world into an increasingly dense and complex network of interorganizational relationships. As a consequence, we are faced with the relative decline in the economic, political, and cultural importance of the nation-state which has become "too small for the big problems of life, and too big for small problems of life" (Bell 1987, 1967; Harvey 1990; Nowak 1990; Sztompka 1990).

At this point it is useful to delineate three analytical dimensions of organizational environments within which global interorganizational relationships/practices take place. *First,* there are three spheres of social/organizational action, each with its own logic/rationality: (1) economic/wealth, (2) political/power, and (3) cultural/symbolic (for the conceptualization of the spheres, see Arnason 1990; Beyer 1990; Etziony-Halevy 1990; Featherstone 1990; Hannerz 1989; King 1990 a,b; Lash and Urry 1987; Morgentau 1967; Sklair 1991; Wallerstein 1990 a,b). *Second,* geographic reach/scope of interorganizational environments can be ranked in an ascending order: (1) subnational, (2) national, (3) international, and (4) global (see Bell 1987; Giddens 1990; Sklair 1991; Nowak 1990; Gill and Law 1988; Worsley 1990). *Third,* complexity of interorganizational relationships can also be ranked in an ascending order: (1) dyadic or pairwise organizational relationships, (2) organization/action sets or a focal agency's dyadic relationships with other organizations (see Hall 1991; Merton 1957; Evan 1966; Caplow 1964; van de Ven and Ferry 1980; Aldrich 1979; Aldrich and Whetten 1981), and (3) interorganizational networks or groups of organizations linked by a particular type of a relationship in the form of teamwork (Aldrich, 1979; van den Ven and Ferry 1980).

I operationalize globalization processes in two interrelated ways. *First,* globalization is operationalized in terms of: (1) the ever faster increasing number of international and global organizations (geographic reach/scope of interorganizational environments), (2) their ever-increasing interconnectedness (complexity of interorganizational relationships), and (3) their ever more weighty influence on the global scale within economic/wealth, political/power, and cultural/symbolic spheres (logic/rationality of social/organizational action). *Second,* globalization is operationalized in terms of the increasingly interconnected processes/flows that link or cut across the three spheres. Put differently, globalization is operationalized as an always shifting configuration of logics/rationalities of social/organizational action, geographic reach/scope of interorganizational environments, and complexity of interorganizational relationships.

Processes of globalization within the three spheres

In the *economic/wealth sphere,* which relies on *instrumental rationality,* multinational/global corporations seem to simultaneously rely on and use all types of organizational interactions available (see Clairmonte and Cavanagh 1982; Kegley, Wittkopf, and Rawls 1988; UN Commission 1991). They range from: (1) free-market, competitive business transactions (Johnston and Lawrence 1988) to (2) different types of interorganizational (sub)contracting (Dore 1983) or teamwork labeled as value-adding partnerships (Johnston and Lawrence 1988), quasifirms (Eccles, 1981; Bradach and Eccles 1989), a "virtual" organization (Morton 1991), global strategic linkages (Nohria and Garcia-Pont 1991), and strategic alliances (Collins and Doorley 1991), to (3) hierarchies of common ownership (Johnston and Lawrence 1988). Consequently, multinational corporations may simultaneously engage in free-market competitive transactions—based on conflicting interests and hoarding of information—and interorganizational subcontracting—based on cooperation, communication/sharing of information, and making implicit or explicit binding agreements—with the same corporate entities.

In the *cultural/symbolic sphere,* which revolves around value or substantive rationality, globalization processes are operationalized in terms of: (1) the ever faster increasing number of subnational, national, organizational, and professional cultures of the nation-state, and international and global cultures of international and global organizations (geographic reach/scope), (2) the ever faster increasing number of interactions between these clusters of cultures (complexity of relationships), and (3) their ever more weighty influence on the global scale (logic/rationality of social/organizational action).

Because of the acceleration of these interactions and the continuous redrawing of symbolic boundaries, not only is the cultural continuity across generations—tradition—seriously threatened, but the distinction between the global and the local is also becoming very complex and dynamic (see Bauman 1990; Featherstone 1990; Bell 1976, 1987; Giddens 1990; Harvey 1990).

In the *political/power sphere,* which depends upon a specific combination of instrumental and substantive rationality, globalization processes are operationalized in terms of: (1) the ever faster rising number of states, and interstate, transgovernmental, and transnational organizations (geographic reach/scope), (2) the ever increasing number of interactions between them (complexity of relationships), and (3) the ever more weighty influence of interstate, transgovernmental, and transnational organizations on the global scale (logic/rationality of social/organizational action) (see Gelb 1992; Hoffmann 1992; Keohane and Nye 1988; Osmanczyk 1985).

The disjointed world as a single place is created and only temporarily reproduced by the unrepeatably complex interplay of institutions and their practices not only within, but also between the three spheres—the economic/wealth, political/power, and cultural/symbolic.

Processes of globalization between the three spheres

Globalization processes between the three spheres are operationalized in terms of five flows which form a disjunctive crisscross pattern. These are flows of: (1) people (tourists, immigrants, refugees, exiles, and guestworkers), (2) technology (the machinery and plants controlled by national and multinational corporations and government agencies), (3) money (in the currency markets and stock exchanges), (4) images and information in mass media (newspapers, magazines, television, and film), and (5) the Western Enlightenment images of democracy, freedom, welfare, rights, etc.). Consequently, the world becomes a single place, though not in a stable, orderly, rational, and clearly defined way (see Appadurai 1990; Featherstone 1990; Mongardini 1990).

To conceive the world as a disjointed, single place, is not to empty it of moral visions ensconced within cultural/symbolic configurations. Such emptying was suggested by three theoretical models of the present condition. *First,* the industrial convergence theory incarcerated the mankind in the world depicted as a single modern society/social structure without cultural differences. *Second,* the postindustrial theory described the world as a place in which instrumental techno-rationality replaced cultures/ideologies. And *finally,* the information society theory offered the vision of the world in which information technology subjugated the whole cultural realm (see Giner 1987; Archer 1990).

Despite the recent upsurge of nationalism in Eastern and Central Europe, social and political control/integration within the nation-state in the form of nationalism's strong bonds of normative consensus, national sovereign political authority, and national economy has been undermined in the currently decentered, postindustrial, postmodern world by both local and international/global organizing principles and "language games" as forms of communication (see Curson 1986; Derrida 1976; Halal 1986; Lash 1988; Lipietz 1987; Lyotard 1984; Offe 1985).

Currently, the single, world capitalist economic system—with the North American, Pacific Asian, and West European regional markets/trading blocks—intersects the international political regime, and the contradictory, fluid and ever-changing pattern of global cultural interactions/flows. The international political regime is currently poised between a global empire (hegemony of the United States) and a new, multistate balance of power/terror, and with no world state or global leviathan in sight (for conceptualization, see Gill and Law 1988).

My conceptualization and operationalization of globalization processes attempts to capture the intersection(s) of two basic levels of relationships between organizations as social agents. *First,* organizations as organized social subsystems of roles are produced and re-produced by concrete, immediate/direct, and contextualized face-to-face interactions in the form of interpersonal and small group communicative practices based on role expectations/explicit norms. *Second,* anonymous, selfless agents—through mediated communica-tive practices—act in terms of their preferences within abstract, distant/indirect, de-contextualized, and nonorganized subsystems of interdependence (for conceptual distinctions, see Boudon and Bourri-caud 1989). In this view, organizational communicative practices *link* organizations as organized role subsystems to their environments/nonorganized subsystems of interdependence.

Organizational communicative practices are deployed by organi-zational decision-makers to coordinate internal and external activities. This is achieved by three basic types of cooperation. *First,* different ac-tivities occurring at the same time and at the same place are fitted to-gether through *synchronization* based mainly on the face-to-face communicative practices. *Second,* different activities happening at the same place but at different times are fitted together through *sequential linking* based regularly on both the face-to-face and mediated commu-nicative practices. *Third,* organizations are devoting more and more ef-fort to coordination of activities across time and space (at different places at the same time, and at different places at different times) based mainly on mediated communicative practices (for conceptualization, see Blau 1993). Globalization processes require that organizations si-multaneously use all three types of cooperation/coordination and/or rapidly switch from one to another.

Intersections between new intellectual developments and processes of globalization: Implications for the new approaches to organizational communication

To many organizations globalization processes represent turbulence in the form of an ever *increasing uncertainty.* Organizations are faced with managing their own slice of the fast-changing configuration of (inter)organizational linkages/interdependencies. In such conditions, organizational communicative practices exploit strategically new information/communication, transport, and production technologies to create new, temporarily advantageous forms of organizations. New approaches to organizational communication, in order to conceptually articulate these processes, deploy new types of theoretical forms/genres and theoretical accounts.

New information/communication, transport, and production technologies

In order to cope with increasing uncertainty, corporations are putting many of their information/communication eggs in the basket of telecommunications systems. Whether public or private, worldwide telecommunications systems integrate—via wire lines, radio signals, and space satellites—the existing technical communication media such as radio, television, telephone, telegraph, fax machine, and computer. The purpose is to transmit large volumes of messages in the form of texts, videos, and voice at high speed over long distances. Nevertheless, it is estimated that roughly 70 percent of 400 billion paper documents, processed annually by 15 million U.S. business establishments, are not digitized. Many drawings, signatures, and images still cannot be translated into the computer alphabet of ones and zeroes (see Markoff 1992 a,b,c,d; Rifkin 1992; Saffo 1992; Schwartz 1992; Zachary 1992 a,b; Powel 1991).

These telecommunications systems form a backbone of three types of private, organizational information and communication systems: (1) management-oriented information and communication systems, (2) administration-oriented MIS systems, and (3) operation/production and service-oriented information and communications systems. These private organizational information and communication systems are pertinent to new forms of organizational design, and new organizational practices (see Berleur and Drumm 1991; Williams 1991; Culnan and Markus 1987; Rogers 1988; Tushman and Nelson 1990).

New forms of work organization: Voluntarism vs. structural constraints

The integrative character of the new, *flexible* communication, transport, and production technologies can be translated into an expanding domain of voluntaristic action in the form of new types of cooperative work organization, and an increasing choice between different technological solutions. Rather than creating a new universal model of work organization, new technologies tend to encourage a divergent organizational development in a number of different directions. Within the domain of expanded voluntaristic action, generative ability of the most successful organizations—their capacity to develop a number of different organizational patterns simultaneously and to change rapidly from one pattern to another—implies local creations of (in principle) an infinite number of patterns of organization rather than a "diffusion"/replication of a finite number of already proven organizational patterns.

For example, in Western industrialized nations new technologies, coupled with a shift of power in favor of management, enabled, since the 1970s, new forms of work organization—structuring of task interdependencies through teamwork—at the level of (1) workshops or departments, (2) establishments, (3) enterprises, and (4) industries and their respective markets.

Work organization on the shopfloor took the form of organization-specific combinations of the following design elements: (1) job rotation (workers periodically perform different jobs), (2) job enrichment (workers are given tasks of different quality), (3) job enlargement (workers perform an increased number of tasks), and (4) multiskilled work teams or autonomous groups. The overall establishment and/or enterprise organization—despite an ever wider range of organizational patterns—seems to have shifted from the *hierarchy* and its inward-oriented control based on formal positions to transitional forms composed of overlapping work teams or groups to the "*clotheshanger*" with most organizational tasks integrated on the production level by "internal" and "external" teams (see Grootings 1991; Gustavsen and Hethy 1991).

Theoretical genres/forms and accounts deployed by new approaches to organizational communication

New forms of work organization and organizational practices threw in sharp relief the inadequacy of the "old" approaches to organizational communication. These approaches provided two types of theoretical forms/genres—explanations and interpretations—and three types of theoretical accounts—economic, political, and cultural—of organizational structures, processes, and (communicative) actions. *Theoretical forms/genres* are configurations of concepts and propositions or general statements of relationships between concepts. While explanations consist of categories/concepts and relationships between them as postulated by theorists, interpretations are more complex in that they include perspectives of multiple communicators on the relevant "texts" as well as perspectives of the interpreter(s)/theorist(s). *Theoretical accounts* specify the nature of the regularities—relationships between concepts—based on a particular type of rationality/logic governing the spheres of organizational action. I will briefly examine each type of theoretical account.

The economic account is based on the "undersocialized" (Wrong 1961; Granovetter 1985; Swedberg 1991; Zelizer 1978, 1983, 1985, 1988, 1989) conception of the atomized, utilitarian, self-interested actor/communicator. The actor's—individual, dyad, group, organization, network of organizations, industry, nation-state, and regional, international and/or global alliance—strategic and utilitarian action consists of a "rational choice" of the appropriate means—organizational (communicative) strategies, structures, and actions—to generating wealth (see Weber 1951, 1978; Parsons 1961, 1977; Schutz 1964; Pareto 1935; Boudon and Bourricaud 1989; Turner 1991; Eder 1990). Organizational communication is viewed as a straightforward use of coherent, unambiguous symbolic codes—whose relations to external reality are assumed to be unproblematic—in order to create economic wealth.

The "oversocialized" (Wrong 1961; Granovetter 1985) passionate actor/communicator who follows the dictates of generalized morality is assumed by *the cultural account*. The "oversocialized" actor/communicator allegedly acts coherently as a unit by simply implementing cultural definitions of substantive rationality—symbolic classifications/definitions of social bonds and practices in terms of moral strictures, religious commandments, and solidarity (see Mongardini 1990; Weber 1951, 1978; Parsons 1961, 1977; Habermas 1975). Organizational communication is seen as a simple use of ready-made symbolic codes expressing taken-for-granted cultural interpretations of social reality in order to acquire legitimacy.

The actor/communicator whose main goal is the acquisition and/or preservation of power based on unequal distribution of political, economic, and cultural resources is a character privileged by *the political account* (see Mongardini 1990; Rueschemeyer and Rueschemeyer 1990; Morgentau 1967; Habermas 1975). The political actor/communicator is supposed to act coherently as a unit by following political rationality—ideally a coherent combination of the instrumental/formal rationality (i.e., realpolitik) and substantive/value rationality in the form of ethical principles and/or ideologies such as socialism, communism, anarchism, fascism, nationalism, liberalism, conservatism, and Islamic fundamentalism. Organizational communication is defined as a deliberate use of symbolic codes to acquire, preserve, and legitimate such unequal distribution of power.

The inadequacy of the theoretical accounts offered by old approaches to organizational communication is fundamental. Such accounts not only reduce the actor/communicator to a single, stable, coherent, and homogeneous motive and principle of action—the ecnomic, the political, and the cultural—but also eliminate any combination and/or conflict between the three dominant motives and principles of action. These ahistorical and context-blind accounts privilege one type of rationality under all conditions, and reduce communication to an unproblematic, simple, and perfect exchange of explicit information.

In contrast, as will become obvious in the following chapters, new approaches to organizational communication are rooted in a wide range of broader intellectual currents and alternative conceptions of theory, and disjointed globalization processes within and between the three spheres of organizational action. The new approaches to organizational communication stress rapid change, incoherence, fluidity, and only partial, transient and local organizational order. They share a loosely connected set of conceptual moves. *First,* narrative as a unique set of connections between particular events is legitimized as a third theoretical genre/form, as an alternative or addition to explanation and interpretation. *Second,* each of the theoretical positions articulated by the contributors to the book is a constellation of theoretical genres/forms. Although each position privileges a single genre/form, fluid boundaries between explanation, interpretation, and narrative stake out a considerable common "space." And *finally,* they all articulate their own version of the *"embeddedness account"* (Granovetter 1985) of organizational (commnicative) structures, processes, and actions. The actor/communicator—individual, dyad, group, organization, network of organizations, industry, nation-state, and regional, international and/or global alliance—is always embedded in concrete systems of relations/networks. Any particular interaction is defined as a complex conjuncture of economic, political, and cultural rationalities which are themselves fragile, problematic, and unstable. Interactions are inseparable from language and other symbolic systems which simultaneously constitute and express "external" realities in a complex and problematic fashion (for a critical analysis of theories of language, see Taylor 1981, 1992).

Critical review of new theoretical positions

It is now time to put all the pieces of the theoretical mosaic together. In doing so, I will first adumbrate similarities and differences between theoretical positions formulated by the contributors to the book. Then,

I will present three major contributions of the book: (1) reformulated standards used to evaluate organizational communicative practices, (2) new vital mechanisms of organizational communication, and (3) practical consequences of the evaluative criteria and new mechanisms of organizational communication.

Similarities and differences between new theoretical positions on organizational communication

The new approaches to organizational communication articulated by the contributors to this book can tentatively be classified according to three criteria. First, the contributors privilege a certain conception of theory. However, each general theoretical position offered in the book is more fruitfully described as a particular, dominant core delineated by fluid overlaps between foundationalist/empiricist, "institutional," and poststructuralist/postmodernist orientations. Second, although the authors subscribe to a single genre/form, fluid boundaries between explanation, interpretation, and narrative stake out a considerable common "space." And finally, they all articulate their own version of the embeddedness account in terms of a complex conjuncture of economic, political, and cultural rationalities which are themselves fragile, problematic, and unstable.

All of this singles out communicative practices in general, and organizational communicative practices in particular as the single most important source of temporary social order/patterned stability. Because the current condition is described as a major social—economic, political, and cultural—transformation, mechanisms of social regularities are unstable, heterogeneous rather than homogeneous, multiple rather than single, interdependent rather than independent, and subject to multiple and contradictory interpretations. This means that the consensus underlying "creative social action" becomes ever more important. Antecedents of social (communicative) action are relevant only insofar as they serve as temporary starting points. First, since cultures are unstable, fluid, and constantly overlap, socialization becomes highly problematic. Clusters of multiple, interacting heterogeneous rules cannot simply be followed—because stable rules are not available—to conduct purposive action. Second, social actors as fragmented selves—bundles of shifting identities—cannot simply rely on personal "values" or homogeneous intentions in the form of durable preferences as antecedents of the "undersocialized," "rational choice" action.

Mead (1932) may be of help here. If social actors acquire meanings from historical/past sequences of communicative practices, future goals compel the actors to modify constellations of these sequences. Consequently, standardized tasks with their standardized vocabularies give way to future visions and new tasks, and creative/new vocabularies. Such creative (communicative) social action can be described in terms of following of rules in a novel way (a temporary recombination of rules), and/or acting independently of the old rules. Communication thus becomes a means to form temporary alliances as institutional frameworks within which social actors negotiate specific sequences of communicative practices in order to forge temporarily the consensus necessary for the accomplishment of specific tasks, and to mint temporary personal and group identities. Organizational communicative practices that weave together economic/instrumental, political/power, and cultural/value rationales of organizational action—within the general condition of changing pluralism, difference, multiplicity, and disagreement—serve to create temporary unity, agreement, and consensus, and to accomplish specific tasks. Since historical antecedents give way to future visions and new tasks as sources of temporary social (communicative) regularities/orders, theorists become "conceptual strategists" who permanently reinvent these future visions/tasks. They resort to either incremental, short-term fine-tuning, or longer-term, transformational redefinitions of the future visions/tasks.

The contributors to the book offer alternative formulations of such new organizational communicative practices. Six chapters can be said to significantly contribute to new approaches to organizational communication within "institutional" theoretical orientation. These are contributions by Contractor (chapter 2), Yu (chapter 3), King and Cushman (chapter 4), Horvath and Fulk (chapter 5), Seibold, Heller, and Contractor (chapter 6), and Finet (chapter 7). Three chapters are innovative contributions within poststructuralist/postmodern conceptions of theory. These are contributions by Huspek (chapter 8), Deetz (chapter 9), and Natalle, Papa, and Grahama (chapter 10).

In a concluding chapter (11), Poole offers his views of the theoretical "territory" this book attempts to stake out.

Contractor's (chapter 2) conceptualization of organizations as self-organized systems undergoing sudden qualitative transformations implies context-specific combinations of rationalities—economic/instrumental, political/power, and cultural/value—organizational members can draw on while engaged in communicative practices. He privileges a mix of the genres/forms of a context-bound explanation and interpretation. On the other hand, Yu (chapter 3) privileges a combination of instrumental/economic and substantive/cultural rationality, and uses the genres of explanation and interpretation in tackling the issues of success and stability of Japanese organizations. Navigating between the extremes of sudden transformations and organizational stability, King and Cushman (chapter 4) privilege instrumental/economic rationality at the expense of both political/power and substantive/cultural rationality by grounding significant organizational communication behaviors in organizational strategy which favors competitive advantage based on *speed of response*. They use the genre of explanation.

Horvath and Fulk (chapter 5) propose a *social-influence model of* computerized information and communication *technology use* in organizations. They favor a context-bound combination of instrumental/economic, political/power, and substantive/cultural rationalities, and use the genre of explanation. In a more concrete fashion, Seibold, Heller, and Contractor (chapter 6) privilege a flexible combination of instrumental/economic and cultural/substantive rationalities, and use the genre of explanation while examining Group Decision Support Systems (GDSSs)—a new generation of coordinating technologies—and their use by organizational work groups or teams.

Finet (chapter 7) privileges a combination of political/power and substantive/cultural rationality, and uses a mix of the genres of explanation, interpretation, and narrative while examining interest advocacy. Focusing on the power-resistance opposition, Huspek (chapter 8) privileges a combination of political/power and substantive/cultural rationality, and uses the genre of interpretation. His point of departure is a contradiction within political rationality between *liberal democracy* (civic life in liberal society) and *authoritarian* organization and control of workplace institutions (the wage-capital relation). In a related but more complex manner, Deetz (chapter 9) somewhat ambiguously privileges substantive/cultural rationality, the genre of narrative while articulating a vision of distortions induced by power inequalities within a self-referential, multilayered organizational discourse. Similarly, Natalle, Papa, and Graham (chapter 10) privilege a combination of political/power and substantive/cultural rationalities, but use the genre of interpretation. However, they examine a concrete dimension of the political environment of the American workplace—the ways the women's movement has been trying to transform organizations to become more responsive to women.

Standards/criteria for the evaluation of organizational communicative practices

The contributors to this volume propound three standards/criteria to be used for the evaluation of organizational communicative practices.

First, organizational communicative practices can be evaluated in terms of their contribution to organizational survival or some other type of success. The contributors articulate three such standards by evaluating contributions of organizational communicative practices to: (1) organizational survival in general; (2) economic organizational success in general; and (3) economic success of specific organizations.

Contractor (chapter 2) argues that organizations—"selfish" self-organized systems—through communication import a large amount of energy from outside, and use this energy to renew their own structures (*"autopoeisis"*) and survive. Self-organized systems expel, rather than accumulate, the accruing disorder/entropy into the environment. Consequently, organizational communicative practices are evaluated in terms of their contribution to organizational rejuvenation and coherence at the expense of the vitality, stability, and predictability of their environments. In a less abstract fashion, Yu (chapter 3) posits that organizational communication practices be evaluated the Japanese way, that is, by their contribution to organizational size, scope, market share, and profit—all measures of organizational success. This means privileging interpersonal face-to-face communication over sophisticated information/communication technologies. Yu argues that there is an extremely high overlap between two levels of relationships between members of Japanese organizations. Face-to-face interactions (guided by still strong, stable norms), and "abstract" interdependencies (based on "anonymous" actors' preferences) are said to be at the minimal variance. High-context interpersonal communication, rather than sophisticated information/communication technologies, is evaluated in terms of its contribution to the transformation of intra- and inter-organizational interdependencies into interpersonalized relationships. This internal and external "interrelatedness" is what Yu labels human relationships. An alternative is to evaluate organizational communicative practices by their contribution to the formulation and implementation of strategies of specific organizations. King and Cushman (chapter 4) claim *speed of response*—rapidly getting products to market—is the crucial time-based, communication-oriented organizational competitive strategy.

Second, organizational communicative practices can be evaluated in terms of their impact on internal and external organizational structures and performance. The contributors outline two distinct arguments: (1) how to evaluate the effects of new information/communication technologies on organizational structures in general; and (2) how to evaluate the effects of a particular type of information/communication technology on small group performance.

Horvath and Fulk (chapter 5) take issue with theories that simply link the declining costs (labor, time, and information inaccuracy) of handling and communicating information of various kinds—information exchange and processing—to a shift from *vertical integration* toward *horizontal cooperation*. These internal and external transformations allegedly lead towards the new, counter-hierarchical organizational structure. Internally, hierarchies/bureaucracies (distinct and stable organizational, interunit, and power boundaries) are said to be transformed via adhocracies/integrated decentralism/distributed-networked organizations (distinct and stable organizational boundary, but blurred boundaries between organizational units) into organizations as markets (splitting of the firm into smaller units having only temporary, contractual relations with each other blurs the boundary between the organization and the outside world). Externally, two major types of transformations are said to be taking place. First, the hierarchy-to-market transition leads from hierarchies to networked-distributed organizations (internal organizational boundaries are blurred) to "biased markets" (the distinction between organizations and the outside world is blurred) and finally to traditional markets of individual, independent firms (the distinction between organizations and the outside world is erased). Second, we may be witnessing the evolution of the market from itself in the form of ever increasing level of "interrelatedness" of firms within the market/industry through horizontal cooperation among networks of competitors and among noncompetitors making compatible/complementary products. Horvath and Fulk argue that the relationships between new information/communication technologies and organizational structural configurations are mediated and/or moderated by the *quality* of information defined not only in terms of its cost but also its qualitative distinctions. The quality of information is product of employees' evaluations or social constructions of the information/communication technology. Consequently, both the effects of the use of information/communication technologies, and the criteria for their evaluation, are organization-specific rather than general and/or universal. At a more specific level, Group Decision Support Systems (GDSS)—a new generation of coordinating, interactive computer-based/computer-mediated systems/technologies—are intended to be used for group collaboration. Seibold, Heller and Contractor (chapter 6) argue that, since collaborative group practices are more inclusive than a simple sharing of information, GDSS systems should be evaluated in terms of their contribution to group performance defined mainly as decision-making at meetings.

Third, organizational communicative strategies can be evaluated by political and moral standards. The contributors evaluate organizational communicative practices in terms of how they: (1) advance and/or eliminate competing views of legitimate organizational practices; (2) expose the internal contradictions of power as they relate to multiple subordinate groups; (3) help create a tentative organizational metacode necessary for a principled critique of organizational power and domination; and (4) help transform the underprivileged position of women in organizations.

Interest advocacy—a series of strategic efforts at normative influence—induces sociopolitical normative change (introduces competing views of what is socially good and appropriate) in organizational sociopolitical environments. Consequently, Finet (chapter 7) proposes that organizational communicative practices—interest advocacy—be evaluated in terms of who is more successful in struggles over social legitimacy—social movements/change advocates or business corporations/change targets—and why and under what conditions are they more successful? Social legitimacy is intrinsically related to power. Organizational communicative practices can thus be evaluated in terms of their contribution to unmasking of the internal contradictions of power, and power-induced inefficiencies and distortions. This can be done, argues Huspek (chapter 8), without privileging one set of values (resistance) over another (power). Documenting the very multiplicity of organizational communicative practices would reveal oppositional and potentially undermining values and norms, diminish power's expanse, and amplify the voice of resistance. Such relatively straightforward opposition between power and resistance is contested by Deetz (chapter 9), who argues that communicative practices in corporate sites result in the skilled production of chaos. Shattered normative hierarchies such as values (political/power rationality), money (instrumental/economic rationality), and the hyper-real production of signs/discourses (substantive/cultural rationality) commingle in such a way as to make almost impossible any principled critique of organizational power, domination, and inefficiencies/distortions. Productive organizational communicative practices cannot be grounded in a preexisting, common organizational communication metacode, not even in one split into its power and resistance poles. However, productive organizational communicative practices should provide a temporary ground for principled critique of organizational power and domination. In contrast to Deetz, Natalle, Papa, and Graham (chapter 10) argue that organizational communicative practices can be used to eliminate the inequality of power in cross-sex communication relationships. They view communication as a means of removing the oppressive gender-based power relationships. The result would be a transformation of organizations based on male ideology into organizations based on a male-female ideology. Such a transformation would change the way women and men think, talk, and act toward one another, and promote true equality between men and women in the workplace.

Vital new mechanisms of organizational communication

The contributors to this volume make a significant contribution to the field of organizational communication by articulating, more or less explicitly, the vital new mechanisms of organizational communication.

Contractor (chapter 2) emphasizes *historicity, time-irreversibility,* and especially *discontinuity,* which occur only in "far-from-equilibrium," nonlinear systems. In such organizations, implies Contractor, mechanisms of communicative practices—dyadic, group, and interorganizational—ultimately cannot escape the fate of far-from-equilibrium, nonlinear systems. Such a fate is brought about by multiple processes, two of which are historicity as nonlinear sequences, and discontinuity as a sudden qualitative change or sudden shifts between *random* behavior and self-organized *systematic* patterns. In contrast to Contractor, who underlines instability and sudden transformation, Yu (chapter 3) singles out high-context communication, which, by reducing information overload through trust, subtlety, and intimacy between organizational members, increases the overall effectiveness and stability of Japanese corporations. By doing so, Yu places a strong emphasis on *forward policing* within Japanese organizations—where still strong norms guide and police actions—rather than on *backward policing,* whereby the product is controlled at each stage of production, or *positional viability* with organizational positions arranged in supplier-customer relations and each position providing excess value with as many as possible of other positions (see Coleman 1990; 44, 427–35, 448, 943). Interorganizational relationships of Japanese corporations—six bank-centered, horizontal *keiretsus* which cut across industries, and numerous vertical, integrated *keiretsus* along a supplier chain dominated by a major manufacturer within a certain industry—are also based on high-context interpersonal communication practices. Although horizontal *keiretsus* are large in scope, size, and economic power, joint consultation, policy-making, and the monitoring of activity in the form of interpersonal interdependencies allow a general trader and a bank to achieve interorganizational coordination and cohesion. Conversely, in each vertical *keiretsu* several layers of subcontractors form a long-term, stable relationship. *Keiretsu* organization members exchange personnel, form joint product-development teams, and share sensitive information. King and Cushman (chapter 4) meander between sudden transformations and organizational stability by singling out *high-speed management* (HSM) as the central communication process in rapidly getting products to market. HSM consists of (1) environmental scanning or monitoring of external economic forces, and (2) value chain processes or monitoring of a firm's internal resources. The most successful firms simultaneously engage in significant cross-organizational activities, and implement time-based, communication-oriented organizational strategies. These activities unfold within four small group communication processes: (1) a linking and negotiation process, (2) a New England town meeting process, (3) a cross-functional teamwork process, and (4) case studies in world-class benchmarking processes. HSM theory operationalizes three fundamental organizational processes in terms of communicative practices: (1) organizational integration achieved through leadership, corporate climate, and teamwork, (2) organizational coordination accomplished through information-based value chain linking, and (3) organizational control entailing planning of organizational goals and targets, their continuous monitoring in real time, and a series of short-term assessments of possible improvements.

Horvath and Fulk (chapter 5) operationalize the *quality of information* as a link between new information/communication technologies and organizational structures in terms of *medium richness*. This ability of a communication medium to carry important nonverbal information that supplies the social context of the communication is "constructed" by the user's perceptions. Since co-workers provide the evaluations or social constructions/cues of the information/communication technology, media richness is group- and organization-specific. The information/communication technology is thus examined within the context of the perceptions, images, and feelings of organization members; the dynamics of interpersonal interaction and decision-making; and the prior social characteristics of individuals and groups *within* organizations. More specifically, Seibold, Heller, and Contractor (chapter 6) offer the "emergent perspective" on context-specific combinations of the three dimensions/factors that are said to account for widely divergent outcomes of the use of the same type of GDSS in similar settings. Different outcomes of the GDSS use—the authors argue—are to be expected since the uses and consequences of information technology emerge unpredictably from complex social interactions guided by the group pragmatics and norms. The three dimensions/factors are: (1) GDSS characteristics such as physical configuration, adaptability or appropriateness of support, level of user friendliness, and who drives the system; (2) GDSS use characteristics such as task differences, time constraints, channel selection, and training; and (3) GDSS user characteristics such as group composition, group size, group structure/hierarchy, history of interacting together, training, attitude/degree of respect toward use of new technologies, level of computer expertise, and past experience of adapting to new technologies.

By focusing on reciprocal relations between organizations and their external environments, Finet (chapter 7) examines "macro" political and sociopolitical features of organizational communication as the predominant form of organizations' institutional agency. Interest advocacy is an interplay of communication practices of two types of agency: (1) social movements which proffer competing views of what is socially good and appropriate, and (2) business corporations which are motivated and frequently justify their actions in terms of self-interest. Interest advocacy involves both the interactional dynamics, and mediated communicative practices. While "mature" change advocates—about whose goals and practices there is a societal consensus—can draw on repertoire of both confrontational and cooperative message strategies aimed at business corporations as change targets, "emerging" change advocates—whose goals and practices are not endorsed yet by a societal consensus—rely almost exclusively on confrontational message strategies. Consequently, change targets use predominantly cooperative message strategies, and resort to confrontational message strategies only when attacked by emerging change advocates. Huspek's critical communication theory (chapter 8)—*nonfoundationalist critical hermeneutics*—does not explicitly focus on social legitimacy. However, he dissects dimensions of the power-resistance oppositions as discursive formations. In such a formation, discourses of resistance, expressing the oppositional "other," define the limits of power, and demonstrate that power is something other than its truth claims. Huspek thus draws the lessons learnt from a comparison of power and resistance discourses— meanings and values that point to potentially new forms of social and political life. In contrast to Huspek, Deetz (chapter 9) views organizations as a political site where the traditional/early modernity, rational/late modernity, and chaotic/postmodernity organizational types and their corresponding simulacra/representational practices simultaneously exist. Since the representational practices/simulacra, which produce and reproduce the organizational forms, eradicate any solid ground for critique, potentially new forms of social and political life can be defined only in abstract terms of equal participation of all organizational stakeholders/ audiences in communicative practices. This amounts to Habermas's (1987) "ideal speech situation" undistorted by power inequalities. In a more optimistic manner, Natalle, Papa, and Graham (chapter 10) outline how three types of feminism account for the inequality of power in cross-sex communication relationships, and present different solutions the three feminisms offer to remedy the inequality. *Liberal feminism* calls for the sharing of power within the existing social structure between men and women as equal partners in the corporation. It argues that differences in male and female communication behavior have no detrimental effect on management effectiveness, and advises women to behave like women and simply increase participation in the management ranks. *Radical feminism* calls for the separation of women and men as a means of removing the oppressive power relationships. Claiming that women are superior to men, radical feminists argue that the "women-identified women" should rely on a matriarchal kinship network in order to form women-owned-and-operated businesses. The separatist philosophy of radical feminists contends that the independent business women entrepreneurs must forge the gender-exclusive (business) networks. This program is justified by the women's alleged superiority in leadership communication behavior such as decision-making and gender-based models of influence. As a third alternative, *materialist feminism,* drawing on Marxist and socialist theory, calls for a complete redefinition of gender in terms of intricate interactions between race, class, and gender. Within the materialist camp, *radical humanists* blame oppressive and privileged discourse/ language for male hegemony and domination, and *radical structuralists* point to male monopoly on power, male-dominated group participation, and privileged control of tangible resources by males.

Practical consequences of evaluative standards and new mechanisms of organizational communication

Theoretical contributions to the volume are also new and relevant in that they articulate—more or less explicitly—consequences of evaluative standards and new organizational communicative mechanisms and practices. In that sense the new theoretical approaches are practical/pragmatic.

It is rather uncertain, implies Contractor (chapter 2), which organizational communicative mechanisms and practices, and under what conditions, enable far-from-equilibrium, self-organizing, nonlinear systems/organizations to survive. Since such organizations are characterized by discontinuity—sudden qualitative changes or sudden shifts between random behavior and self-organized systematic patterns—predictions of the future do not have a solid basis in the past organizational behavior—its history, tradition, and culture. To put it differently, Contractor implies that organizational communicative mechanisms and practices have a limited strategic—future oriented—value. However, they are useful for the analysis of current and past organizational behaviors/practices. At the other end of the continuum, Yu claims (chapter 3) that an accommodating Japanese culture, by enhancing an almost complete conversion of abstract intra- and interorganizational interdependencies into person-to-person interdependencies or human relationships, contributes to the success and stability of Japanese corporations. The lesson seems to be a simple one: high-context interpersonal communication—through mechanisms such as exchange of personnel, joint product-development teams, and contractor-subcontractor relationships—reduces the discrepancies between interpersonal interactions and abstract organizational interactions and, consequently, contributes to organizational success and stability. King and Cushman (chapter 4) articulate a theoretical "space" delineated by the extremes of sudden transformations and organizational stability. Co-alignment, the paradigmatic organizational communication activity, which is constantly evaluated by the existing world-class benchmarks, and management styles that transcend local differences in order to develop a global perspective are necessary, although not sufficient, conditions of corporate success. In contrast to Contractor's position, King and Cushman stress the strategic—future oriented—relevance of the general high-speed management theory. They operationalize co-alignment as a simultaneous, tight, and efficient integration, coordination, and control of environment scanning and organizational value chain processes. Co-alignment is a systematic, communication-based process of continuous improvement of effectiveness in managing organizational interdependencies or linking internal and external resources. This is a paradigmatic communication problem since it requires taking into account the position of the "other"—it is necessarily based on integration, coordination, and control of each unit's needs, concerns, and contributions. The authors, however, leave one question open: Is co-alignment cooperative or domineering? Be this as it may, if the two conditions are not met by a corporate strategy, organizations cannot compete and, ultimately, fail. While stressing strategy, King and Cushman are, however, silent on the issue concerning other necessary characteristics of a successful com-

pany. For example, can successful organizations combine global orientation, high-speed orientation, and a "co-alignment" orientation,
given their local conditions, or must they always tightly integrate all
three of them?

By arguing that both the effects of the use of information/
communication technologies, and the criteria for their evaluation, are
organization-specific, Horvath and Fulk (chapter 5) imply that the relationship between information/communication technologies and organizational structure is not "automatic." Rather, it is mediated and/or
moderated by social and cultural characteristics of individuals and
groups within organizations as well as by the dynamics of interpersonal interaction and decision-making. In a similar fashion, Seibold,
Heller, and Contractor (chapter 6) suggest that there are no simple theoretical recipes for productive uses of Group Decision Support Systems. Consequently, if GDSSs are to improve group performance
defined mainly as decision-making at meetings, their users must forge
context-specific combinations of GDSS characteristics, GDSS use characteristics and GDSS user characteristics.

Finet's (chapter 7) theoretical articulations of interest advocacy
have practical/pragmatic implications for both advocacy move-
ments/organizations, and organizations and organizational communication in general. The success and/or failure of both social move-
ments/change advocates, and corporations/change targets hinges on
their strategic use of the mix of interactional dynamics and mediated
communicative practices, as well as on the use of the mix of confrontational and cooperative message strategies to promote or hinder
alternative definitions of social legitimacy. Such definitions are justifications of different power arrangements. Consequently, it is the role of
a critical theorist, implies Huspek (chapter 8), to act simultaneously as
a "public" analyst and ambiguously (dis)interested consultant who describes and critiques organizational communicative practices, and then
creates a "portfolio" of the lessons learnt from a comparison of power
and resistance discourses. Oppositional discourses, warns Huspek,
may promote either "positive" agenda such as values of solidarity,
equality, and cooperation, or "negative" agenda such as political inaction. Although Huspek simply opposes antilanguage of resistance to
dominant discourse, a critical theorist/researcher, however, may en-
counter empirical situations in which there is a "negotiated code"—a
substantial overlap between discourses of resistance and power. In a
related fashion, Deetz (chapter 9) portrays a more complex role for the
theorist. He/she is sort of a "multicultural" conversationalist, "public"
analyst, and (dis)interested consultant who moves *sequentially* from

one representational practice/simulacrum to another or participates in all three types of simulacra *simultaneously*. The theorist then critiques organizational power and domination by comparing representational practices/simulacra, and suggests courses of action aimed at eliminating power distortions in organizations. One such distortion is the inequality of power in cross-gender communicative relationships. Only the integrated efforts of the three feminisms, argue Natalle, Papa, and Graham (chapter 10), can bring about a meaningful transformation in such organizational structure and communication. When strategically integrated—*liberal* persuasion-based strategies, *radical* calls for the female self-reliance and solidarity in organizational life in order to promote equality, and *materialist* programs for the transformation of capitalist society in order to reconcile democracy (equality and opportunity) and capitalism (competition and domination)—the three feminisms may transform the inequality of power in cross-sex communication relationships.

Let me summarize. It is useful to think of the received theory as a complex, multilayered—philosophical, theoretical, and practical—argument backed by more or less supportive evidence. New theories, however, not only lack evidential base but also offer germen, inceptive, rather than elaborate arguments. With this in mind, what is the significance of the new theories of or arguments about organizational communication presented in this book?

King and Cushman's theory of high-speed management (chapter 4) offers an elaborate argument at all three levels. At the philosophical level, they argue that the faster relevant coalitions of stakeholders coordinate, integrate, and control their activities—that is, communicate—the more likely they are to reap high profits. At the theoretical level, they specify four small-group communicative processes through which relevant coalitions of stakeholders coordinate, integrate, and control organizational activities. At the practical level, King and Cushman specify skills necessary to carry out rapid organizational coordination, integration, and control. As evidence they present case studies of corporations whose success depended on high-speed management as organizational communication. Horvath and Fulk (chapter 5) contend, at the philosophical level, that the effect of new communication technologies on organizational structures and processes is mediated by symbolic and political struggles over definitions of organizational reality. However, at the theoretical level they do not clearly specify communicative practices that constitute symbolic and political struggles of stakeholders to construct organizational reality. Consequently, they do not elaborate communicative skills which stakeholders can deploy in symbolic and political struggles. In a similar fashion, Huspek (chapter 8) argues at the philosophical level that justice in organizations depends on a specific interplay of communicative practices of stakeholders who wield power, and communicative practices of stakeholders resisting this power. Like Horvath and Fulk, Huspek, at the theoretical level, does not differentiate between mechanisms that link power-holders and resisters or the consequences of their struggles. Understandably, he does not offer an elaborate list of communicative skills that power-holders and resisters use as resources.

It is worth noting that Deetz, Finet, and Natalle, Papa, and Graham elaborate the theoretical level of their argument, but leave the philosophical and practical level relatively undifferentiated. Deetz (chapter 9), at the philosophical level, defines organizational success in terms of just communicative processes and outcomes. At the theoretical level he offers the ideal speech situation—structural symmetry or equality of all organizational stakeholders—as a forum for free expression of all "voices." At the practical level, however, Deetz does not provide us with a list of communicative skills and resources necessary to sustain organizational practices demanded by the ideal speech situation. At the philosophical level, Finet (chapter 7) simply assumes that there are constant struggles over standards of social legitimacy. At the theoretical level she specifies communicative strategies that both new social movements and large corporations use in struggles over social consensus. However, she does not specify the communicative skills necessary to successfully engage in such "symbolic and political wrestling." Similarly, Natalle, Papa, and Graham (chapter 10) at the philosophical level define organizational success in terms of just cross-gender communication. Male and female stakeholders are to mutually agree upon standards of equality and equity. At the theoretical level, the authors specify mechanisms, based on three types of feminist politics, that could transform organizations and bring about gender equality. However, the authors pay scant attention to the required communicative skills and resources for such a project.

Contractor, Ju, and Seibold, Heller and Contractor do not distinguish, in a differentiated fashion, the philosophical, theoretical, and practical level of their theoretical argument. At the philosophical level, Contractor (chapter 2) depicts organizations as selfish, open, self-organizing systems that exploit their environment in order to survive. At the theoretical level Contractor, relying on mathematical reasoning, specifies "boundary conditions" of such systems. When the boundary conditions hold, organizations are stable and their behavior is predictable. However, Contractor argues that sudden changes of these boundary conditions cannot be predicted and that, consequently, organizational transformations cannot be engineered. Thus, he leaves us without practical communicative tools to deal with dramatic organizational changes. In a similar fashion, Ju (chapter 3) at the philosophical level defines Japanese giant corporations as relatively open systems that favor long-term survival over short-term profits. At the theoretical level he also specifies boundary conditions of such organizations. Using humanistic rather than mathematical reasoning, he specifies the boundary conditions in terms of close, long-term, face-to-face interactions between all stakeholders that provide for organizational stability rather than change. Ju, however, does not analyze in great detail skills and resources that constitute high-context communication in Japanese organizations. Finally, Seibold, Heller, and Contractor (chapter 6) at the philosophical level define organizational success in terms of high-quality decision-making by organizational groups/teams. At the theoretical level they attempt to specify practices of successful cooperative decision-making through the use of new group decision support systems. But they also pay scant attention to practical communicative skills necessary to successfully use new group-based communication technologies.

As this short critical review makes obvious, new theoretical positions on organizational communicative practices are at different stages of conceptual articulation. The new theoretical positions, consequently, provide different degrees of closure regarding new mechanisms of organizational communicative practices and their practical implications/consequences. Future tasks of theorists and/or researchers lie, then, predominantly in these two areas.

References

Agger, B. 1991. Critical theory, poststructuralism, postmodernism: Their sociological relevance. *Annual Review of Sociology* 17:105–31.

Aldrich, E. H. 1979. *Organizations and environments.* Englewood Cliffs, NJ: Prentice Hall.

Aldrich, E. H., and D. Whetten. 1981. Organization-sets, action-sets and networks: Making the most of simplicity. In *Handbook of organizational design,* vol. 1, ed. P. C. Nystrom and W. H. Starbuck. New York: Oxford University Press.

Alexander, C. J. 1990. Between progress and apocalypse: Social theory and the dream of reason in the twentieth century. In *Rethinking progress: Movements, forces, and ideas at the end of the 20th century,* ed. J. C. Alexander and P. Sztompka. Boston: Unwin Hyman.

———. 1991. Sociological theory and the claim to reason: Why the end is not in sight. *Sociological Theory* 9:147–53.

Antonio, J. R. 1991. Postmodern storytelling versus pragmatic truth-seeking: The discursive bases of social theory. *Sociological Theory* 9:154–63.

Appadurai, A. 1990. Disjuncture and difference in the global cultural economy. In *Global culture: Nationalism, globalization and modernity,* ed. M. Featherstone. London: Sage.

Archer, S. M. 1990. Theory, culture and postindustrial society. In *Global culture: Nationalism, globalization and modernity,* ed. M. Featherstone. London: Sage

Arnason, P. J. 1990. Nationalism, globalization and modernity. In *Global culture: Nationalism, globalization and modernity,* ed. M. Featherstone. London: Sage.

Bauman, Z. 1990. Modernity and ambivalence. In *Global culture: Nationalism, globalization and modernity,* ed. M. Featherstone. London: Sage.

Bell, D. 1976. *The cultural contradictions of capitalism.* New York: Basic Books.

———. 1987. The world and the United States in 2013. *Daedalus, 116.*

Berleur, J., and J. Drumm. 1991. *Information technology assessment.* Amsterdam, Holland: Elsevier S.

Beyer, F. P. 1990. Privatization and the public influence of religion in global society. In *Global culture: Nationalism, globalization and modernity,* ed. M. Featherstone. London: Sage.

Blau, J. 1993. *Social contracts and economic markets.* New York: Plenum Press.

Blunt, P. 1989. Strategies for human resource development in the Third World. Opening address at the International Human Resource Development Conference, University of Manchester, June 25–28.

Boudon, R., and F. Bourricaud. 1989. *A critical dictionary of sociology.* Chicago: University of Chicago Press.

Bradach, J. L., and R. G. Eccles. 1989. Price, authority, and trust: From ideal types to plural forms. *Annual Review of Sociology,* 97–118.

Burns, T. 1992. *Erving Goffman.* London: Routledge.

Caplow, T. 1964. *Principles of organization.* New York: Harcourt Brace Jovanovich.

Criss, J. J. 1992. Habermas and Goffman: Some suggestions for future research. *Perspectives* 15 (3):6.

Clairmonte, F., and J. Cavanagh. 1982. Transnational corporations and global markets: Changing power relations. *Trade and Development: An UNECTAD Review* 4:149–82.

Clegg, R. S. 1990. *Modern organizations: Organization studies in the post-modern world.* London: Sage.

Coleman, J. 1990. *Foundations of social theory.* Cambridge, MA: The Belknap Press of Harvard University Press.

Collins, M. T., and T. Doorley. 1991. *Teaming up for the '90s: A guide to international joint ventures and strategic alliances.* Homewood, IL: Business One Irwin.

Cooper, R., and G. Burrell. 1988. Modernism, postmodernism, and organizational analysis: An introduction. *Organization Studies* 9:91–112.

Culnan, M. J., and M. L. Markus, 1987. Information technologies. In *Handbook of organizational communication: An interdisciplinary perspective,* ed. F. M. Jablin, L. L. Putnam, K. H. Roberts, and L. W. Porter. Newbury Park: Sage.

Curson, C. (ed.). 1986. *Flexible patterns of work.* London: Institute of Personnel Management.

Daniels, T. D., and Spiker, B. K. 1991. *Perspectives on organizational communication* (2nd ed.). Dubuque, IA: Wm. C. Brown Publishers.

D'Andrade, G. R. 1986. Three scientific world views and the governing law model. In *Metatheory in social science,* ed. D. W. Fiske and R. A. Schweder. Chicago: University of Chicago Press.

Davidow, W. H., and M. S. Malone. 1992. The virtual corporation. New York: Harper Collins.

Deetz, S. A. 1992. *Democracy in an age of corporate colonization: Developments in communication and the politics of everyday life.* Albany, NY: SUNY Press.

Derrida. J. 1976. *Speech and phenomenon.* Evanston, IL: Northwestern University Press.

Dore, R. 1983. Goodwill and the spirit of market capitalism. *British Journal of Sociology* XXXIV(4): 459–82.

Eccles, R. G. 1981. The quasifirm in the construction industry. *Journal of Economic Behavior and Organization* 2:235–57.

Eder, K. 1990. The cultural code of modernity and the problem of nature: A critique of the naturalistic notion of progress. In *Rethinking progress: Movements, forces, and ideas at the end of the 20th century,* ed. J. C. Alexander and P. Sztompka. Boston: Unwin Hyman.

Eisenberg, E. M., and Goodal, H. R. 1993. *Organizational communication: Balancing creativity and constraint.* New York: St. Martin's Press.

Etziony-Halevy, E. 1990. The relative autonomy of elites: The absorption of protest and social progress in western democracies. In *Rethinking progress: Movements, forces and ideas at the end of the 20th century,* ed. J. C. Alexander and P. Sztompka. Boston: Unwin Hyman.

Evan, W. 1966. The organization set: Toward a theory of interorganizational relations. In *Approaches to organizational design,* ed. J. Thompson. Pittsburgh: University of Pittsburgh Press.

Featherstone, M. 1990. Global culture: An introduction. In *Global culture: Nationalism, globalization and modernity,* ed. M. Featherstone. London: Sage.

Gambrell, J. 1993. Art and the great utopia. *The New York Review of Books,* 40 (8): 52–59 (April 22).

Gelb, H. L. 1992. The curse of nations. *The New York Times,* Sunday, July 5: E11.

Giddens, A. 1990. *The consequences of modernity.* Stanford, CA: Stanford University Press.

Gill, S., and D. Law. 1988. *The global political economy: Perspectives, problems and policies.* Baltimore, Johns Hopkins University Press.

Giner, S. 1987. Sociology and moral philosophy. *International Review of Sociology,* n.s., 3.

Goldhaber, G., and G. Barnett. (eds.). 1988. *Handbook of organizational communication.* Norwood, NJ: Ablex.

Goffman, E. 1981. *Forms of talk.* Philadelphia: University of Pennsylvania Press.

———. 1983. The interaction order. *American Sociological Review* 48:1–17

Granovetter, M. 1985. Economic action and social structure: The problem of embeddedness. *American Journal of Sociology* 91:481–510.

Grootings, P. 1991. New forms of work organization in Europe: East-West comparisons. In *New forms of work organization in Europe,* ed. P. Grootings, B. Gustavsen, and L. Hethy. New Brunswick: Transaction Publishers.

Gustavsen, B., and L. Hethy. 1991. New forms of work organization: An overview. In *New forms of work organizations in Europe,* ed. P. Grootings, B. Gustavsen, and L. Hethy. New Brunswick: Transaction Publishers.

Habermas, J. 1975. *Legitimation crisis.* Boston: Beacon Press.

———. 1984. *The theory of communicative action.,* vol. 1. Boston: Beacon Press.

———. 1987. *The theory of communicative action,* vol. 2. Boston: Beacon Press.

Halal, W. 1986. *The new capitalism.* New York: Wiley.

Hall, R. 1991. *Organizations: Structures, processes and outcomes.* Englewood Cliffs, NJ.: Prentice Hall.

Hannerz, U. 1989. Notes on the global ecumene. *Public culture* 1(2).

Harvey, D. 1990. *The condition of postmodernity: An enquiry into the origins of cultural change.* Oxford Blackwell.

Hoffmann, S. 1992. Delusions of world order. *The New York Review of Books,* April 9:37–43.

Jablin, F., L. Putnam, K. Roberts, and L. Porter (eds.). 1987. *Handbook of organizational communication.* Newbury Park, CA: Sage.

Jacques, E. 1989. *Requisite organizations.* Arlington, VA: Casson Hall.

Jencks, C. 1987. *Post-Modernism: The new classicism in art and architecture.* New York: Rizzoli

Johnston, R., and P. R. Lawrence. 1988. Beyond vertical integration—The rise of the value-adding partnerships. *Harvard Business Review* 88(4): 94–101.

Kegley, E. C. Jr., E. R. Wittkopf, and L. W. Rawls. The multinational corporation: Curse or cure? " In *The global agenda: Issues and perspectives,* ed. Charles W. Kegley, and E. R. Wittkoph. New York: Random House (2nd ed.).

Keohane, O. R., and J. S. Nye. 1988. Complex interdependence, transnational relations, and realism: Alternative perspectives on world politics. In *The global agenda: Issues and perspectives,* ed. C. W. Kegley and E. R. Wittkoph. New York: Random House.

King, A. 1990a. *Global cities.* London: Routledge.

———. 1990b. Architecture, capital and the globalization of culture. In *global culture: Nationalism, globalization and modernity,* ed. M. Featherstone. London: Sage.

Kinsella, W. J. 1993. Communication and information technologies: A dialectical model of technology and human agency. *The New Jersey Journal of Communication* 1, no. 1 (Spring): 2–18

Lash, S., and J. Urry. 1987. *The end of organized capitalism.* Oxford: Polity Press.

———. 1988. Postmodernism as a regime of signification. *Theory, Culture and Society* 5:311–36.

Lemert, C. 1991. The end of ideology, really. *Sociological Theory* 9: 164–72.

Lipietz, A. 1987. *Miracles and mirages: The crisis of global fordism.* London: Verso.

Lyotard, J. F. 1984. *The postmodern condition: A report on knowledge.* Minneapolis: University of Minnesota Press.

Markoff, J. 1992a. Foray into mainstream for parallel computing. *The New York Times,* Monday, June 15: D1, D3.

———. 1992b. A media pioneer's quest: Portable electronic newspapers. *The New York Times,* Sunday, June 28: F11.

———. 1992c. Serving no chip before its time. *The New York Times,* Thursday, July 23: D1, D21.

———. 1992d. In a world of instant copies, who pays for original work? *The New York Times,* Sunday, August 9: E18.

McPhee, R., and P. Tompkins (eds.). 1985. *Organizational communication: Traditional themes and new directions.* Beverly Hills, CA: Sage.

Mead, G. H. 1932. *The philosophy of the present.* Edited by A. E. Murphy, with prefatory remarks by J. Dewey. Chicago: Open Court.

Merton, K. R. 1957. *Social theory and social structure.* Glencoe, IL: Free Press.

Mills, C. W. 1959. *The sociological imagination.* New York: Grove.

Mongardini, C. 1990. The decadence of modernity: The delusions of progress and the search for historical consciousness. In *Rethinking progress: Movements, forces, and ideas at the end of the 20th century,* ed. J. C. Alexander and P. Sztompka. Boston: Unwin Hyman.

Morgentau, H. J. 1967. *Politics among nations: The struggle for power and peace.* New York: Knopf (4th ed.).

Morton, M. S. 1991. "Introduction." In *The corporation of the 1990s: Information technology and organizational transformation,* ed. M. S. Morton. New York: Oxford University Press.

Mumby, D. K. 1987. The political function of narrative in organizations. *Communication monographs* 54:113–27.

———. 1988. *Communication and power in organizations: Discourse, ideology, and domination.* Norwood, NJ: Ablex.

Nohria, N., and C. Garcia-Pont. 1991. Global strategic linkages and industry structure. *Strategic Management Journal* 12 (Special Issue): 105–24.

Nowak, S. 1990. Models of directional change and human values: The theory of progress as an applied social science. In *Rethinking progress: Movements, forces, and ideas at the end of the 20th century,* ed. J. C. Alexander and P. Sztompka. Boston: Unwin Hyman.

Offe, K. 1985. *Disorganized capitalism.* Oxford: Polity Press.

Osmanczyk, E. J. 1985. International organizations. In *The encyclopedia of the United Nations and international agreements.* Philadelphia and London: Taylor and Francis.

Pareto, V. 1935. *The mind and society.* New York: Harcourt, Brace and Jovanovich.

Parsons, T. 1961. An outline of the social system. In *Theories of society,* ed. T. Parsons et al. New York: Free Press.

———. 1977. *The evolution of societies*. Englewood Cliffs. NJ: Prentice Hall.

Powel R. 1991. Digitizing TV into obsolescence. *The New York Times,* Sunday, October 20: F11.

Putnam, L. L. 1982. Paradigms for organizational communication research: An overview and synthesis. *Western Journal of Speech Communication* 46: 192–206.

Putnam, L. L., and M. Pacanowsky (eds.). 1983. *Communication and organizations: An interpretive approach*. Beverly Hills, CA: Sage.

Richardson, L. 1991. *Postmodern social theory: Representational practices. Sociological Theory* 9:173–79.

Rifkin, G. 1992. Where commercial arts meet computer age. *The New York Times,* July 15: D5.

Rogers, E. M. 1988. Information technologies: How organizations are changing. In *Handbook of organizational communication,* ed. G. M. Goldhaber and G. A. Bakhett, Norwood, NJ: Ablex.

Rorty, R. 1982. *Consequences of pragmatism*. Minneapolis: University of Minnesota Press.

Rueschemeyer, D., and M. Rueschemeyer. 1990. Progress in the distribution of power: Gender relations and women's movements as a source of change. In *Rethinking progress: Movements, forces, and ideas at the end of the 20th century,* ed. J. C. Alexander and P. Sztompka. Boston: Unwin Hyman.

Saffo, Paul. 1992. The electronic future is upon us. *The New York Times,* June 7: F13.

Schwartz, J. 1992. The next revolution. *Newsweek,* April 6: 42–48.

Schutz, A. 1964. *Collection papers*. Vol. 2: *Studies in social theory,* edited by A. Broderson. The Hague: Martinius Nijhoff.

Sciulli, D. 1989. Analytical limits of communicative action: Two requirements of Habermas' critical theory and of societal constitutionalism. *Current Perspectives in Social Theory* 9:55–90.

Scott, W. R. 1992. *Organizations: Rational, natural, and open systems*. Englewood Cliffs, N.J.: Prentice Hall.

Seidman, S. 1991a. The end of sociological theory: The postmodern hope. *Sociological Theory* 9:131–46.

———. 1991b. Postmodern anxiety: The politics of epistemology. *Sociological Theory* 9:180–90.

Sklair, L.1991. *Sociology of the global system: Social change in global perspective*. Baltimore: Johns Hopkins University Press.

Swedberg, R. 1991. Major traditions of economic sociology. *Annual Review of Sociology* 17:251–76.

Sztompka, P. 1990. Agency and progress: The idea of progress and changing theories of change. In *Rethinking progress: Movements, forces, and ideas at the end of the 20th century,* ed. J. C. Alexander and P. Sztompka. Boston: Unwin Hyman.

Taylor, T. J. 1981. *Linguistic theory and structural stylistics.* Oxford: Blackwell.

————. 1992. *Mutual misunderstanding: Skepticism and the theorizing of language and interpretation.* Durham: Duke University Press.

Thayer, L. (ed.). 1985. *Organization and communication: Emerging perspectives.* Norwood, NJ: Ablex.

Turner, S. 1991. Rationality today. *Sociological Theory* 9: 191–94.

Tushman, M. L., and R. R. Nelson. 1990. Introduction: Technology, organizations, and innovation. *Administrative Science Quarterly,* special issue 35:1–8.

The United Nations Commission on Transnational Corporations, 9th session, 5–15 March 1991. Description of the data bases available in the comprehensive information system.

Van de ven, H. A., and D. L. Ferry. 1980. *Measuring and assessing organizations.* New York: John Wiley.

Wallerstein, I. 1990a. Culture as the ideological battleground of the modern world-system. In *Global culture: Nationalism, globalization and modernity,* ed. M. Featherstone. London: Sage.

————. 1990b. Culture in the world system: A reply to Boyne. In *Global culture: Nationalism, globalization, and modernity,* ed. M. Featherstone. London: Sage.

Weber, M. 1951. *The religion of China.* Glencoe, IL: The Free Press.

————. 1978. *Economy and society: An outline of interpretive sociology.* Berkeley: University of California Press.

Williams, F. 1991. *The new telecommunications: Infrastructure for the information age.* New York: The Free Press.

Wittgenstein, L. 1958. *Philosophical investigations:* Oxford: Blackwell.

Worsley, P. 1990. Models of the modern world-system. In *Global culture: Nationalism, globalization and modernity,* ed. M. Featherstone. London: Sage.

Wrong, D. H. 1961. The oversocialized conception of man in modern sociology. *American Sociological Review* 26:183–93.

Zachary, G. P. 1992a. Industries find growth of digital electronics brings in competitors. *The Wall Street Journal,* February 18: A1, A4.

————. 1992b. Coming digital age may transform your living room in many ways. *The Wall Street Journal,* February 18: A4.

Zelizer, V. A. 1978. Human values and the market: The case of life insurance and death in 19th century America. *American Journal of Sociology* 84:591–610.

————. 1983. *Morals and markets: The development of life insurance in the United States.* New Brunswick: Transaction Publishers.

————. 1985. *Pricing the priceless child: The changing social value of children.* New York: Basic Books.

————. 1988. Beyond the polemics and the market: Establishing a theoretical and empirical agenda. *Social Forces* 3:614–34.

————. 1989. The social meaning of money: Special monies? *American Journal of Sociology* 95:342–77.

NOSHIR S. CONTRACTOR

2 Self-Organizing Systems Perspective in the Study of Organizational Communication

The more freedom in self-organization, the more order!

Enrich Jantsch, *The Self-Organizing Universe*

During the 1970s, several communication and organizational theorists advocated a systems perspective to the study of organizational communication (Katz and Kahn 1978; Monge 1977). Theoretical approaches developed in the 1940s and triggered by interest in biological phenomena, resulted in the broad frameworks of General Systems Theory (Bertalanffy 1968; Miller 1978) and cybernetics (Wiener 1954). Inspired by these developments, organizational and communication scholars conceptualized organizations as "open" structural-functional systems that had clearly identified boundaries, through which they transacted information and materials with the environment, including vendors and clients (Monge 1977). In order to accomplish its functions, the organization itself comprised many interrelated "subsystems" such as managerial, technological, and strategic units (Kast and Rosenzweig 1973). This image of the organization spawned a new vocabulary, considerable theorizing, and a modest amount of empirical research.

Scholars operating from a systems perspective rejected the notion that there was one best way of organizing. Instead they offered *contingency* theories. For instance, Burns and Stalker (1961) proposed that the optimum structure for an organization was contingent on its

The preparation of this manuscript was supported by a grant from Apple Computer's Advanced Technology Group and a Beckman Award from the University of Illinois.

39

environment. Woodward (1965) and her colleagues suggested that a fit must exist between the organization's structure and the technology it used. Lawrence and Lorsch (1967) suggested that the degree of differentiation and integration among the organization's subsystems must match the complexity in the organization's environment.

Discontent with traditional systems thinking

In the past two decades, several observers of organizational practice and research scholars have raised serious concerns about the conceptualization of organizations from a traditional systems perspective. Popular literature, inspired by traditional systems theories, had argued that organizational practitioners should respond to crises by being more adaptive, more flexible, more innovative, more quick to react, creating cross-functional organizational structures, and paying more attention to links with the environment. Sheldon (1980) notes that these palliatives represented attempts at incremental or "normal" changes in order to buffer the organization from its environment and preserve the equilibrium.

Contemporary writings in the popular press suggested that, as society enters a new phase of the information age, organizations are in the midst of discontinuous changes (Davis 1987; Davis and Davidson 1991; Ferguson 1980; Handy 1990). Ferguson (1980) describes the "2001 organization" as a network of relationships that are self-generating, self-organizing, sometimes even self-destructing. Further, these writings suggest that in order to be prepared for these discontinuous changes, organizations must recognize and thrive on chaotic changes in the organization and its environment (Peters 1987).

Scholarly concerns with the limitations of traditional systems thinking can be broadly classified into three categories. *First,* Weick (1979) argued that contingency theories erroneously conceptualized organizations as stable *static* structures that had to be buffered from the environment. To emphasize this criticism, Weick (1979) titled his book "The social psychology of organiz*ing*" in contrast to Katz and Kahn's (1978) book, based on a traditional systems approach, titled "The social psychology of organiz*ation.*"

Second, many scholars noted that systems contingency theories viewed "organizations and their environments as being far too concrete." (Morgan 1986, 74). Thus contingency theories tended to reify the material aspects of organizations, ignoring the fact that organizations are also the products of their members' visions, ideas, norms, and beliefs (Pondy and Mitroff, 1979). This criticism of traditional systems thinking precipitated the emergence of interpretive and critical perspectives on organizational communication (Putnam and Pacanowsky 1983). These approaches focus on organizations as cultures and meaning systems (Pondy, Frost, Morgan, and Dandridge 1983). They reject traditional systems theory's assumption that the organization and all its subsystems share a harmonious functional unity. As a result, they do not view the existence of conflicting goals and multiple interpretations as necessarily dysfunctional (Eisenberg 1984; Monge and Eisenberg 1987).

Third, the research methods used in the study of contingency theories were perceived as being sorely inadequate. These studies, commonly characterized as functionalist research (Putnam 1983), were based on a unidirectional causal analysis of covariance among a small set of variables that measured static, easily observable, characteristics of the organization.

These concerns, by theorists and practitioners, prompted some scholars to conceptualize organizations in terms of patterned changes rather than stable, albeit complex, structures (Mohr 1982). For instance, Miller and Friesen (1984) propose that organizations be characterized in terms of momentum and revolution. They distinguish between quantum and piecemeal changes. Pettigrew (1985) describes these as revolutionary and evolutionary eras. Tushman and Romanelli (1985) conceptualize organizations as evolving systems with strategic reorientations punctuating periods of convergence. During periods of convergence, attempts at normal change are often resisted. However, during periods of strategic reorientation, relatively minor disturbances within the organization (or perturbations from the environment) can trigger large qualitative changes in the organization. Recognition of these discontinuities is an important first step in understanding organizational changes. It suggests a research agenda that points to the futility of seeking "predetermined timetables, of ordered and inevitable sequences or stages" (Pettigrew 1990, 270). The remainder of this section reviews and discusses exemplars of this new research agenda at the work group, organizational and occupational levels.

At the *work group* level, Gersick (1988) rejects the received view that groups progress through generalizable phases, such as "forming, storming, norming and performing" (Tuckman 1965). Rather, Gersick (1988) notes, each work group weaves in and out of these "phases," following a trajectory shaped by the work team's initial disposition and ongoing history. Gersick (1991) argues that these apparently random temporal variations in the work group emerge from a stable and coherent "deep structure" (p. 12). Gersick (1991, 12) defines a deep structure as the "basic activity patterns" that provide the group with a "menu" of choices at each point in time. All work teams have the same basic activity patterns, and yet the manner in which they unfold may vary significantly depending on the choices made by the groups—especially their initial choices.

At the *organizational* level, Van de Ven and Poole (1990) note that many studies have examined the antecedents to, or consequences of, innovation (for a review, see Tornatsky et al. 1983). These studies, consistent with the tenets of traditional systems contingency theories, seek to explain organizational innovation in terms of structural characteristics such as centralization, differentiation, and integration. However, Van de Ven and Poole (1990, 313) note that "very few studies have directly examined how and why innovations emerge, develop, grow or terminate over time." They seek to develop a "process theory that may produce some fundamental 'laws of innovating' useful for explaining how a broad class of processes, sequences and performance conditions unfold along the innovation journey" (Van de Ven and Poole 1990, 313).

At the *occupational* level, Barley (1990, 221) notes that studies examining the effects of technology on occupational roles were "wittingly, or unwittingly premised on Marx's notion that shifts in the technical infrastructure transform societies by altering modes and relations of production." Indeed, the sociotechnical perspective (Rice 1958; Trist and Bamforth 1951) is one of the best articulated systems contingency theories in the organizational literature. The sociotechnical systems perspective argues that the introduction of new technologies in the workplace must be accompanied by changes in the organization's manifest structural configurations. However, Barley (1990) argues that in order to understand the interrelationship of technologies with roles and structures, organizations are better conceptualized as manifestations "of a stream of ongoing actions, interactions, and interpretations that gradually define the contours of tasks, roles and relationships" (p. 223). From this standpoint, Barley (1990, 221) seeks to "chronicle the actions, interactions, and interpretations occasioned by specific machines to explain how technically induced changes in an interaction order (Goffman 1983) might lead to organizational and occupational change."

The three research examples, discussed above, do not seek to explain behavior in terms of contingencies predicated on the manifest structural configurations of group, organizational, or societal systems and subsystems. Instead, they focus explicitly on the emergent process of organizing—the deep processes of transformation that produce overt patterns of behavior. Hence, in all three examples, "what is critical is not just events, but the underlying logics that give events meaning and significance . . . logics which may explain how and why these patterns occur in particular chronological sequence" (Pettigrew 1990, 273). Understanding and explicating these underlying "logics of change" (Morgan 1986, 234) require a closer examination of five conceptual issues that were ignored in research guided by traditional systems theory: (i) differences in knowledge claims made by cross-sectional and dynamic research, (ii) mutual causality, (iii) historicity, (iv) time-irreversibility, and (v) discontinuity.

The next section discusses these five conceptual issues and points to the limitations faced by traditional systems theorists in addressing them. In subsequent sections, I will argue that self-organizing systems theory (Prigogine 1980) provides an opportunity to intellectually advance our understanding of organizational communication processes by responding to the limitations of traditional systems theory. Specifically, self-organizing systems theory is offered as an appropriate conceptual framework to explicitly articulate the underlying logics of change and to systematically examine the processes by which these logics of change generate, sustain, and change surface structures.

Issues neglected by traditional systems research

Dynamic inferences

The renewed emphasis on "process thinking" has underscored the importance of understanding the dynamics within organizations—a concern that has not been lost on contemporary functionalist research (Monge et al. 1984). It is therefore not surprising that most contemporary organizational communication researchers either examine dynamic hypotheses or, more likely, suggest that future research must validate their cross-sectional findings in a dynamic context. In this section I will argue, with the help of a research example, that there are fundamental distinctions between the nature of knowledge claims associated with cross-sectional and dynamic hypotheses. These distinctions demonstrate why testing the adequacy of process theories on the basis of cross-sectional hypotheses will, in most cases, lead to misleading conclusions.

With the emergence of interpretive perspectives in the study of organizational communication, there has been a renewed interest in research examining the relationship between communication, shared understanding, and coordinated activity in the workplace. Some organizational researchers (e.g., Van Maanen and Schein 1979) have argued that coordinated activity, including but not restricted to communicative action, is made possible as a result of individuals sharing a common set of meanings and interpretations. Others (e.g., Weick 1979) have proposed that shared meanings, rather than being a precursor of coordinated activity, results from retroactive sense-making.

A third group of organizational researchers (e.g., Barley 1986; Contractor and Ehrlich,1993; Contractor and Eisenberg 1990; Pettigrew 1990; Poole and DeSanctis 1990; Ranson, Hinings, and Greenwood 1980; Riley 1983; Yates and Orlikowski 1992) suggest that coordinated activity and the existence of a common set of shared meanings and interpretations are recursively linked to each other— each shapes the other in an emergent pattern. Their arguments for this recursive model are grounded in Giddens' (1984) metatheory or structuration. According to Giddens (1984, 2), "Human social activities, like some self-reproducing items in nature, are recursive. That is to say, they are not brought into being by social actors but continually recreated by them via the very means whereby they express themselves as actors. In and through their activities agents reproduce the conditions that make these activities possible." The underlying logic generating this recursive process is termed modalities (Giddens 1984) or appropriations (Poole and DeSanctis 1990).

Traditional functionalist research would test the relationship between coordinated activity and shared interpretations by positing the following cross-sectional hypothesis: Organizational members who coordinate their activities with each other are more likely to share common interpretations than members who do not coordinate activities with others.

However, it is important to recognize that lack of empirical support for this cross-sectional hypothesis does *not,* in and of itself, indicate lack of support for the proposed recursive model linking coordinated activity and shared interpretations. The relationships between coordinated activity and shared interpretations described above refer to the *underlying logic*—not its manifestations at a particular point in time. Hence, even though the underlying logic posits a reinforcing recursive relationship between coordinated activity and a shared set of interpretations, organizational members with a diverse set of interpretations *can* in certain situations coordinate their activities— an organizational communication phenomenon described by Eisenberg (1986) as the "unified diversity." Indeed, Donnelon, Gray and Bougon (1986) found that group members were able to coordinate their activities in the absence of a shared set of interpretations by the process of developing equifinal interpretations. Interpretations are said to be equifinal if despite their differences, they lead to similar outcomes.

The arguments presented above indicate that cross-sectional hypotheses are inappropriate to test the adequacy of the proposed recursive model. Instead, consider the following four dynamic hypotheses:

1. The current level of coordinated activity between organizational members will be significantly influenced by their prior level of coordinated activity.

2. The current level of shared interpretations among organizational members will be significantly influenced by their prior level of shared interpretations.

3. Prior levels of coordinated activity between organizational members will influence their current level of shared interpretations, beyond that predicted by their prior levels of shared interpretations alone.

4. Prior levels of shared interpretations between organizational members will influence their current level of coordinated activity, beyond that predicted by their prior levels of coordinated activity alone.

The first and second hypotheses explicitly acknowledge that organizational processes are, in part, self-generating—a process referred to as *autocatalysis* or *self-referencing* by systems theorists (Eigen and Schuster 1979). The third hypothesis posits that variable x (coordinated activity) causes variable y (shared interpretations) in a dynamic context, if and only if, changes in variable x can predict changes in variable y above and beyond those predicted by past values of variable y. Likewise, the fourth hypothesis proposed variable y (shared interpretations) causes variable x (coordinated activity) in a dynamic context, if and only if, changes in variable y can predict changes in variable x above and beyond those predicted by past values of variable x. The definition of dynamic causality employed in the third and fourth hypotheses was first proposed by Granger (1980), and is referred to as *Granger causality*.

The above example serves to underscore the differences in knowledge claims made by cross-sectional and dynamic hypotheses. Notwithstanding its widespread currency, there is *no* substantive reason to believe that support, or lack thereof, for the cross-sectional hypothesis must be consistent with the corresponding dynamic knowledge claims. Indeed, Abell (1971, 2) proves mathematically that causal coefficients obtained from cross-sectional and dynamic knowledge claims would correspond if, and only if, the two variables are in "aggregate equilibrium" (p. 3). Two variables are in aggregate equilibrium if one of two conditions are valid: (i) there is no change over time in the level of coordinated activity *and* the level of shared interpretations, or (ii) the rates of change for the level of coordinated activity and shared interpretations are exactly equal. Both of these assumptions are unlikely to be valid, rarely made explicit, and almost never tested. Abell (1971, 3–4) notes that, "The ease with which correlations between variables are taken as significant parameters without any reason to suppose the variables have reached a joint equilibrium distribution is disturbing."

Like most communication theories, the structurational arguments being forwarded here are fundamentally of a processual nature—and must therefore lead to the test of dynamic knowledge claims. These arguments, therefore, do not offer an intellectual rationale to deduce and expect support for the cross-sectional hypothesis relating the amount of coordinated activity and shared interpretations. The arguments presented above do not discount the significance of cross-sectional research. Rather, they underscore intellectual differences in inferences gleaned from the examination of covariance across cases (such as, individuals) at one point in time, and the covariance across time (that is, change) for each case.

The tenuous connection between cross-sectional and dynamic knowledge claims have long been emphasized by social scientists (Coleman 1964). However, the early practitioners of traditional systems theory, many of who were social demographers interested in cross-sectional knowledge claims, invested considerable efforts in proposing and testing models that posited direct and indirect causal relationships among a large set of cross-sectional variables (Blalock 1960). Abbott (1988) notes that this investment of effort also resulted in the development and commodification (in canned computer packages, such as Statistical Package for Social Sciences SPSS) of sophisticated multivariate statistical techniques, ranging from regression analysis to structural equation modelling. Unfortunately, their efforts also led to the unquestioned deployment of these statistical techniques by researchers who were seeking to test process theories.

Mutual causality

With its emphasis on identifying contingencies, research conducted from a traditional systems framework typically hypothesized and tested unidirectional causal relationships from organizational antecedents to outcomes. However, unidirectional causal models are not appropriate to articulate and test process theories that explicitly posit circular relationships (Monge 1982). The concept of circular relationships has received considerable attention from contemporary systems theorists. Two elements that have a circular relationship are described as being *mutually causal*. Maruyama (1982) described different ways in which mutually causal "loops" can help preserve or change a system. In *cybernetic* systems, the two elements influence each other to preserve the system at some stable state. However, in *morphogenetic* systems, the two elements transform each other and thereby change the system. In the structurational example discussed above, a cybernetic explanation would be appropriate in situations where organizational members engage in stable patterns of coordinated activity guided by stable shared interpretations. In such situations, a departure from existing levels of coordinated activity would be viewed as an aberration, and members would be guided by their stable shared interpretations to reduce any future aberrations. In contrast, a morphogenetic framework would be more appropriate in explaining the emergence of new patterns of coordinated activity and the elaboration of new interpretations (Archer 1982).

Traditionally, functionalist researchers in organizational communication have avoided positing mutually causal relationships, in large part because they are confined to the logic of unidirectional causal modeling. For instance, following the example discussed earlier, structurational arguments explicitly acknowledge a circular relationship between members' coordinated activity and their shared interpretations. However, there have been very few attempts at developing dynamic models that explicate such mutually causal relationships (Erickson 1988; for preliminary work, see Abelson 1979; Coleman 1957).

Historicity

The logic of univariate causal modeling has also limited functionalist researchers' ability to adequately take into account the historicity of organizational communication procsesses. Historicity refers to the time-dependent nature of relationships among a set of variables. For instance, Abbot (1988, 173) notes that functionalist research "seldom take the position, common in historical writing, that 'at time *t*, *x* was important, while later, the conjuncture of things, made *y* more important'." Statements of this form are theoretically intuitive and have long constituted the bedrock of interactionist and ethnomethodological perspectives (Blumer 1956; Sacks, Schegloff, and Jefferson 1974).

In the terminology of systems theory, this problem can be traced to the flawed assumption of linearity in contemporary functionalist research. In a linear system, a unit change in the value of a variable *x* will always cause a specific change in the value of variable *y*. However, in nonlinear systems, the change in variable y resulting from a unit change in variable x will depend on the magnitude of variable x.

As discussed earlier, structurational arguments lead to the dynamic propositions that changes in coordinated activity among organizational members will influence their shared interpretations, and vice versa. In a linear system the magnitude of the mutually causal coefficients would be assumed to be constant. That is, regardless of their history, a unit change in organizational members' coordinated activity will always result in a specific change in their level of shared interpretations, and vice versa. This proposition is not consistent with process arguments nor is it borne out by empirical observations. For instance, several scholars have noted that the processual dynamics at the early stages of organizing are qualitatively different from later stages (Eisenhardt and Schoonhoven, 1990; Gersick 1988, 1991; Stinchcombe 1965). In a nonlinear system, the magnitude of the mutually causal coefficients will themselves vary depending on the existing and prior levels of coordinated activity and shared interpretations. Hence, using nonlinear systems models, it is possible to posit, for instance, that in cases where there is moderate coordinated activity among organizational members, a unit increase in the activity will result in a substantial increase in their shared interpretations; in cases where there is already a high level of coordinated activity among members, a unit increase in activity will have a smaller impact on their shared interpretations.

While, functionalist researchers have not generally hypothesized nonlinear models, there have been some attempts to capture the historicity of organizational processes using transfer function and autoregressive integrated moving average (ARIMA) models (Monge, Cozzen,sand Contractor 1992). These models allow variables to depend on their own past levels and on past random disturbances (Box and Jenkins 1976).

Time irreversibility

The phenomenon of time-irreversible effects have been discussed extensively in thermodynamics (Prigogine 1980) and electromagnetics, where it is referred to as "hysteresis." In general terms, it can be used to describe a wide range of organizational communication processes that take the following form: A unit increase in a variable x will result in an increase in variable y. However, a subsequent unit decrease in variable x will *not* result in a corresponding decrease in variable y.

Structurational arguments, discussed earlier, provide an example of the time irreversibility phenomenon. An increase in the level of coordinated activity among organizational members will influence their shared interpretations. However, it is plausible that organizational members will maintain these shared interpretations even if there is a modest reduction in their level of coordinated activity. Functionalist researchers have, as a rule, not articulated or tested hypotheses that capture this phenomenon (see Oliva, Day, and MacMillan 1988 for an exception). This is because of the implicit assumption in the logic of unidirectional causal modeling that if an increase in variable x results in an increase in variable y, it must follow that a decrease in variable x will always result in a corresponding decrease in variable y.

The phenomenon of time irreversibility, like the notion of historicity discussed earlier, is a characteristic of nonlinear systems and entered the mainstream of systems discourse with the emergence of catastrophe theory (Thom 1975; Zeeman 1977) As mentioned earlier, the magnitude of the mutually causal relationships between variables x and y in a nonlinear system are *not* assumed to be constant. Rather, the magnitude of the causal coefficient varies as a function of the existing and prior levels of the variables. In cases where time-irreversible effects occur, the magnitude of the causal relationships are determined not only by the prior levels of the variables, but also the *direction* in which they are changing, that is, if they are increasing or decreasing. For instance, the causal effect of x on y will have one magnitude if x is increasing, and a different magnitude if x is decreasing.

Discontinuity

In the introduction to this chapter, discontinuous changes were identified as one of the intriguing phenomena observed in contemporary organizations. The term discontinuity is used to characterize sudden qualitative change in the emergence of an organizational process— a discontinuous change in one variable resulting from a continuous change in another variable. In its simplest form, a discontinuity can be used to describe organizational processes that take the following form: "In cases where a variable x is below a certain threshold level, a unit change in variable x has a certain effect on variable y. At values higher than the threshold level, a unit change in variable x has a qualitatively different effect (or no effect whatsoever) on y." The threshold level of x represents the point of discontinuity, sometimes referred to as a bifurcation point (Thom 1972).

Such a discontinuity can occur in the relationship between organizational members' coordinated activity and their shared interpretations. A modest decrease in the level of shared interpretations can prompt organizational members to *increase* their level of coordinated activity—with the expectation that this increase in activity would reduce their differences in interpretation. However, if the decrease in the level of shared interpretations crossed a threshold level, members would, in frustration, drastically *reduce* their level of coordinated activity. A study conducted by Schachter (1951) points to a similar discontinuity in the causal relationship between agreement among individuals and their interpersonal communication. Schachter found that a modest level of disagreement among students in a dormitory prompted them to *increase* their communication with one another— but only to a point. If the disagreement among individuals increased beyond this point, individuals chose to drastically *reduce* their communication with one another.

The systematic study of "discontinuities" from a systems perspective was first articulated by catastrophe theorists (Thom 1972; Zeeman 1977). Catastrophe theory developed a formal model to describe discontinuous changes in a system from one state to another. For instance, Flay (1978) applied catastrophic models to explicate Fishbein and Ajzen's (1975) theory relating attitude and behavior. Flay (1978) employed a catastrophe model to specify conditions under which minimal changes in individuals' attitudes could result in sudden discontinuous changes in their behavior.

Prigogine (1980) proposed a more general form of discontinuity. It extended the concept of discontinuity to include sudden shifts between random behavior and systematic patterns. Thus, according to Prigogine (1980), a discontinuity marks a point where a system of variables that exhibit random behavior are transformed into self-organized systematic patterns.

The phenomenon of discontinuity, like historicity and time-irreversibility, can only be articulated and tested in nonlinear systems models. Not surprisingly functionalist research have neglected examining the nature of discontinuities in organizational processes. Unlike historicity and time irreversibility, discontinuity as conceptualized by Prigogine (1980) only occurs in nonlinear systems that are "far-from-equilibrium." A system is defined as being "far-from-equilibrium" when (i) it imports a large amount of energy from outside the system, (ii) uses the energy to help renew its *own* structures, a process referred to as "autopoeisis" (Varela, Maturana, and Uribe 1974) and (iii) expels, rather than accumulates, the accruing disorder (entropy) back into the environment.

It is important to distinguish between the traditional notion of an "open" system and a "far-from-equilibrium" system. In both cases, the system transacts energy and/or information with the environment. In the case of traditional "open" systems, the energy and information drawn from the environment is used to keep the system at a desired equilibrium state. Thus the order in traditional "open" systems refers to the stable configuration of various structures within the system. However, in "far-from-equilibrium" systems, energy and information are drawn to keep the system in a state of ongoing flux. At a point of discontinuity, this flux takes on an ordered pattern. Thus the order in "far-from-equilibrium" systems, termed " *process structure*" (Jantsch 1980a, 21), refers to the stable patterns associated with the dynamics within the system. Prigogine (1980) suggests that the shift in interest from traditional "open" systems to "far-from-equilibrium" systems reflects a shift in intellectual interests from questions about "being" to questions about "becoming"—a transition reflected in recent organizational scholarship.

Summary

This chapter began with the observation that, in the past decade, there has been widespread disenchantment with the application of traditional systems theory to the study of organizational communication. This section has described five classes of organizational phenomena that are consistent with many of the arguments proposed in process theories, but have been virtually ignored by functionalist research in the area of organizational communication. *Contemporary,* in contrast to traditional, systems perspectives, offer a vocabulary to precisely conceptualize these phenomena. It therefore seems appropriate for scholars to reevaluate the utility of systems perspectives in the study of organizational communication. The next section describes the theoretical assumptions and requirements of one of the most influential systems perspectives to emerge in the past decade—self-organizing systems theory.

Theoretical requirements for self-organizing

Broadly speaking, self-organizing systems theory seeks to explain the emergence of patterned behavior in systems that are initially in a state of disorganization. From the start of this century, researchers in many of the physical and life sciences had observed that systems initially in a state of disorganization (high entropy) would under certain conditions *spontaneously* demonstrate patterned behavior.

In 1900, the French physicist Henri Benard reported that heating a thin layer of liquid wedged between two glass plates can cause organization to appear in the form of a honeycomb consisting of hexagonal cells of convecting liquid. In the early 1950s, Belousov, a biophysicist at the Soviet Ministry of Health, and a fellow Russian Zhabotinsky were studying how enzymes helped the body's metabolic processes. While studying a set of chemical reactions they noticed that as they continued to add reactancts and agitate the mixture, the solution started to oscillate between being colorless and of a yellow hue. The oscillations were extremely stable and the reaction was dubbed as a "chemical clock." Both of these studies were perceived by the scientific community as curiosities. After all, the laws of thermodynamics predicted that the addition of energy to a system should *increase* the system's state of disorder.

Starting in the late 1950s, systematic investigations into the processes of self-organization were undertaken by Ilya Prigogine and his colleagues at the Free University of Brussels and Heinz von Foerster and his colleagues at the Biological Computer Laboratory at the University of Illinois (Jantsch 1980a). The critical breakthrough occurred when Prigogine and his colleagues mathematically derived four key features that were common to all systems that exhibited the emergence of spontaneous order (Glansdorff and Prigogine 1971):

1. At least one of the components in the system must exhibit autocatalysis.

2. At least two of the components in the system must be mutually causal.

3. The system must be open to the environment with respect to the exchange of energy and matter.

4. The system must operate in a far-from-equilibrium condition.

Prigogine and his colleagues mathematically proved that these four characteristics were necessary, but not sufficient, theoretical requirements for a system to self-organize. Further, Prigogine mathematically deduced that the emergence of spontaneous order was *not* theoretically inconsistent with principles of nonequilibrium thermodynamics—a landmark accomplishment that earned him the Noble Prize in 1977 (for technical discussions of self-organizing systems theory, see Nicolis and Prigogine 1977, 1989; Prigogine 1980; Schieve and Allen 1982; for nontechnical overviews, see Briggs and Peat 1989; Coveney and Highfield 1990; Jantsch, 1980b; Prigogine and Stengers 1984).

During the past decade, the notion of self-organizing systems have galvanized scholars interested in a wide range of issues. Researchers have drawn on self-organizing systems theory to describe heart rhythms (Noble 1979; Glass and Mackey 1988), creation of biological shapes (Meinhardt 1982), population dynamics among species (May 1976), the epidemiological spread of diseases (Schaffer, Olsen, Truty, and Fulmer 1990), the physiology of perception (Freeman 1991), the psychology of optimal experiences (Csikszentmihalyi 1990; Eisenberg 1990), strategies for collective action in social systems (Garfinkel 1987), cultural evolution (Loye and Eisler 1987), the dynamic evolution of urban centers (Allen and Sanglier 1980), the redistribution of wealth across nations (Gierer 1980), the evolution of economies (Boldrin 1990; Radzicki 1990), the pattern of business cycles (Sayers 1990), the dynamics of international security (Grossman and Mayer-Kress 1989; Mayer-Kress 1990; Saperstein 1990), the emergence of civilizations (Iberall 1987), theories on the evolution of life (Gould 1987; Dawkins 1987), the "Gaia" theory of earth as a living system (Lovelock 1979, 1990; Margulis and Sagan 1986), and the design of self-organizing technological networks (Bellman and Roosta 1987).

In addition, there have been calls for the application of self-organizing perspectives in management (Malik and Probst 1984; von Foerster 1984); organizational change (Ford and Backoff 1988; Gersick 1991; Goldstein 1988), the appropriation of new communication technologies (Contractor and Seibold 1993), communication and societal development (Braman, in press; Krippendorf 1987), communication and cultural evolution (Kincaid 1987), and mass communication technologies and society (Batra 1990). The theory of self-organizing has also caught the attention of humanists. Hayles (1990, 291) investigating the parallels between postmodernism and the theory of self-organizing systems, notes that they share a "a deeply ingrained ambivalence toward totalizing structures!" The next section provides an example of how structurational arguments to study the emergence of shared meaning in organizations can be articulated in a self-organizing systems framework.

Explicating a theory in a self-organizing systems framework

The first two of the four dynamic hypotheses, presented earlier in this chapter, proposed that organizational members' coordinated activity and their shared interpretations are, in part, self-generating. The third and fourth hypotheses proposed mutually causal relationships between members' coordinated activity and their shared interpretations. This section begins by casting these hypotheses in a self-organizing systems framework.

(i) Shared interpretations (*Shared Interp*) are sustained and developed among organizational members who coordinate their activity (*Coord. Act.*).

$$K_1$$

Coord. Act. + *Shared Interp* $\Rightarrow$ Increase in *Shared Interp*   (1)

(ii) Coordinated activity (*Coord. Act.*) is sustained and developed among organizational members who share their interpretations (*Shared Interp.*).

$$K_2$$

Coord. Act. + *Shared Interp* $\Rightarrow$ Increase in *Coord. Act.*   (2)

where, K_1 and K_2, the nonlinear causal coefficients, are referred to as the system's parameters.

According to self-organizing systems theory, the underlying logics described in equations 1 and 2 do *not,* by themselves, meet the four theoretical requirements necessary to describe the emergent processes suggested by structurational arguments. This is because, equations (1) and (2) meet only two of the four theoretical requirements for self-organizing. In equation (1), shared interpretation among organizational members is hypothesized to reproduce itself, while in equation (2) coordinated activity is hypothesized to reproduce itself. These two hypotheses meet the requirement of *autocatalysis.* Further, equations (1) and (2) indicate a *mutually causal relationship* between coordinated activity and shared interpretation among individuals, meeting the requirement of mutual causality. However, equations (1) and (2) do not met the third and fourth theoretical requirements for self-organizing. The equations do not specify how the system is *open* to the environment; further, the equations do not specify the mechanisms under which the system can operate in a *far-from-equilibrium* condition.

In terms of organizational theory, the underlying logics offer an incomplete characterization, because they do not explicitly posit that demand and supply from the organization's environment provide the rationale for members' coordinated activity. Even though this observation is not inconsistent with structurational arguments, it has not been explicitly discussed by theorists as a key element of the underlying logics of change. Equation (3), below, is one attempt at responding to this limitation. Specifically, it posits that material and symbolic resources from the organization's environment (*Environmental Resources*) influence the levels of coordinated activity (*Coord. Act.*) among organizational members.

$$K_3$$

$$Environmental\ Resources \Rightarrow Coord.\ Act. \tag{3}$$

where, K_3, a nonlinear causal coefficient, is a system parameter.

The three equations offer one possible representation of the underlying logics of change that are based on structurational arguments *and* meet the theoretical requirements of a self-organizing systems model. As mentioned in the previous section, the four theoretical requirements for self-organizing articulated by Glansdorff and Prigogine (1971) are necessary, but not sufficient conditions. This implies that the underlying logics described in the three equations do not ensure the emergence of a self-organized meaning system. Rather, they describe the "design of the playing field and the rules of the game," while the emergent patterns that may arise from these logics might be "compared loosely to a game in play" (Gersick 1991, 16).

Even though the system is relatively simple—three variables (coordinated activity, shared interpretations, and environmental resources) in three equations—it is well nigh impossible for any human to mentally construe the wide variety of long-term dynamics that can be generated by the underlying logic (Poole 1990). Further, because the system of equations are nonlinear, they do not, as a rule, have closed form solutions and are therefore not analytically tractable. However, recent developments in computational science make it possible to use simulations as a tool to observe the long-term dynamics implied by the proposed underlying logics. Simulations help the researcher add precision to the verbal descriptions of the underlying logics in three areas.

First, verbal descriptions of the structurational process posit that coordinated activity and shared interpretations influence each other in a recursive process. In the self-organizing model proposed here, these influences are represented by the system parameters (the nonlinear causal coefficients, K_1, K_2, and K_3). Due to the lack of precision in the verbal formulation, a researcher can only make an educated guess on the nature of these coefficients. Simulations help the researcher examine if, and how, changes in the specification of the system's parameters will qualitatively alter the structurational processes.

Second, verbal descriptions of the structurational process do not offer precise predictions of how the initial levels of coordinated activity, shared interpretations, and environmental resources would influence the self–organizing process. Simulations help the researcher explore transient and long-term effects, if any, of these initial conditions.

Third, though verbal descriptions of the structurational process suggest that the dynamics of coordinated activity and shared interpretations display the effects of historicity, time irreversibility, and discontinuity, they do not offer specific conditions for their occurrence. Simulations provide the researcher an opportunity to precisely identify conditions under which the dynamics implied by the underlying logics would display historicity, time irreversibility, and discontinuity.

The information obtained in these three areas will help researchers deduce precise hypotheses about the transient and long-term dynamics implied by the proposed underlying logics of change. Empirical support for these hypotheses would indicate that the self-organizing system reformulation of the structurational arguments were not falsified. Notice that the goal is to deduce hypotheses based on the observation of *qualitative* changes in the long-term dynamics, not to make numeric predictions about the level of coordinated activity or shared interpretations among organizational members. Hence, the absolute values of the parameters used in the simulation are not in and of themselves consequential. Using simulations to help social scientists better comprehend and appreciate the process structures implied by the proposed underlying logics was first proposed by Forrester (1973) and more recently advocated by Hanneman (1988) and Poole (1990). It represents the use of simulation for theory building, as compared to its conventional use in the physical sciences for model predictions and forecasting.

It must be emphasized that the model described above, while illustrating the process by which structuration theory can be reformulated in terms of a self-organizing system, is exceedingly simplified. Two limitations warrant special mention. *First,* the equations imply that the set of coordinated activities and shared interpretations are treated homogeneously. That is, shared interpretations on issue A are assumed to have the same influence as shared interpretations on issue B. Likewise, coordination on activities P and Q are considered to have the same impact on the self-organizing process. While this assumption helps simplify the illustration above, it is inconsistent with the tenets of structuration theory, and must be discarded in any rigorous implementation of the self-organizing systems model. *Second,* the model illustrated above is wholly deterministic and does not allow for external random disturbances. This simplifying assumption is problematic on two counts. It violates our social sensibilities of naturally occurring systems. More importantly, from a self-organizing systems framework, the absence of external random variations imply that the model can only describe the persistence or change in shared interpretations and activity. It precludes the ability to model the emergence or elaboration of new interpretations or activity.

Conclusion

There is widespread consensus that traditional systems theory failed to realize its promise as an appropriate framework for the study of organizational communication. There are intellectual as well as pragmatic reasons that contributed to this failure. In this chapter I have described many of the *intellectual* shortcomings of traditional systems theory. In many instances, these shortcomings were first brought to the attention of the field by interpretive and critical researchers. Their conceptual contributions have motivated proponents of systems perspectives to reexamine the theoretical assumptions of traditional systems theory. In retrospect, traditional systems theory was appropriate in understanding how to stabilize and control systems with a large number of components. This made it very useful in the domain of technology. However, it proved less useful to scholars who were interested in examining process structures in systems where equilibrium was not a desirable goal.

The self-organizing systems perspective outlined in this chapter has the potential of renewing interest in systems approaches to the study of organizational communication. More importantly, and perhaps more controversially, it bears the promise of building on insights gained from contemporary interpretive and critical research. Many of the central concepts in interpretive-critical research (such as intersubjectivity, structure, production and reproduction, symbolic convergence, and interpretive schemes) are richly evocative but highly abbreviated verbal descriptions that are inadequate both in defining the concepts and articulating their interrelationships. Poole (1990) characterizes this as the interpretive-critical version of a "reductionist" problem. Contemporary systems perspectives, such as self-organizing systems theory, offer the vocabulary and the mechanisms to add precision to many of the concepts and relationships of interest to interpretive-critical research.

In closing, it is also instructive to review some of the *pragmatic* issues that contributed to the failed promise of traditional systems theory. When it was first introduced, many researchers in organizational communication embraced the systems metaphor in their work. However, as Poole (1990, 6) notes, "Most often, systems theory became a metaphor, rather than an instrument of analysis." In a review of social science systems models, Berlinksi (1976) observed that several of them lacked precision and tended to use systems terminology in a ceremonial way.

One potential reason for this lack of precision was the lack of easily accessible computational resources. This obstacle has been overcome in the past decade, with the development of several easy-to-use simulation and modeling programs for the personal computer including DYNAMO (Richardson and Pugh 1981), STELLA (Richmond and Peterson 1990) and MATHEMATICA (Wolfram 1992).

Another potential reason for the ceremonial use of systems concepts may be due to researchers' lack of training in systems methodology. As Poole (1990, 17) observes, "Communication researchers must grapple with modelling software, learn the necessary mathematics and computer languages, and struggle with shaping the formalisms to our needs." It would be a tragedy if the intellectual promise of contemporary systems perspectives in the study of organizational communication were stymied because of our inability to overcome these pragmatic hurdles.

References

Abell, P. 1971. *Model building in sociology.* London: Widenfeld & Nicolson.

Abelson, R. P. 1979. Social clusters and opinion clusters. In *Perspectives on social networks research*, ed. P. W. Holland and S. Leinhardt. New York: Academic Press.

Abbott, A. 1988. Transcending general linear reality. *Sociological Theory,* 6:169–186

Allen, P. M., and M. Sanglier. 1980. Order by fluctuation and the urban system. In *Autopoiesis, dissipative structures and spontaneous social orders,* ed. M. Zeleny. Boulder, CO: Westview Press.

Archer, M. S. 1982. Morphogenesis versus structuration: On combining structure and action. *British Journal of Sociology* 33:455–83.

Barley, S. R. 1986. Technology as an occasion for structuring: observations on CT Scanners and the social order of radiology departments. *Administrative Science Quarterly,* 31, 78–108.

Barley, S. R. 1990. Images of imaging: Notes on doing longitudinal field work. Organization Science 1:220–47.

Batra, N. D. 1990. A self-renewing society: The role of television and communications technology. Lanham, MD: University Press of America.

Bellman, R., and R. Roosta. 1987. On a class of self-organizing communication networks. In Self-organizing systems: The emergence of order, ed. F. Yates. New York: Plenum Press.

Berlinski, D. 1976. On systems theory. Cambridge, MA: MIT Press.

Bertalanffy, L. von 1968. General system theory: Foundations, development, applications. New York: Brazillier.

Blalock, H. M. 1960. Social statistics. New York: McGraw-Hill.

Blumer, H. 1956. Sociological analysis and the 'variable.' American Sociological Review 21:683–90.

Boldrin, M. 1990. Dynamic competitive equilibria and chaos. In The Ubiquity of Chaos, ed. P. Krasner. Washington, DC: American Association for the Advancement of Science.

Box, G. E. P., and G. M. Jenkins. 1976. Time series analysis. San Francisco: Jossey-Bass.

Braman, S. (in press). Entering chaos: Designing the state in the information age. In Civil society and information society, ed. S. Splickel, A. Calabrese, and C. Sparks. New York: Ablex.

Briggs, J., and F. D. Peat. 1989. Turbulent mirror: An illustrated guide to chaos theory and the science of wholeness. New York: Harper & Row.

Burns, T., and G. M. Stalker. 1961. The management of innovation. London: Tavistock.

Coleman, J. S. 1957. Community conflict. Glencoe, IL: Free Press.

———. 1964. Introduction to mathematical sociology. New York: Free Press.

Contractor, N. S., and M. C. Ehrlich. 1993. Strategic ambiguity in the birth of a loosely coupled organization: The case of the "$50 million experiment." Management Communication Quarterly 6:251–281

Contractor, N. S., and E. M. Eisenberg. 1990. Communication networks and new media in organizations. In Organizations and communication technology, ed. C. Steinfield and J. Fulk. Newbury Park CA: Sage.

Contractor, N. S., and D. R. Seibold. 1993. Theoretical frameworks for the study of structuring processes in group decision support systems: Adaptive structuration theory and self-organizing systems theory. Human Communication Research 19:528–63.

Coveney, P., and R. Highfield. 1990. *The arrow of time: A voyage through science to solve time's greatest mystery.* New York: Fawcett Columbine.

Csikszentmihalyi, M. 1990. *Flow: The psychology of optimal experience.* New York: Harper/Collins.

Davis, S. M. 1987. *Future perfect.* New York: Addison-Wesley.

Davis, S., and B. Davidson. 1991. *2020 Vision.* New York: Simon & Schuster.

Dawkins, R. 1987. *The blind watchmaker.* New York: Norton.

Donnelon, A., Grey, B., and Bongon, M. 1986. Communication, meaning, and organized action. Administrative Science Directory, 31: 43–55.

Eigen, M., and P. Schuster. 1979. *The hypercycle: A principle of natural self-organization.* New York: Springer.

Eisenberg, E. M. 1984. Ambiguity as strategy in organizational communication. *Communication Monographs* 51:227–42.

———. 1986. Meaning and interpretation in organizations. *Quarterly Journal of Speech* 72:88–97.

———. 1990. Jamming: Transcendence through organizing. *Communication Research* 17:139–64

Eisenhardt, K. M., and C. B. Schoonhoven. 1990. Organizational growth: Linking founding team, strategy, environment and growth among U.S. semiconductor ventures (1978–1988). *Administrative Science Quarterly* 35:504–29.

Erickson, B. 1988. The relational basis of attitudes. In *Social structures: A network approach,* ed. B. Wellman and S. Berkowitz. New York: Cambridge University Press.

Ferguson, M. 1980. *The Aquarian conspiracy: Personal and social transformation in our time.* Los Angeles: Tarcher.

Fishbein, M., and I. Ajzen. 1975. *Belief, attitude, intentions and behavior: An introduction to theory and research.* Reading, MA: Addison-Wesley.

Flay, B. R. 1978. Catastrophe theory in social psychology: Some applications to attitudes and social behavior. *Behavioral Science* 23:335–50.

Ford, J. D., and R. H. Backoff. 1988. Organizational change in and out of dualities and paradox. In *Paradox and Transformation: Towards a theory of change in organization and management,* ed. R. E. Quinn and K. S. Cameron. Cambridge, MA: Ballinger.

Forrester, J. W. 1973. *World dynamics.* Cambridge, MA: MIT Press.

Freeman, W. J. 1991. The physiology of perception. *Scientific American* 264:78–85.

Garfinkel, A. 1987. The slime mold dictyostelium as a model of self-organization in social systems. In *Self-organizing systems: The emergence of order,* ed. F. E. Yates. New York: Plenum Press.

Gersick, C. J. 1988. Time and transition in work teams: Toward a new model of group development. *Academy of Management Journal* 31: 9–41.

———. 1991. Revolutionary change theories: A multilevel exploration of the punctuated equilibrium paradigm. *Academy of Management Review* 16:10–36.

Giddens, A. 1984. *The constitution of society.* Berkeley, CA: University of California Press.

Gierer, A. 1980. Socioeconomic inequalities: Effects of self-enhancement and depletion. In *Autopoiesis, dissipative structures, and spontaneous social orders,* ed. M. Zeleny. Boulder, CO: Westview Press.

Glansdorff, P., and I. Prigogine. 1971. *Thermodynamic study of structure, stability and fluctuations.* New York: Wiley.

Glass, L., and M. Mackey. 1988. *From clocks to chaos: The rhythms of life.* Princeton, NJ: Princeton University Press.

Goffman, E. 1959. *Presentation of self in everday life.* New York: Anchor.

Goffman, E. 1983. The interaction order. *American Sociological Review,* 48, 1–17

Goldstein, J. 1988. A far-from-equilibrium systems approach to resistance to change. *Organizational Dynamics,* 17:16–76.

Gould, S. J. 1987. Is a new general theory of evolution emerging? In *Self-organizing systems: The emergence of order,* ed. F. E. Yakes. New York: Plenum Press.

Granger, C. W. J. 1980. Testing for causality. *Journal of Economic Dynamics & Control* 2:329–52

Gray, B., M. Bougon, and A. Donnelon. 1985. Organizations as constructions and deconstructions of meaning. *Journal of Management* 11: 83–98.

Grossman, S., and G. Mayer-Kress. 1989. Chaos in the international arms race. *Nature* 337:701–05.

Handy, C. 1990. *The age of unreason.* London: Arrow.

Hanneman, R. A. 1988. *Computer-assisted theory building: Modeling dynamic social systems.* Beverly Hills, CA: Sage.

Hayles, N. K. 1990. *Chaos bound: Orderly disorder in contemporary literature and science.* London: Cornell University Press.

Iberall, A. S. 1987. On rivers. In *Self-organizing systems: The emergence of order,* ed. F. E. Yates. New York: Plenum Press.

Jantsch, E. 1980a. *The self-organizing universe: Scientific and human implications of the emerging paradigm of evolution.* New York: Pergamon.

————. 1980b. The unifying paradigm behind autopoiesis, dissipative structures, hyper- and ultracycles. In *Autopoiesis, dissipative structures and spontaneous social orders*, ed. M. Zeleny. Boulder, CO: Westview Press.

Kast, E., and J. E. Rosenzweig. 1973. *Contingency views of organization and management.* Chicago: Social Research Associates.

Katz, D., and R. L. Kahn. 1978. *The social psychology of organizations.* New York: Wiley.

Kincaid, D. L. 1987. The convergence theory of communication, self-organization and cultural evolution. In *Communication theory: Eastern and Western perspectives*, ed. D. L. Kincaid. San Diego, CA: Academic Press.

Krippendorf, K. 1987. Paradigms for communication and development with emphasis on autopoiesis. In *Communication theory: Eastern and Western perspectives*, ed. D.L.Kincaid. San Diego, CA: Academic Press.

Lawrence, P. R., and J. W. Lorsch. 1967. Differentiation and integration in complex organizations. *Administrative Science Quarterly* 12:1–47.

Lovelock, J. E. 1979. *Gaia: A new look at life on earth.* New York: Oxford University Press.

————. 1990. *The ages of Gaia: A biography of our living earth.* New York: Bantam.

Loye, D., and R. Eisler. 1987. Chaos and transformation: Implications of non-equilibrium theory for social science and society. *Behavioral Science* 32:53–65.

Malik, F., and G. Probst. 1984. Evolutionary management. In *Self-organization and management of social systems: Insights, promises, doubts, and questions*, ed. H. Ulrich and G. J. B. Probst. Berlin: Springer-Verlag.

Maryulis, L., and Sagen, D. 1986. Microcosmos. New York: Summit Books.

Maruyama, M. 1982. Four different causal metatypes in biological and social sciences. In *Self-organization and dissipative structures: Applications in the physical and social sciences*, ed. W. C. Schieve and P. M. Allen. Austin: University of Texas Press.

Maturana, H. R. 1980. Autopoiesis: reproduction, heredity and evolution. In *Autopoiesis, dissipative structures and spontaneous social orders*, ed. M. Zeleny. Boulder, CO: Westview Press.

May, R. M. 1976. Simple mathematical models with very complicated dynamics. *Nature* 261:459.

Mayer-Kress, G. 1990. A nonlinear dynamical systems approach to international security. In *The ubiquity of chaos*, ed. P. Krasner. Washington, DC: AAAS Press.

Meinhardt, H. 1982. *Models of behavioral pattern formation.* London: Academic Press.

Miller, D., and P. M. Friesen. 1984. The longitudinal analysis of organizations: A methodological perspective. *Management Science* 28: 1013–34.

Miller, G. 1978. *Living systems*. New York: McGraw-Hill.

Mohr, L. B. 1982. *Explaining organizational behavior: The limits and possibilities of theory and research*. San Francisco: Jossey-Bass.

Monge, P. R. 1977. The systems perspective as a theoretical basis for the study of human communication. *Communication Quarterly* 25:19–29.

———. 1982. Systems theory and research in the study of organizational communication: The correspondence problem. *Human Communication Research* 8:245–61.

Monge, P. R., M. D. Cozzens, and N. S. Contractor. 1992. Communication and motivational predictors of the dynamics of innovation. *Organization Science* 2:1–25.

Monge, P. R., and E. M. Eisenberg, 1987. Emergent communication networks. In F. M. Jablin, L. L. Putnam, K. H. Roberts, and L. W. Porter (Eds.) *Handbook of Organizational Communication* (pp. 304–342). Newbury Park, CA: Sage.

Monge, P. R., R. V. Farace, E. M. Eisenberg, K. I. Miller, and L. L. White. 1984. The process of studying process in organizational communication. *Journal of Communication* 34:22–43.

Morgan, G. 1986. *Images and organization*. Beverly Hills, CA: Sage.

Newcomb, T. M. 1953. An approach to the study of communicative acts. *Psychological Review* 60:393–404.

———. 1956. The prediction of interpersonal attraction. *American Psychologist* 11: 575–87.

Nicolis, G., and I. Prigogine. 1977. *Self-organization in non-equilibrium systems*. New York: Wiley.

———. 1989. *Exploring complexity*. New York: Freeman.

Noble, D. 1979. *The initiation of the heart beat*. London: Oxford University Press.

Oliva, T. A., D. L. Day, and I. C. MacMillan. 1988. A generic model of competitive dynamics. *Academy of Management Review*, 13:374–89.

Peters, T. 1987. *Thriving on chaos*. New York: Harper & Row.

Pettigrew, A. M. 1985. *The awakening giant: Continuity and change in ICI*. Oxford: Blackwell.

———. 1990. Longitudinal field research on change: Theory and practice. *Organization Science* 1:267–92.

Pfeffer, J., and G. R. Salancik. 1978. *The external control of organizations*. New York: Harper & Row.

Pondy, L., P. Frost, G. Morgan, and T. Dandridge. (eds.). 1983. *Organizational symbolism.* Greenwich, CT: JAI Press.

Pondy, L., and I. I. Mitroff. 1979. Beyond open systems models of organization. In *Research in organizational behavior,* vol. 1., ed. L. L. Cummings and B. M. Staw. Greenwich, CT: JAI Press.

Poole, M. S. 1990. *A Turn of the wheel: The case for a renewal of systems inquiry in organizational communication research.* Paper presented at the Arizona State University Conference on Organizational Communication, Tempe, AZ, February 1990.

Poole, M. S., and G. DeSanctis. 1990. Understanding the use of group decision support systems: The theory of adaptive structuration. In *Organizations and communication technology,* ed. C. Steinfield and J. Fulk. Newbury Park, CA: Sage.

Prigogine, I. 1980. *From being to becoming: Time and complexity in the physical sciences.* New York: Freeman.

Prigogine, I., and I. Stengers. 1984. *Order out of chaos: Man's new dialogue with nature.* New York: Bantam.

Putnam, L. L. 1983. The interpretive perspective: An alternative to functionalism. In *Communication and organizations: An interpretive perspective,* ed. L. L. Putnam and M. Pacanowsky. Beverly Hills: Sage.

Putnam, L. L., and M. E. Pacanowsky (eds.). 1983. *Communication and organizations: An interpretive approach.* Beverly Hills, CA: Sage.

Radzicki, M. 1990. Institutional dynamics, deterministic chaos, and self-organizing systems. *Journal of Economic Issues* 24:57–103.

Ranson, S., C. R. Hinings, and R. Greenwood. 1980. The structuring of organization structures. *Administrative Science Quarterly* 25:1–18.

Rice, A. K. 1958. *Productivity and social organization: The Ahmedabad experiment.* London: Tavistock.

Richardson, G. P., and A. L. Pugh. 1981. *Introduction to system dynamics modeling with DYNAMO.* Cambridge: MIT Press.

Richmond, B., and S. Peterson. 1990. *STELLA II user's guide* (Computer program manual). Hanover, NH: High Performance Systems.

Riley, P. 1983. A structurationist account of political culture. *Administrative Science Quarterly* 28:414–37.

Sacks, H., E. A. Schegloff, and G. Jefferson. 1974. A simplest systematics for turntaking in conversation. *Language* 50:696–735.

Saperstein, A. M. 1990. Chaos and the making of international security policy. In *The ubiquity of chaos,* ed. P. Krasner. Washington, DC: American Association for the Advancement of Science.

Sayers, C. 1990. Chaos and the business cycle. In *The ubiquity of chaos,* ed. P. Krasner. Washington, DC: American Association for the Advancement of Science.

Schachter, S. 1951. Deviation, rejection, and communication. *Journal of Abnormal Social Psychology* 46:190–207.

Schaffer, W. M., L. F. Olson, G. L. Truty, and S. L. Fulmer. 1990. The case for chaos in childhood epidemics. In *The ubiquity of chaos,* ed. P. Krasner. Washington, DC: American Association for the Advancement of Science.

Schieve, W. C., and P. M. Allen. 1982. *Self-organization and dissipative structures.* Austin: University of Texas Press.

Sheldon, A. 1980. Organizational paradigms: A theory of organizational change. *Organizational Dynamics, 9* 61–80.

Smircich, L. 1983. Studying organizations as cultures. In *Beyond method: Strategies for social research,* ed. G. Morgan. Beverly Hills, CA: Sage.

Stinchcombe, A. 1965. Social structure and organizations. In *Handbook of organizations,* ed. J. March. Chicago: Rand McNally.

Thom, R. 1975. *Structural stability and morphogenesis.* Reading, MA: Benjamin.

Tornatsky, L. G., J. D. Eveland, M. G. Boylan, W. A. Hetzner, E. C. Johnson, D. Roltman, and J. Schneider. 1983. *The process of technological innovation: Reviewing the literature.* Washington, DC: National Science Foundation.

Trist, E. L., and K. W. Bamforth. 1951. Some social psychological consequences of the Longwall method of coal getting. *Human Relations,* 4:3–38.

Tuckman, B. 1965. Developmental sequences in small groups. *Psychological Bulletin* 63:384–99.

Tushman, M. L., and P. Anderson. 1986. Technological discontinuities and organizational environments. *Administrative Science Quarterly* 31:439–65.

Tushman, M. L., and E. Romanelli, 1985. Organizational evolution: A metamorphosis model of conveyence and reorientation. In L. L. Cummings and B. M. Staw (Eds.), *Research in organizational behavior* (vol. 7, pp. 171–222). Greenwich, CT: JAI Press.

Van de Ven, A., and M. S. Poole. 1990. Methods for studying innovation development in the Minnesota innovation research program. *Organization Science* 1:313–35.

Van Maanen, J., and E. Schein. 1979. Toward a theory of organizational socialization. In *Research in organizational behavior,* vol. 1, ed. B. Staw and L. Cummings. Greenwich, CT: JAI Press.

Varela, F. G., H. Maturana, and R. Uribe. 1974. Autopoiesis: The organization of living systems, its characterization and a model. *Bio Systems 5.*

Von Foerster, H. 1984. Principles of self-organization—in a socio-managerial context. In *Self-organization and management of social systems: Insights, promises, doubts, and questions,* ed. H. Ulrich and G. J. B. Probst. Berlin: Springer-Verlag.

Weick, K. 1979. *The social psychology of organizing.* 2nd ed. Reading, MA: Addison-Wesley.

Wiener, N. 1954. *The human use of human beings: Cybernetics and society.* New York: DeCapo.

Wolfram, S. 1992. Mathematica: A system for doing mathematics by computer. 2nd ed. Reading, MA: Addison–Wesley.

Woodward, J. 1965. *Industrial organization: Theory and practice.* Oxford: Oxford University Press.

Yates, J., and W. J. Orlikowski. 1992. Genres of organizational communication: An approach to studying communication and media. *Academy of Management Review* 17:299–326.

Zeeman, E. C. 1977. *Catastrophe theory: Selected papers, 1972–1977.* Reading, MA: Addison-Wesley.

Zeleny, M. 1980. Autopoiesis: A paradigm lost? In *Autopoiesis, dissipative structures and spontaneous social orders,* ed. M. Zeleny. Boulder, CO: Westview Press.

YANAN JU

3 Supremacy of Human Relationships: A Japanese Organizational Model

Western interest in the Japanese organizational management and communication philosophies and models has very much been generated by the remarkable economic success of Japan over the last two decades or so (see, for example, Vogel 1979; Pascale and Athos 1981; Ouchi 1981; Whitley 1990). Abegglen and Stalk (1985) note that most of the explanations of the Japanese success come from one of two basic theories, benign conspiracy and sinister conspiracy. The benign conspiracy theory attributes the success of the Japanese to such factors as cultural homogeneity, a nonconfrontational mode of communication, participative decision-making, workers' commitment to their jobs, and paternalistic corporate cultures. The sinister conspiracy theory, which has recently become popular, claims that "the Japanese government, corporations, and groups cooperate closely to further their shared interests," and "these shared interests are conspiring to achieve worldwide dominance of industry. The participants, managed by the Ministry of International Trade and Industry (MITI), target segments of industry and subsidize the efforts of companies with grants, tax relief, tariff protection, and market sharing agreements, then press forward into Western markets until all effective opposition has been destroyed" (Abegglen and Stalk 1985, 5). An economic recession-spurred Japan bashing in the early 1990s brought the sinister conspiracy theory to an emotional extreme. Not satisfied by either the benign or the sinister conspiracy theory, Abegglen and Stalk (1985, 5) suggest something else: the Japanese companies that succeed do so principally because of their choice of competitive fundamentals including a growth bias, a preoccupation with actions of competitors, the creation and ruthless exploitation of competitive advantages, and the choice of corporate financial and personnel policies that are economically consistent with all of the preceding. These cultural-general competitive fundamentals, according to Abegglen and Stalk (1985), can be readily adopted by determined Western competitors. The Abegglen and Stalk approach is among the many culture-free structural approach advocates who believe that the so-called Japanese management system is very much based on business and organizational structures and has little to do with the nation's traditional culture (cf. Jain 1990). This structural approach stands in contrast to the two conspiracy theories, benign or sinister, which take a special interest in culture.

No theories are perfect; each has an element of truth. Even in Kuhn's (1970) "paradigm shift" thinking, in which an entire field of knowledge is conceptualized in a radically different fashion, the new excitement may soon be frustrated by an even newer approach. However, new thinking is still a luxury. This chapter is an attempt to develop a new angle from which to look at the secret of the Japanese success in organizational management and communication. We will examine a consistently enduring organizational phenomenon which had been in existence in Japan even before its modern success story. This has been the phenomenon of the supremacy of human relationships in organizations, their thickness and paramount importance in daily organizational life. We believe that the supremacy of human relationships as a Japanese organizational model is rooted in Japanese management philosophies and the nation's traditional culture. It is important to remember that once cultural variables are involved, one is not supposed to copy the model, no matter how effective it has been, and apply it in a new cultural environment without examining its unique cultural background. We mean to suggest that any culture-specific model has only limited applications. Therefore, instead of recommending that the Japanese organizational model be copied in other parts of the world, we encourage reflection on the serious handling of human relationships in an organizational setting, which we believe will be crucial to the successful functioning of modern organizations in both East and West.

To accomplish this task, we will first review various management and communication practices in Japanese organizations, both at intra- and inter-organizational levels, in which the supremacy of human relationships is upheld as of paramount importance. A description and analysis of human relationships-based organizational practices is followed by our suggestion that the managing of human relationships is a central part of Japanese organizational theories and management philosophies, rooted in Japanese "interrelatedness" in economic behavior (Helou 1991). This Japanese interrelatedness further finds its origins in traditional Japanese culture. However, instead of emphasizing that Japanese culture has played a significant role in their economic success, we argue that the satisfaction of one of the most important requirements of human organization—managing human relationships, which has been facilitated by an accommodating culture—has been key to the notable success of the Japanese. In other words, our argument rests on the supremacy of human relationships as a success factor in organizational functioning logically rooted in the Japanese management philosophy of interrelatedness; culture is viewed as that which happens to be accommodating and supportive. We suggest that the serious treatment of human relationships is not a Japanese creation; it is, rather, a universal mandate of all modern organizations, even though the way or the degree to which human relationships are handled may vary from nation to nation or from culture to culture. The notion of "universal mandate" is emphasized in a brief discussion of human relationships as a defining characteristic of human organization and how classic Western theories of organization have neglected this part of the essence of organizational life.

Supremacy of human relationships: A Japanese organizational practice

Given the limitations of space, we will restrict our discussion of the supremacy of human relationships in Japanese organizations to the intra- and inter-organizational levels only. Whereas differences in managing human relationships among Japanese organizations are many, our emphasis is nevertheless on their commonalities. At the intra-organizational level, we will focus on some of the typical Japanese management and organizational communication practices. Though our discussion is not exhaustive, we try to include those fundamentals which are relationships-biased. At the inter-organizational level, we will mainly take a look at how the *keiretsu* system works in Japan.

Intra-organizational relationships

We discuss six management and communication fundamentals with our focus on how human relationships are related or managed. These are relationships-based organizational structures; the *ringi* system; life-time employment; seniority as a key factor in the reward system; non-specialized career paths; and high-contexting communication.

Relationships-based organizational structure. Forms of organizational structure, such as functional, divisional, or matrix, that are seen in the West also exist in Japan. However, formal organizational structure is only secondary in importance in Japan. In the United States or other Western countries, formal organizational structure tends to be defined in terms of allocation of authority, division of labor, and task flow. In Japan, "it is the company's pattern of relationships and formal arrangement of roles and relationship of people so that work is directed toward meeting the goals of the company" (Namiki and Sethi 1988, 79). This means that it is the pattern of human relationships, not the ideally established formal structure, which dictates how work is directed toward achieving the goals of an organization. "Internal communication is also based mainly on personal relationships and factions rather than on the formal arrangement. The internal working of a Japanese corporation is therefore strongly influenced by Japan's traditional cultural traits such as groupism, rank consciousness, and vertical interpersonal relationships. The processes, rather than the formal organizational structure, are the essence of the form in Japan" (Namiki and Sethi 1988, 79–80).

Namiki and Sethi (1988) discuss the role of middle and top management from a human relationship perspective. They argue that middle managers perform an essential role in the decision-making-by-consensus (*ringi*) system, but how effectively they can play this role depends largely on a middle manager's personal relationships and ties with other managers of both lower and higher levels. Middle managers must not only play an essential role in bridging the gap between the lower and higher management levels, but be competent in putting decisions into practice. Both tasks would require him or her to nurture personal relationships with other managers at various levels and with people whom he or she manages. Effective top management is also made possible by effective managing of human relationships. "Most of the working hours of the top management in Japanese corporations are occupied with establishing and maintaining 'private' relations with responsible men in policymaking positions in other corporations and government departments" (p. 81).

Harmonious relationships, a guarantee for ringisei. Ringisei, or decision-making by consensus, is one of the most important management systems in Japanese organizations. *Ringisei* means obtaining approval on a proposed matter through the vertical, and sometimes horizontal, circulation of documents to the concerned members in the organization (Namiki and Sethi 1988, 75). Defined as such, *ringisei* may be viewed as a basically bottom-up communication process which involves a series of meetings. It is possible that a certain matter could concern a number of sections or departments, or even the whole organization. If this is the case, meetings are first conducted in the group where a certain proposal is initiated. Such meetings may be relaxed, intimate, and less structured face-to-face interactions. An official decision-making meeting is often followed by after-meeting social interactions. Such informal social interactions may help reach unanimous agreement which is crucial for defining the success of *ringisei* (cf. Hayashi 1988). It is therefore argued that harmonious interpersonal relationships are crucial for the effective handling of such meetings. The initiating group would also be responsible for getting coordination and promoting informal consensus from other concerned groups. The second round of meetings tend to be more formal, ritualistic, and better structured. It is likely that the proposal of an initiating group will be turned down at a meeting involving functional groups which the head or members of the initiating group do not enjoy a good interpersonal relationship with. It is known to all organization members in Japan that harmonious intergroup relationships are a major guarantee for the success of the *ringisei* system.

What is really interesting is the role that "men of influence" (Namiki and Sethi 1988, 78) play in the running of the *ringisei* system. These organizational "men of influence" may not hold formal hierarchical positions, but enjoy good personal relations with other opinion leaders in various groups. These "men of influence," with relationships that have established over the years with other organization members based on common bonds of school, age, or organizational membership, determine to a large extent whether consensus will be reached on a proposal. Therefore, harmonious human relationships are a guarantee for the functioning of *ringisei*.

Lifetime employment. It needs to be pointed out at the beginning that lifetime employment, which is mainly practiced in large Japanese organizations, has a significant impact on how organization members perceive and manage human relationships in organizations, even though nearly half of all Japanese between the ages of twenty and twenty-nine now expressed a preference for an "employment changing" job environment to the assurance of lifetime employment (Mroczkowshi and Hanaoka 1989). Ouchi (1981), in his *Theory Z,* lists lifetime employment as one of the seven major differences between Theory Z organizations (organizations that follow Japanese management practices) and Theory A organizations (American organizations). A typical employment practice in a large Japanese organization is that a college graduate gets hired right from school and stays with the company until he or she retires at the age of 55. This practice generates tremendous employee loyalty to the company, makes the company willing to invest in employee training, and facilitates high-context communication among organization members, which is crucial to the effective managing of human relationships in a highly complex organizational context.

One of the most important implications of lifetime employment, relating to high-context communication, is that one cannot afford not to deal with interpersonal relationships with great caution. In one's lifetime employment, he or she is likely, over the years, to build extensive interpersonal relationships with colleagues at various levels who have come to join the same "big family." As an organization member moves up the organizational hierarchy from shopfloor worker to supervisor, to section chief, to department manager, and possibly, to the top management, he or she will have established an intricate web of human relationships, which will soon become the last thing he or she can afford to lose in an organization. As all members have their own networking of interpersonal relationships, each being different based on different "common bonds," the organization becomes indeed an enormously complicated system of human relationships interlocked within an extremely sophisticated high-context communication system.

Seniority as a key factor in reward system. Closely related to lifetime employment is seniority as a key factor in an organization's reward system. Mroczkowski and Hanaoka (1989) note that even though it is broadly believed that the principle of seniority governs the Japanese system of motivating employees, rewarding loyalty, and maintaining group harmony, the pure seniority principle has been systematically eroding in Japan. They report that between 1978 and 1987, the contribution of the seniority factor to pay raises systematically declined from an average of 57.9% to 46% while the contribution of the performance factor increased from 42.1% to 54% (p. 46). However, the fact that seniority accounts for 46% of all pay raises is still impressive. And it remains to be seen whether the increase of performance as a contribution factor to determining reward is likely to continue. We argue that seniority is still perceived and practiced as more important in Japanese organizations than in their Western counterparts.

One of the big advantages of upholding seniority as important is its tendency to discourage destructive competition among organization members. In a sense this is a more equal system; each and every organization member has a chance to move up as he or she continues to work for the organization. In other words, you don't have to beat your colleagues to get there; you will get there when your time comes. This helps generate a spirit of comraderie among group members in which a senior person is more willing to share his or her information and experience with a junior person, and the latter will show more respect for the former. Harmonious, family-like relationships are more likely to be formed amidst such a spirit. One possible drawback on an overemphasis on seniority, however, is to discourage performance and creativity mainly on the part of junior members.

Nonspecialized career paths. One of the major differences between Japanese organizations and their Western counterparts is that there are more generalists in the former than in the latter. A Japanese employee keeps on training as a regular part of his or her job until he or she retires; at the same time he or she is trained not only in his or her job but in all other jobs at his or her job level. On-the-job training by rotation creates flexibility in the work force and also helps make of each middle or upper manager a generalist with a broader perspective and experience of the company's business. And over the years, a manager or worker builds wider interpersonal relationships and friendships which are vital for the practice of *ringisei* (Namiki and Sethi 1988, 87). Again this relates back to lifetime employment, where an employee has the luxury of time to do the job rotation and develop his or her cross-functional interpersonal networking.

High-contexting communication. Modern organizations are complex information processing systems. Technological and communication revolutions and breakthroughs have brought with themselves an organizational epidemic: information overload. No organization, no matter how advanced and sophisticated its information processing system is, can possibly handle the huge volume of information that keeps coming in at an increasing speed. Indeed, today's managers in many Western organizations have become willing or unwilling slaves of their own desks which are stacked with piles upon piles of linguistic codes their computers and secretaries never seem tired of supplying. They are the true slaves of linguistic codes. What is worse is that the information overload seems to be getting more and more uncontrollable.

The only way to solve this human-created nonhuman problem is through human beings themselves. The Japanese (and probably other East Asians as well) have been doing a truly remarkable job in solving the problem. The secret is the use of high-contexting communication which occurs in close human relationships. In high-contexting communication often the mass of information or meaning is not in the explicit linguistic codes, but in the context of communication, in the reading of nonverbal messages, in the subtlety of human relationships (Hall 1991). According to Hall, contexting, which is a screening process by which humans determine what they pay attention to and what they do not attend to, involves two entirely different but interrelated processes—one inside the organism and the other outside. "The first takes place in the brain and is a function of either past experience (programmed, internalized contexting) or the structure of the nervous system (innate contexting), or both. External contexting comprises the situation and/or setting in which an event occurs (situational and/or environmental contexting)" (Hall 1991, 50–51). A group of workers who have been working together for, say, twenty years could understand each other perfectly without even saying or doing anything; their past years of experiences working together have programmed them such that they will be able to communicate without resorting too much to linguistic codes. And this is also possible for a manager and the person that he or she manages after they have established a close interpersonal relationship.

Human relationships are always complex and changing, and often so much so that explicit linguistic communication can do very little in helping people understand, explain, or predict each other's behavior. Such complexities in organizations, however, can effectively be handled by using high-contexting communication. Ouchi (1981) discusses three lessons from Theory Z: trust, subtlety, and intimacy. We argue that the reason these three lessons are really worth learning is because they capture the essence of high-contexting communication in Japanese organizations. Trust, subtlety, and intimacy are all variables that belong to the larger category of human relationships. Some of the discussions of trust, subtlety, and intimacy in Ouchi's *Theory Z,* although a decade old, still sound fresh and informative and are worth quoting.

On trust:

"[T]he central feature of [a] trading company [such as Mitsui, or Mitsubishi, or Sumitomo] is an extensive management system that maintains a sense of trust between employees in the trading company. Japanese employees, just like American counterparts, want to get ahead. They want to make deals beneficial to both their departments and themselves. They work in an environment of tremendous uncertainty, buying and selling copper ore, crude oil, wheat, and televisions. On a typical day, the central office of one of the major trading firms will receive 35,000 telex messages, each one with an offer to buy or sell. Often, the firm's overall profitability will be maximized if an office takes a loss, which will be more than made up in another office so that the company benefits overall. The success of the trading company depends critically upon the willingness of individual offices and employees to make these sacrifices. That willingness exists because the Japanese trading firm uses managerial practices that foster trust through the knowledge that such sacrifices will always be repaid in the future. Equity will, in the end, be restored. (Ouchi 1981, 5)

What might be added to this passage is the fact that "the knowledge that such sacrifices will always be repaid in the future" does not exist in the form of writing; this knowledge comes from the employees' past experiences.

On subtlety:

A foreman who knows his workers well can pinpoint personalities, decide who works well with whom, and thus put together teams of maximal effectiveness. These subtleties can never be captured explicitly, and any bureaucratic rule will do violence to them. If the foreman is forced, either by a bureaucratic management or by an equally inflexible union contract, to assign work teams strictly on the basis of seniority, then that subtlety is lost and productivity declines. (p. 6)

On intimacy:

The common thread in Japanese life is intimacy. The caring, the support, and the disciplined unselfishness which make life possible come through close social relations. The loss of closeness in modern life concerns many social observers. . . . In the Japanese example, we find a successful industrial society in which intimacy occurs in the place of work as well as in other settings. (p.8)

The trust, subtlety, and intimacy that permeate human relationships in Japanese organizations form the basis of high-contexting communication, which has proved to be one of the most effective means of solving information overload and, in turn, increasing overall organizational effectiveness.

The "keiretsu": A network of inter-organizational relationships

Inter-organizational relationships carry an importance equal to intra-organizational relationships in Japan. We will discuss how inter-organizational relationships are handled through the *keiretsu* system.

The *keiretsu,* or a Japanese industrial group, simply defined, is a network of inter-organizational relationships. It is an inter-organizational system of coordination and teamwork. The origins of the *keiretsu* go back to the rise of Japan's great banking families in the nineteenth century. By the 1930s the nation's bankers had built vast mining-to-manufacturing conglomerates, called *zaibatsu,* which controlled much of Japan's industry. The member firms of each *zaibatsu* were bound by a central holding company and a vast network of interlocking directorships. After World War II, the *zaibatsu,* which played a central role in supporting Japan's militarism, were disbanded by the American Occupation authorities. But soon after the Americans left in the early 50s, companies of the former *zaibatsu* regrouped themselves into new clusters, taking a new name called *keiretsu.* The main difference between the pre–World War II *zaibatsu* and the present *keiretsu* is that the latter are no longer controlled by holding companies. Instead, the ostensibly independent companies of a *keiretsu* organized themselves around a core commercial bank which guarantees the companies' long-term viability by supplying corporate capital and coordinating other key management strategies among member firms of the group. This is called a bank-centered, or horizontal, *keiretsu.* For example, the Sumitomo group, one of the six largest bank-centered *keiretsu* in Japan, is organized around the Sumitomo Bank. In contrast to horizontally related, bank-centered *keiretsu,* there are also vertical *keiretsu,* which are industrial groups of companies integrated along a supplier chain dominated by a major manufacturer. A good example of vertical *keiretsu* is the Toyota Motor Company.

The six major horizontally related, bank-centered *keiretsu* in Japan, which include Mitsui, Mitsubishi, Sumitomo, Dai-ichi Kangyo, Fuyo, and Sanwa, group together some 12,000 companies which between them have sales equivalent to a quarter of Japan's GNP. A *keiretsu* typically cuts through a wide range of industries. The Mitsui group, for example, includes companies in fibre and textiles, foodstuffs, construction, retailing, finance and insurance, chemicals, pulp and paper, mining, steel and metals, transportation and warehousing, electricity and machinery, and automobiles (Wright 1989, 20). Helou (1991) identifies four key features of the *horizontal keiretsu* in Japan:

1. The scope, size, and economic power. For example, the subsidiaries and affiliates of key *keiretsu,* as well as their branch offices, domestic and overseas, tend to be of a size more representative of an economy than an institution.

2. A common tendency of *keiretsu* is to bring together representatives of their member companies for joint consultation, policy-making, and the monitoring of activity developments. A good example is the Presidents' Association, constituted of top executives of key *keiretsu* companies.

3. The central role played by a *keiretsu's* general trader and bank. The general trader performs a special organizing function and leads in bringing the group's firms together in joint ventures, domestically or overseas. A core *keiretsu* bank assumes an essential role in pooling resources, maintains a control power on the basis of provision of funds and shareownership, and provides guidance to corporate investment behavior and opportunities.

4. Drive toward a general objective. This is reflected in a *keiretsu's* co-alignment of industrial policy objectives, resource flow, competing strategies, and promotion of cohesion. Thus the *keiretsu* may be viewed as a nexus of relationships.

It seems clear that what underlies the four identifiable features of the *keiretsu* is, again, the supremacy of human relationships. It is hardly possible for a *keiretsu* to function without harmonious human relationships among member companies. First, the enormous size and range of businesses involved in a *keiretsu* presuppose the necessity of managing of interlocking human relationships among participating firms. Second, such relationships are negotiated by representatives of various member companies. The Presidents' Association provides a convenient occasion where chief executives exchange personal messages as well as business information at both the informal and formal levels. In the case of Mitsui, for example, the presidents of twenty-five or so most strategically important firms meet every second Thursday; so the group is called the "Second-Thursday Group" (Wright 1989, 21). Third, close human relationships are a precondition for the functioning of the central role that the general trader and core commercial bank play in each *keiretsu*. Wright (1989) reports that the relationship between banks and industrial firms is a far more intimate, supportive one than that in most other countries. It is not rare for the general trader or core commercial bank to send senior financial or other management personnel to assist member companies in trouble. The high-level personnel exchange promotes inter-organizational coordination and cohesion. Fourth, the achieving of a *keiretsu's* general objective is very much guaranteed by the co-alignment of key business success factors through a nexus of human relationships. Therefore, it would not be an exaggeration to claim that the effective functioning of the bank-centered *keiretsu* is impossible without the subtlety and intimacy of horizontal inter-organizational human relationships.

The *vertical keiretsu*, or supplier *keiretsu*, are composed of several layers of subcontractors, which usually have interlocking directorates. The principal manufacturer generally owns some of its subcontractors' stock and provides financial and technological assistance. This may involve transfers of sophisticated new equipment or the training required to help the supplier produce next-generation products (Anchordoguy 1990, 59). Supplier *keiretsu* are most developed in the automobile, electronics, and machinery industries, where the product is composed of various parts. The best example, as mentioned previously, is the Toyota Motor Company.

As early as in the 1950s, Toyota divided its suppliers into several tiers with different responsibilities. First-tier suppliers were each assigned a major component such as car seats or the electrical system. Second-tier suppliers would supply individual parts or subsystem components to the first-tier companies. Second-tier suppliers, in many cases, developed a third-level of suppliers which supplied what the former needed. Toyota only dealt directly with the first-tier suppliers. The companies of various tiers work together to form an integral whole of the product-development team and were well informed of a car model's performance specifications. The relationship between Toyota and its first-tier suppliers has always been close as both expect the relationship to be a long-term and stable one. In the spirit of teamwork, Toyota is provided with the most sensitive information about the suppliers' operations, including costs and quality levels. Information sharing also occurs at meetings of first-tier and second-tier supplier associations, where advances in manufacturing techniques are discussed. As a rule, Toyota's design engineers would visit first-tier plants to observe and take part in the production planning for the new model (Ju 1993). From the example of Toyota, it is clear that harmonious human relationships between the main manufacturer and its suppliers through such mechanisms as interlocking directorates and frequent exchange of personnel are an important guarantee of the successful functioning of a vertical *keiretsu*.

Human relationships: Organizational inter-relatedness at the human level

What is the underlying philosophy, or the essence, of the so-called Japanese management and organizational communication system? Helou (1991, 100) argues that the competitive nature of the Japanese individual firm is, in an effective manner, the subject-matter of the principle of "Japanese relativity" and its appreciation of inter-relatedness in economic behavior. Thus if a certain economic unit (e.g. a firm) is to function in the optimum manner, it has to exist and be maintained in an expedient relative status, in principle contrasted with its standing and behavior under laissez-faire economics. Accordingly, the modus operandi in the Japanese case represents a state of interactive behavior among economic units and a state of interdependence between each and the whole.

Helou goes on to suggest that the *keiretsu*—we might add intra-organizational behavior as well—should "be interpreted to be reflective of the nature of the Japanese own precepts and principles of industrial organization and economic management which stem from a Japanese industrial rationality and economic mind."

Helou calls such industrial rationality "economic cohesion" (p. 102) or "cohesion economics" (p. 105). This is "the Japanese way of bringing parts together" (p. 102). Whereas Helou sees the issue from an economics perspective, we may well treat such industrial rationality as originated from a Japanese management philosophy deeply rooted in its traditional culture. Such a philosophy is either what Helou calls "interrelatedness," or what may be said, in a more concrete term, to be the mandate of organizational interdependencies, which reflects the very nature of human organization. Interdependences as an omnipresent organizational phenomenon, within the larger socioeconomic context, must be managed at various levels both intra- and inter-organizationally, including the level of human relationships. The managing of organizational interdependencies at the level of human relationships, or the level of materials, or other functional levels, simply stated, is to "bring parts together." However, "the Japanese way of bringing parts together," viewed in the light of our previous discussions of organizational practices in Japan, seems to be characterized by the supremacy of human relationships.

Human organizations are collections of human beings who have come together for whatever objective they have set to achieve. It is always important to remember that it is organization members who control organizational processes, and it is organization members who manage organizational interdependencies at various levels. It is hardly imaginable that organizational interdependencies, at whatever levels, can be effectively managed before humans figure out how to manage their own interdependencies. Therefore the supremacy of human relationships in Japanese organizations as a premiere management approach is theoretically logical. It is not only theoretically logical, but it fits well with Japanese economic and organizational set-ups as exemplified in both the horizontal and vertical *keiretsu*. It not only fits well with the established structures, but finds its "homeland" in traditional Japanese culture.

An accommodating Japanese culture

"There is no such thing as Management with a capital "M" and the art of managing and organizing has no homeland" (Laurent 1986, 96). In this section, instead of arguing that the competitiveness of Japanese organization is attributable to traditional Japanese culture, we view the larger cultural milieu as accommodating and supportive. This is to say that it is the satisfaction of the fundamental requirements of managing and organizing including the managing of organizational interdependencies that generates the competitiveness of Japanese organizations, not the culture. However, this does not mean that culture becomes an irrelevant variable. The fact is that traditional Japanese culture accommodates and supports the practice of the supremacy of human relationships in the country's organizations.

Human relationships are a system in which an individual self relates to another person one way or another. All human relationships including those in an organizational setting originate from this self-other relatedness. So it is crucial, first of all, to know how the Japanese view "self." "For the Japanese, 'self' means the portion which is *distributed* [emphasis added] to him [her], according to the situation he [she] is in, from the living space shared between himself [herself] and the other person with whom he [she] had developed a mutually dependent relationship . . . . A reason why this self-consciousness of the Japanese is formed this way is probably that self and others are in a symbiotic relationship, and that they believe that their beings depend largely on other beings . . . This relativistic 'self' can easily be mistaken for being unindependent . . . . However, here, selves are 'mutually dependent,' and their spontaneous fulfillment of the needs intentionally controlled" (Markus and Kitayama 1991, 142). This Japanese concept of self, which has a tremendous impact on the formation of human relationships in Japanese society, can be better understood when contrasted with the typical American view of self. For Americans, "an 'individual' . . . holds a conviction that he [she] is a firmly established substance which is solely independent, and, therefore, cannot be invalidated by others. Also, he [she] is convinced that he [she] is the master of himself [herself], but at the same time he [she] is liable for his [her] own deeds. The individual objectifies such an assertion (that he [she] is undoubtedly himself [herself] and the sense of autonomy" (pp. 140–141).

The relativistic self, which has its psychological anchorage in another individual, generates a feeling of dependence, which is called *amae* in the Japanese language. *Amae* is a state of mind that describes a desire to be passively loved, and a desire to be protected, as in a mother/child relationship, from the world of objective reality (Namiki and Sethi 1988, 56). In Japan, " *amae* is vitally important to the individual's psyche and emotional stability, the entire social structure is set to fulfill this need" (ibid.). When two persons involved in a relationship share the same feeling of dependence, mutual dependence or interdependence is logically generated. It is therefore argued that interdependencies in an organizational setting are culturally rooted in person-to-person interdependence.

"The basic single-unit interpersonal relationship between two Japanese persons is *oyabun-kobun* (*oya*, father; *ko*, child), in vertical system. Members in a work-related group or in any Japanese organization are tied together by this kind of relationship. . . . The structure of a group in Japan, including the corporate group, is based on the *accumulation of such relationships*" (p. 58; emphasis added). The absoluteness of authority in Japanese organizations and father-childkind of superior-subordinate relationships have no parallels in the West.

We assume that it is a coincidence that the emphasis of person-to-person interdependency in Japanese traditional culture matches perfectly with the mandate of effective managing of interdependencies, including those at the level of human relationships, for successful organizational functioning. Whereas it is fortunate to have an accommodating culture by which the managing of interdependencies, and human interdependencies in particular, has been made easier, how about running organizations and doing business in a sociocultural milieu where self-actualization is deemed more important than upholding human relationships? What if the necessary nurturing of human relationship is missing in the larger sociocultural environment? To answer the two self-imposed, seemingly unanswerable questions, we want to emphasize, once again, human relationships as a defining characteristic of human organization, and suggest that the fact that it has received somewhat light treatment in Western organizational theorizing needs to be seriously addressed.

*Human relationships: A defining characteristic of
human organization but a missing focus in western
organizational theorizing*

Organizations are not Western creations, nor are they the result of Eastern civilizations. Organizations, traditional or more modern, are
groupings that human beings, wherever they are from, create to accomplish whatever tasks they could not accomplish individually. As
Goldhaber, author of a popular textbook on organizational communication in the West, points out, such groupings are "a network of interdependent relationships" (Goldhaber 1990, 33). When an organization
is viewed as a network of interdependent relationships, Goldhaber goes
on to say, "we can focus on the underlying structure that generates and
guides the relationships; we can focus on the people who actually do
the relating; or we can focus on how the various relationships contribute to the organizations as a whole" (ibid.) These three concerns
have led to the development of three major schools of organizational
theorizing in the West, namely, the classical theory, the human relations
theory, and the social systems theory. The interesting thing is that, although "interdependent relationships" have been said to be important,
none of the three major schools of thought whose essence is represented
in the three ways of examining organizational relationships as indicated
in the above quote really focuses on "human relationships." The classical theory of organization puts its emphasis on order, logic, and efficiency, and view organization members as replaceable human cogs
(Weber 1947; Fayol 1949; Taylor 1919). The human relations theory
of organization, despite the seemingly suggestive term of "human relations," really says little about human "relations" or "relationships." Its
emphasis is the satisfaction of individual member needs in an organization, based on the assumption that satisfied, participating, and self-
actualized individuals are more productive (Roethlisberger and
Dickson 1939; MacGregor 1960; Miles 1965). The social systems theory of organization does talk about relationships, but again the main
focus is not human relationships; what it is most concerned about is the
interdependent nature of activities of an organization's functional units
(Katz and Kahn 1978; Miller 1972).

It is interesting to note that despite the fact that human relationships are one of the most important defining characteristics of organization, they have never been seriously addressed in any of the
above-mentioned theories of organization. Later theories of organization including Weick's model (Weick 1969, 1979) and the cultural approach (cf. Conrad 1990) also do not highlight human relationships or

make them a major focus. Whereas each of the more influential theories of organization has its own strengths and weaknesses, we want to indicate that all of them have been developed by Western scholars presumably based on the realities of Western organizations. These strongly Western-based theories can be useful tools with which to describe and predict workings of Western organizations, but they are inadequate when faced with contrasting realities in non-Western organizations, organizations in Japan or other East Asian countries for example.

Recent Western interest in non-Western organizational behaviors, as we pointed out previously, was generated by the remarkable economic success of Japan and, more recently, of other East Asian nations, but then we heard arguments over benign conspiracy vs. sinister conspiracy, or whether culture or structure has been a dominant contributing factor. Japanese or East Asian organizational studies appear more like an academic fad than a serious search for some universal truth, for something larger than a mere so-called East Asian model or Japanese management model.

This chapter was intended to be mainly descriptive and analytical; it is not designed to be prescriptive. We only want to stress the fact that the competitiveness of Japanese organizations comes, among other factors, from the priority given to human relationships in corporate life. We by no means wish to suggest that "the Japanese way of bringing parts together" or the "supremacy of human relationships" should be accepted as a universally applicable way. Indeed, Western society could never embrace the Japanese-style pattern of paternal superior-subordinate relationships in organizations. Nor could it adopt many other Japanese management practices. We do want to suggest, however, that a more serious treatment of human relationships needs to be put on the agenda in both Western organizational practices and organizational theorizing, even though the sociocultural milieu is less accommodating to and probably less supportive of close human relations.

References

Anchordoguy, M. 1990. A brief history of Japan's keiretsu. *Harvard Business Review* 90 (4): 58–59.

Abegglen, J. C., and G. Stalk, Jr. 1985. *Kaisha, the Japanese corporation.* New York: Basic Books.

Conrad, C. 1990. *Strategic organizational communication.* Orlando, FL: Holt, Rinehart and Winston.

Fayol, H. 1949. *General and industrial management.* Translated by C. Storrs. London: Pitman & Sons.

Goldhaber, G. M. 1990. *Organizational communication.* Dubuque, IA: Wm. C. Brown Publishers.

Hall, E. T. 1991. Context and meaning. In *Intercultural communication: A reader,* ed. L. A. Samovar and R. E. Porter. Belmont, CA: Wadsworth Publishing Company.

Hayashi, S. 1988. *Culture and management in Japan.* Translated by F. Baldwin. Tokyo: University of Tokyo Press.

Helou, A. 1991. The nature and competitiveness of Japan's keiretsu. *Journal of World Trade* 25 (3): 99–131.

Jain, H. C. 1990. Human resource management in selected Japanese firms, their foreign subsidiaries and locally owned counterparts. *International Labour Review* 129:73–84.

Ju, Y. 1993. Organizational teamwork: A high-speed management perspective. In *High-speed management: An organizational communication perspective,* ed. D. P. Cushman and S. S. King. Albany, NY: SUNY Press.

Katz, D., and R. Kahn. 1978. *The social psychology of organizations.* New York: Wiley.

Kuhn, T. S. 1970. *The structure of scientific revolutions.* Chicago: University of Chicago Press.

Laurent, A. 1986. The cross-cultural puzzle of international human resource management. *Human Resources Management* 25 (1): 91–102.

MacGregor, D. 1960. *Human side of enterprise.* New York: McGraw-Hill.

Markus, H. R., and S. Kitayama. 1991. Culture and self: Implications for cognition, emotion, and motivation. *Psychological Review* 98:224–53.

Miles, R. 1965. Keeping informed—human relations or human resources? *Harvard Business Review* 43:148–63.

Mroczkowshi, T., and M. Hanaoka. 1989. Continuity and change in Japanese management. *California Management Review* 31 (2): 39–53.

Miller, J. G. 1972. Living systems: The organization. *Behavioral Science* 17:1–182.

Namiki, N., and P. Sethi. 1988. Japan. In Comparative Management — A Regional View, ed. R. Nath. Cambridge, MA: Ballinger Publishing Company.

Ouchi, W. G. 1981. *Theory Z: How American business can meet the Japanese challenge.* Reading, MA: Addison-Wesley.

Pascale, R. T., and A. G. Athos. 1981. *The art of Japanese management.* New York: Harper & Row.

Roethlisberger, F., and W. Dickson. 1939. *Management and the worker.* Cambridge, MA: Harvard University Press.

Taylor, W. F. 1919. *Principles of scientific management.* New York: Harper & Row.

Vogel, E. F. 1979. *Japan as number one: Lesson from America.* Cambridge, MA: Harvard University Press.

Weber, M. 1947. *The Theory of Social and Economic Organizations.* Translated by A. M. Henderson and T. Parsons; edited by T. Parsons. New York: Oxford University Press.

Weick, K. 1969; 2nd ed. 1979. *The social psychology of organizing.* Reading, MA: Addison-Wesley.

Whitley, R. D. 1990. Eastern Asian structures and the comparative analysis of forms of business organization. *Organization Studies* 11 (1): 47–74.

Wright, R. W. 1989. Networking—Japanese style. *Business Quarterly* 54 (2): 20–24.

SARAH S. KING
DONALD P. CUSHMAN

4 High-Speed Management as a Theoretical Principle for Yielding Significant Organizational Communication Behaviors *

Until recently the search for theoretical principles capable of yielding significant organizational communication behaviors has been rather barren. The reason has been simple. Organizational strategy, the prime candidate for locating powerful cross-organizational theoretical principles has had at its core non-communicational activities. For example, if an organization pursues a strategy of *competitive advantage based on product cost,* the central organizational process yielding cross organizational theoretic activity is *production or manufacturing activities.* On the other hand if an organization pursues a strategy of obtaining *competitive advantage based on product differentiation,* then the central organizational process yielding cross organizational theoretical activity is product uniqueness or *research and development activities.*

While human interaction or communication is involved in both organizational manufacturing and research and development activities, the primary cross-organizational theoretic activities are organizational manufacturing and technological innovations in creative engineering in research and development processes, not communication processes. Communication processes function as second-level support activities and are given their regularities based on the primary organizational activities of production and innovation.

However, when *speed of response or time* becomes the primary source of competitive advantage, this all changes and effective communication becomes the primary cross-organizational theoretic activity and other organizational processes such as research and development, manufacturing, sales, and servicing products become support activities to the primary process of speed in getting a product to market (Stalk 1988).

It will be the purpose of this paper to explore speed of response or time as the primary source of competitive advantage in the 1990s and to trace out the theoretic principles involved in effective organizational communication or speed in getting a product to market. In so doing we shall (1) explore the business environment which makes rapid response or time the primary source of competitive advantage; (2) examine high-speed management as the central theoretic communication process involved in rapidly getting products to market; and (3) discuss the transformations which high-speed management has made theoretically in the traditional organizational communication processes of integration, coordination, and control.

The business environment which makes rapid response or time the primary source of competitive advantage

Prior to examining time as the primary basis for organizational competitive advantage and high-speed management as the primary theoretical perspective of effective organizational communication processes, we shall explore four trends whose convergence has led to the restructuring of the global economic environment, placing new demands on corporate management, and giving rise to high-speed management systems.

1. A series of breakthroughs has taken place in information and communication technologies which have dramatically changed organizational manufacturing, marketing, and management.

2. This information and communication revolution has helped generate a dramatic increase in world trade, the emergence of a global economy, and the development of three large core markets.

3. These technological breakthroughs and increases in world trade have created a volatile business climate characterized by rapidly changing technology, quick market saturation, and unexpected competition, making succeeding in business difficult (Fraker 1984).

4. To compete successfully in such an environment requires that executives employ management theories and practices which emphasize innovation, adaptation, flexibility, efficiency, and rapid response.

Breakthroughs in information and
communication technologies

A series of technological breakthroughs have taken place which make possible the generation, processing, and instant delivery of information and communication throughout the world, creating a revolution in organizational manufacturing, marketing, and management. At the center of this revolution is a constellation of new management tools based on computers and telecommunications and classified as (*a*) *new manufacturing*, (*b*) *marketing*, and (*c*) *management technologies*. Taken collectively, these tools provide a new way of thinking and acting in regard to all the problems which confront management in dealing with a rapidly changing economic environment.

New manufacturing technologies employ computer aided and telecommunication linked engineering, manufacturing, and resource planning processes to allow for the rapid development, production, sales, and service of customized new products at low cost, high quality, and easy service throughout the world (Young 1990). Allen-Bradley, a Milwaukee manufacturer of industrial controls, possesses one of the world's most modern computer-aided and telecommunication-linked engineering, manufacturing, and resource-planning facilities. This facility can produce one of a product or 100,000 of the same product at the same per unit cost. This plant can receive the specifications for an order one day and deliver the product at its destination the next, cutting the average turnaround time on orders from four weeks to two days. Under such a system, engineering and manufacturing costs decreased 40 percent while profits increased by 32 percent and product quality increased by 200 percent (Port 1986, 100–108).

New marketing information technologies employ computer-aided and telecommunication-linked environmental scanning, electronic test marketing, and real-time merchandising for speed in providing customers with world-class products when and where they want them in order to increase market share (Young 1990). Campbell Soup Company, for example, can scan the environment to determine customer desire for a new soup; then computer model its contents; simulate its production; calibrate its cost, price, profit, and sales potential; develop an artificial intelligence system to control its rate and quality of production; pretest its name, taste, shelf placement, the type and content of its advertising; and run its test markets—reducing a management decision process which used to take years to a matter of two or three days. These new marketing technologies cut the cost of this process by 30 percent while increasing product success rates by 80 percent (Russell, Adams, and Boundy 1986).

New management information technologies employ computer-aided and telecommunication-linked decision support, operational research, artificial intelligence, and group technology systems to integrate, coordinate, and control management processes in order to create competitive advantage. American Express recently implemented an artificial intelligence system which provides decision support for managers making authorization decisions on individual purchases from 400,000 shops and restaurants throughout the world. This expert system reduced by 20 percent the turn around time per transaction, reduced by 50 percent the number of authorizations in trouble ninety days after approval, while providing annual savings of $27 million (Feigenbaum, McCorduck, and Nii 1988). New manufacturing, marketing, and management information technologies when appropriately employed allow for more effective integration, coordination, and control of all organizational processes creating the potential for competitive advantage (Young 1990).

These then are some of the new information and communication tools which when taken collectively are creating a new way of thinking and acting in regard to all management problems. They have in common the technology that allows organizations to track and respond in real time to the interests of managers, stockholders, workers, customers, and competitors throughout major portions of the globe. Similarly, such a world-class information and communication capability allows organizations to track and respond in real time to international changes in the cost of capital, labor, raw materials, consumer taste, and competitor response.

Breakthroughs in information and communication technologies are increasing world trade

The ability of corporations to track in real time the needs of customers and changes in the cost of capital, labor, and raw materials throughout the world has led to (a) a rapid increase in world trade, (b) the emergence of a global economy, with (c) strong regional markets. Driven by information and communication technologies and the comparative advantage they create, world trade over the past four decades has grown much faster than the world's gross national product. International exports and imports were about one-fifth the world GNP in 1962, one-fourth in 1972, one-third in 1982, and are projected to approach one-half in the world GNP by 1994 (Wall Street Journal 1990).

Over the past decade a single model of economic development has emerged which is influencing economic policies throughout the nations involved in the emerging global economy.

The generalization of such a model does not imply that all governments or all economies are alike; it merely suggests broad central tendencies in the economic policies of most nations as they begin to participate in the global economy. This model includes seven general features: (1) control of inflation through fiscal austerity and monetary restrictions; (2) reduction of labor costs as a percentage of product cost; (3) increased productivity and profitability through the effective use of information and communication technology; (4) restructuring of industrial and service sectors by disinvesting from low-profit areas and investing in high-growth, high-profit areas; (5) privatization and deregulation of some aspects of the economy by withdrawing from state ownership and control in favor of open market forces; (6) relative control over the pricing of raw materials and energy assuring the stability of pricing systems and exchange flows; and (7) opening up gradually to world markets and increased internationalization of economies.

As Castells (1986, 300) argues:

> Such a model is not necessarily linked to a particular political party or administration, or even to a country, even though the Reagan or Thatcher governments seem to be the closest examples of the fulfillment of these policies. But very similar policies have developed in most West European countries, in those governed by Socialists, and even in Communist-led regions (Italy) or Communist-participating governments (France, for a certain period). At the same time, in most Third World countries, austerity policies, inspired or dictated by the International Monetary Fund and world financial institutions, have also developed along the same lines, establishing not without contradictions and conflicts (Walton 1985) a new economic logic that is not only capitalistic but a very specific kind of capitalism.

With the emerging global economy, comparative advantage is shifting towards those regions of the world with (1) a large core market, (2) a strong scientific and technological work force, and (3) a private and public economic sector which can attract the capital necessary to provide the infrastructure needed for increased growth and technological changes. The U.S./Canadian core market, the EEC core market, and the Japanese area of influence in Asia appear to meet these criteria (Baig 1989).

*The information and communication revolution and the rise
in world trade has created a volatile business climate*

"Rapidly changing technology, quick market saturation, unexpected
global competition—these all make succeeding in business, particularly a high technology business, harder than ever today" (Fraker
1984). The volatile business climate engendered by the information
technology and communication revolution and the globalization of
economic forces has led to a significant realignment of individual corporate resources. In order to understand this corporate realignment we
will (*a*) explore the unique problem this realignment creates for individual corporations, and (*b*) outline the new corporate perspective for
responding to this problem.

The unique problem of the shrinking product life cycle. Most of the environmental forces precipitating the need for rapid change in corporate
operations arise from a single problem—namely the fact that firms are
confronted by shrinking product life cycles. The product life cycle is
the period of time available from the inception of an idea for a product until the market for that product is saturated or disappears due to
new product development. A product life cycle normally involves several stages—product conceptualization, design, testing, refinement,
mass production, marketing, shipping, selling, and servicing.

Dominique Hanssens, a professor in UCLA's Graduate School of
Management, has studied the product life cycle in electrical appliances
for years. He reports (Fraker 1984) that years ago the product life cycle for refrigerators took over thirty years to mature, providing considerable time for each phase of the product life cycle to develop.
However, all of this has changed. The market for microwave ovens has
taken ten years to mature; shortwave radios, four years; computer
games, three years, and so on. Perhaps the most dramatic example of
shrinking product life cycles as a result of rapidly changing technology,
quick market saturation, and unexpected competition, can be found in
the computer industry (Berlant, Browning, and Foster 1990).

The first commercially successful computer, containing an 8-bit
memory chip, came to market in 1977; four years later in 1981 the 16-
bit memory chip appeared; two years later in 1983 came the 32-bit
memory chip; and one year later in 1984 came the 64-bit memory chip.
By 1987 we witnessed the appearance of the one-megabyte memory
chip, by 1989 the four megabyte memory chip, and by 1990 the development of a sixteen-megabyte memory chip was well underway.
The industrial shakedown from such rapid changes has taken its toll.

Large U.S. companies, once dominant in their respective markets such as Hewlett Packard, Apple, and DEC, who were unable to respond effectively to the end of one product life cycle and the beginning of a new one, lost their market position, with still other firms going out of the computer business.

How can a company manage to avoid these unpleasantries and prosper? What new techniques and skills must managers master to respond to this challenge? Only recently have executives who have responded successfully to this challenge began to report a consistent pattern of attack which shows promise of providing a foundation for a new corporate perspective on how to respond to rapid environmental change.

A new corporate perspective on rapid change. Fraker (1984) argues that a rapidly changing technology, quick market saturation, and unexpected competition have led to the emergence of a new corporate perspective for coping with a volatile business climate.

1. *Companies must stay close to both their customers and their competitors.* Successful companies always know what the customer needs and attempt to provide it. When products and manufacturing processes change rapidly, it is crucial to keep up with the investment strategies and product costs of rival companies. In order to accomplish this, companies must develop and maintain a rapid and accurate intelligence system capable of preventing surprises.

2. *Companies must think constantly about new products and then back that thinking with investment fast.* A good new product strategy requires a large, active, and focused research and development team with ready access to and the prudent use of large amounts of capital.

3. *Rapid and effective delivery requires close coordination between design, manufacturing, testing, marketing, delivery, and servicing systems.* The interdependence of these systems combined with the short lead time in product delivery makes certain that any error within or between systems will delay product delivery, endangering market penetration. Close cooperation between these systems requires strong, quick, and responsive integration, coordination, and control systems.

4. *Product quality, user friendliness, ease of service, and competitive pricing are essential for market penetration.* In an environment where consumer and investor representatives compare, rate, and effectively communicate product differences, market penetration depends on quality, utility, and readily serviceable products. This in turn re-

quires the active monitoring, testing, and checking the servicing of one's own and one's competitors products.

5. *Companies which introduce new products must consider the processes and costs required to cannibalize their own products and to retrench the workers involved.* Companies faced with rapidly changing technology, quick market saturation, and unexpected competition must be prepared to change or withdraw their own products rather than let their reputation and market shares be eroded by a competitor. Corporate planning for new products must include contingencies for shifting, retraining, or retrenching large product sectors rapidly.

6. *A corporate vision must be developed which emphasizes change, allows for the assimilation of new units with alternative values, and encourages members to learn from mistakes without reprisal.* Corporate cultures which cannot change rapidly will impede market adaptation. Corporations faced with stiff competition will often acquire other corporations with alternative values which will have to be integrated without delay into their corporate culture. Finally, a certain number of new initiatives are doomed to failure for all the reasons previously cited. Talented members of an organization must learn quickly from their failures and press on to new projects.

7. *A corporate strategy must be developed which scans the globe for potential acquisitions, joint ventures, coalitions, value-added partnerships, and tailored trade agreements which can give a corporation a technological edge, market access, market control, and/or rapid response capabilities.* Such a pooling of corporate resources is necessary for survival in a rapidly changing, highly competitive, international economic environment.

Each of these seven issues form the basis for a new set of corporate assumptions and practices.

High-speed management as the central communication process in rapidly getting products to market

"Rapidly changing technology, quick market saturation, unexpected global competition—these all make succeeding in business . . . harder than ever today" (Fraker 1984). These volatile economic forces, when combined with regional core market recessions and sector economic recessions such as automotive and real estate, are placing considerable stress upon organizations participating in the global economy.

The fallout in the form of bankruptcies, consolidation, rationalization, and precipitous drops in income, profits, and stockholder values have been significant.

However, several so called "well managed" global corporations such as General Electric, Asea, Brown and Boveri, and Toyota have not only avoided this stress, but have watched their sales and profits increase and have flourished. We believe that high-speed management played an important role in the adjustment of these successful global corporations to environmental change. More specifically, we argue that the fundamental problem confronting organizations who participate in the global economy is one of carefully monitoring in real time the major economic forces, market forces, and competitor plans throughout the globe, and then rapidly reorienting of an organization's units in such a manner as to obtain value-added advantage relative to one's competitors throughout the world.

High-speed management is the effective communication system employed by these so called "well managed" companies. Let us examine high-speed management in several stages.

First, we shall delineate high-speed management's communication characteristics and the effect such characteristics have upon organizational performance.

Second, we shall explore the two chief theoretic components of high-speed management—environmental scanning and value chain theory—and their effect upon organizational performance.

Third, we shall investigate organizational co-alignment as the paradigmatic theoretic communication activity in high-speed management and explore its effect on organizational performance.

Successful organizations are employing new management assumptions

Rapid environmental change creates organizational problems, but it can also create organizational opportunities. An organization's management system, with its integration, coordination, and control processes must have certain specifiable characteristics in order to respond to the opportunities created by successive, rapid, environmental change. A management system which capitalizes on environmental change must be (*a*) innovative, (*b*) adaptive, (*c*) flexible, (*d*) efficient, and (*e*) rapid in response . . . a high-speed management system (Cushman and King 1987).

Innovative management refers not only to product development, but innovation in corporate structure, manpower utilization, outsourcing, inventory control, manufacturing, marketing, servicing, and competitive positioning.

Adaptive management refers to an organization's appropriate adjustment to change in employee values, customer tastes, investor interests, government regulations, the availability of global economic resources, and the strategic positioning of competitors.

Flexible management refers to the capacity of an organization to expand, contract, shift direction on products and competitive strategy; to assimilate acquisitions, joint ventures, and coalitions, and to excise unproductive or underproductive units.

Efficient management refers maintaining the industry lead in world-class products, productivity, investors' equity, return on investment, employee satisfaction, customer support, product quality, and serviceability.

Rapid response management refers to setting and maintaining the industry standard in speed of response to environmental change (Pepper 1989).

The organizational benefits which flow from a high-speed management system can be breathtaking.

First, order of magnitude changes occur in response time. General Electric reduced from three weeks to three days the amount of time required to deliver a custom-made circuit breaker. Motorola used to turn out electronic pagers three weeks after the factory order arrived, now the process takes two hours (Ruffin 1990).

Second, order of magnitude changes occur in productivity, product quality, and market share. A recent survey of fifty major U.S. corporations by Kaiser and Associates, a large consulting firm, found that all listed time-based management strategies at the top of their priority list (Dumaine 1989, 54). Why? Because speed of response tends to provide order of magnitude improvements in productivity, profits, product quality, and market shares.

Third, order of magnitude changes occur in profits. McKinsey & Company management consulting group demonstrates that high-tech products that come to market six months late earn 33 percent less profit over five years than those coming out on time, while 50 percent overbudget increase in product development cuts profits only 4 percent when the product is on time (Vesey 1991, 25).

The focus of this new corporate perspective and thus the goal of high-speed management is the use of the new information technologies and human communication process to rapidly develop, test, and produce a steady flow of low-cost, high-quality, easily serviced, high-value products which meet the customers' needs and to quickly get these products to market before one's competition in an effort to achieve market penetration and large profits.

An outline of the theory of high-speed management

Competitive advantage in a rapidly changing economic environment will depend upon a corporation's capacity to monitor accurately changes in *external economic forces* and then to rapidly reorder a firm's *internal resources* to effectively respond to these external economic forces. In order to accurately monitor changes in external economic forces, an organization must have a world-class information and communication capability. A world-class information and communication capability would allow an organization to track and respond in real time to international changes in the cost of capital, labor, and raw materials as well as changes in consumer taste and competitor response.

Similarly, sustainable competitive advantage in the 1990s will depend upon a corporation's capacity to rapidly orient and reorient a firm's product development, purchasing, manufacturing, distribution, sales, and service systems in response to volatile environmental change. To understand and systematically employ a high-speed management system, we are in need of a theoretic framework to guide the development and maintenance of such a world-class information and communication capability. It is the purpose of this portion of our essay to explicate such a general theoretic framework. Our explication of this framework will proceed in two stages: (1) we shall explore a theory of environmental scanning as an information and communication framework for monitoring and evaluating rapid changes in an organization's external economic forces, and (2) we shall explore value chain theory as an information and communication framework for rapidly orienting and reorienting an organization's internal resources in response to changing external environmental forces.

A theory of environmental scanning. Environments create both problems and opportunities for organizations. Organizations must cope with changes in the cost of capital, labor, raw materials, shifts in consumer taste, governmental regulations, political stability, and unexpected competition. Similarly organizations depend upon the environment for scarce and valued resources, for developing strategic alliances such as coalitions, licensing, acquisitions, joint ventures, consortiums, value-added partnerships, and tailored trade agreements aimed at improving a firm's research and development, manufacturing, distribution and service, and sales capabilities. An organization's environment, perhaps more than any other factor, affects organizational strategy, structure, and performance. However, whether changes in organizational strategy, structure, and performance lead to positive or negative consequences rests almost entirely upon the speed, accuracy, and interpretation of the information and communication regarding various environmental changes and the rapid reorientation of an organization's strategy, structure, and resources in order to take advantage of such changes.

Each industry and market in which a firm operates will contain its own unique underlying competitive dynamic based upon what one's competitors are doing to influence sales and the influences to which one's customers are responding in buying products. Thus environmental scanning of industry and market forces must track the organizational strategies, structures, and resources employed by one's competitors and the tasks, inclinations, products, and potential products which one's customers will want or demand. This information and communication analysis is normally performed by the product divisions operating in the industry and market.

Once the competitive dynamics of an industry and market are understood, then top management normally scans the economic, technical, political, and social forces at work in the global economy which might be employed by one's competitors or oneself to influence these competitive dynamic. For example, capital can frequently be borrowed from Japanese banks at 3 to 5 percent less than other sources; skilled labor can be obtained in Singapore, Taiwan, and Korea at 30 to 60 percent less than in the U.S.-Canadian and European Economic Community core markets; parts and manufacturing processes can frequently be subcontracted from other firms less expensively than provided in house. These global forces can significantly influence the competitive dynamics of an industry and market and are central to reorienting one's own firm to achieve a competitive advantage.

Environmental scanning is at once a simple and complex process. It is simple in that the critical information required to analyze the underlying dynamics of an industry and market are frequently readily available by all the competitors. It is complex in that the number of areas monitored to effect this dynamic may be large. Let us explore the elements in this process in a concrete example.

Jack Welsh, CEO of General Electric, a very successful global competitor, describes the two levels of environmental scanning and their effect on corporate alignment in his firm. Once a year at the annual meeting of GE's top 100 executives, each of the firm's fourteen business leaders is required to present an environmental scanning analysis of his or her respective businesses. Each business leader is asked to present one page answers to five questions:

1. What are your business' global market dynamics today and where are they going over the next several years?
2. What actions have your competitors taken in the last three years to upset those global dynamics?
3. What have you done in the last three years to effect those dynamics?
4. What are the most dangerous things your competitors could do in the next three years to upset those dynamics?
5. What are the most effective things you could do to bring about your desired impact on those dynamics?

Welsh concludes:

> Five simple charts. After those initial reviews, which we update regularly, we could assume that everyone at the top knew the plays and had the same playbook. It doesn't take a genius. So when Larry Bossidy is with a potential partner in Europe, or I'm with a company in the Far East, we're always there with a competitive understanding based on our playbooks. We know exactly what makes sense; we don't need a big staff to do endless analysis. That means we should be able to act with speed.
>
> Probably the most important thing we promise our business leaders is fast action. Their job is to create and grow new global businesses. Our job in the executive office is to facilitate, to go out and negotiate a deal, to make the acquisition, or get our businesses the partners they need. When our business leaders call, they don't expect studies, they expect answers.
>
> Take the deal with Thomson, where we swapped our consumer electronics business for their medical equipment business. We were presented with an opportunity, a great solution to a serious strategic problem and we were able to act quickly. We didn't need to go back to headquarters for a strategic analysis and a bunch of reports. Conceptually, it took us about 30 minutes to decide that the deal made sense and then maybe two hours with the Thomson people to work out the basic terms.(Tichy and Charzon 1989, 115)

Environmental scanning allows us to focus on the forces external to an organization which significantly influence its internal relationships. Value chain theory allows us the opportunity to reorient an organization's internal relationships in an effort to influence an organization's response to external forces.

An explication of value chain theory. We are in need of a theoretic framework for analyzing the kinds of international markets, the types of competitive advantage, and the issues involved in configuring and linking a firm's activities relative to one's competitors so as to obtain a sustainable competitive advantage. Particularly useful in this regard is *value chain theory.* We shall therefore: (*a*) explicate value chain theory, and (*b*) draw out the implications of this analysis for high-speed management.

The basic unit of analysis in understanding international competition is the industry, because it is in the industry that market shares are won or lost. In order to analyze how international competition functions, we must explore various market strategies, types of competitive advantage, and who value chain theory can serve as a theoretic approach for developing the sources of competitive advantage within an organization's functioning.

The forms of international competition within an industry range from *multidomestic* to *global.* A *multidomestic approach* to markets treats each country or core market as a unique arena and adjusts a firm's strategy for obtaining a competitive advantage to the specific issue in that market. When a firm takes this market-by-market approach, its international strategy is multidomestic. A multidomestic firm views its industry as a collection of individual markets. In such instance, a firm normally operates relatively autonomous subsidiaries in each market.

A *global approach* to markets is one in which a firm's competitive position in one country or core market is significantly affected by the firm's competitive position in other countries or core markets. International competition in a global industry is more than a collection of independent subsidiaries located in individual markets with unique strategies for obtaining competitive advantage in each market. A global approach rests on a series of interdependent activities which are integrated, coordinated, and controlled so that competitive advantage in one part of the world can be leveraged to obtain competitive advantage throughout the linkage system.

Competitive advantage can be viewed conceptually as emanating from time, when due to the high demand for certain products or services the first producer into the market with a quality product can dominate the market, and obtain high-end pricing and maximized profits based on speed of response creating a time-competitive advantage. The Chrysler Corporation's development, production, and marketing of minivans beat its competitors to market by one year, allowing Chrysler to capture all of the market for minivans for one year and get high end pricing for maximum profits, and to hold a majority of the market (51 percent) for the next two years due to its time-competitive advantage.

Most top international firms seek to exploit competitive advantage from various sources. To diagnose where the sources of a firm's competitive advantage are and how each organization's functional units and business processes add value or fail to add value to products, we are in need of a theoretic framework for disaggregating a firm's discrete activities and evaluating their value-added contribution to an organization's products. Particularly useful in this regard is value chain theory. Managers term the discrete activities involved in producing a product or service the value chain and arrange them into *functional unit* activities and *business processes* (see figure 4.1).

In examining an organization's *functional unit level* of the value chain, notice that the two circles which denote suppliers and customers are normally found *outside* the organizational structure, while the square boxes denote functional activities performed *within* an organization's structure. In examining an organization's business process level, note how each process includes some activities unique to each business process and some activities which overlap with other business processes.

Functional units and business processes may be located anywhere on the globe where they can gain competitive advantage from their location. *Product development processes* are normally located in regions where firms have access to a steady supply of state-of-the-art engineers such as Silicon Valley in California near the University of California–Berkeley, Stanford University, and California Technological University or Route 128 in Massachusetts near Harvard, MIT, and other schools where competitive advantage can be obtained from product differentiation. *Product delivery processes* are normally located near sources of inexpensive and skilled labor and automated production facilities such as Korea, Singapore, and Taiwan, where competitive advantage can be obtained from low-cost production. *Customer service and management* teams are normally located in the core markets a firm services in order to obtain competitive advantage from rapid response time. A firm may obtain competitive advantage and/or value-added contributions from one or more of these sources. However, competitive advantage and value-added activities gained in one functional unit or business process can be added to or

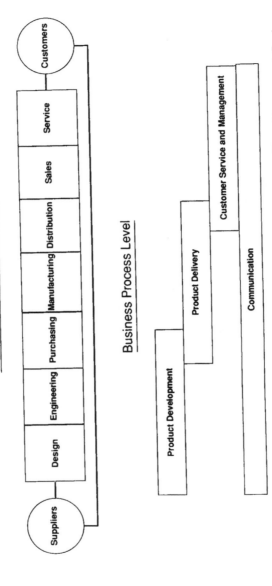

AN ORGANIZATION'S VALUE CHAIN

Functional Business Unit Level

| Design | Engineering | Purchasing | Manufacturing | Distribution | Sales | Service |

Suppliers — Customers

Business Process Level

Product Development

Product Delivery

Customer Service and Management

Communication

FIG. 4.1. Source: Revised from J. Rockart & J. Short, IT in the 1990s, *Sloan Management Review*, 30 (1989): 12.

cancelled out by an organization's performance in other functional units or business processes. This is what is meant by value-added or value-diminishing chains of activities.

Implications for high-speed management. While environmental scanning and value chain theory appear to be useful as analytic tools for exploring the types and sources of competitive advantage two questions arise regarding the framework's generalizability.

First, can the appropriate use of environmental scanning and value chain theory to analyze change in the environment and quickly adjust an organization's value chain to meet these changes separate successful from unsuccessful international competitors based on configuration and linking processes irrespective of industry?

Second, can environmental scanning and value chain theory demonstrate that firms which have a competitive advantage based on time also have improved performance ratings on all forms of competitive advantage?

Marquise Cvar (1984) attempted to answer the first question when he undertook a study at twelve international corporations in 1984. For his research, Cvar selected eight successful and four unsuccessful firms for study. Four of the successful firms were American, while one each was Swiss, British, Italian, and French. Three of the four unsuccessful firms were American and one was Swiss. These twelve firms each competed in separate industries. Successful firms were distinguished from unsuccessful firms by their high investment in information and communication technology and by the effective use of information and communication to analyze and evaluate quickly changes in the external organizational environment and then to reorient rapidly its internal resource in responding to those changes.

Smith, Grimm, Chen, and Gannon (1989) attempted to answer our second question in their study of twenty-two top-level managers from high-technology electronics firms. They explained major portions of the variance in organizational performance or increases in profits and sales on the basis of decreases in response time to environmental change. They found that an external orientation by a firm, a rapid response to competitor threat, and the radicalness of the change initiated in the organization were all positively related to increased profits, sales, and the general performance of an organization. Decreases in response time to external change were highly correlated with communication systems improvements in an organization's research and development, manufacturing, and marketing.

Value chain theory does appear to be capable of (1) separating successful from unsuccessful international firms, and (2) revealing how competitive advantage based on integration, coordination, and control improves overall organizational performance. We are now in a position to explore the transformations the general theory of high-speed management has brought about in the traditional conceptualization of organizational communication processes.

Co-alignment as the paradigm theoretic high-speed management organizational communication activity

Such environmental scanning and organizational adaptation processes confront what many management experts have come to see as management paradoxes. An organization to be successful at this adaptation process must be at the same time global and local, big and small, centralized and decentralized, fast and slow, achieve economics of scale and produce highly specialized products. Caught in this swamp of seemingly paradoxical environment demands, the management systems of most organizations have become disjointed, sluggish, fat, and unresponsive.

However, once again for a very small set of globally successful organizations, the opposite has been true. They have met these seemingly paradoxical demands with an organizational management system which manifests a slimmed down administrative system characterized by tight and efficient integration, coordination, and control of environmental scanning and organizational adaptation processes. It is the central claim of this paper that what characterizes the management systems in those successful, as opposed to the unsuccessful, global corporations is a new understanding and implementation of the uniquely communication component in effective management systems and organizational co-alignment processes.

Fortunately, several well-documented studies have explored in detail how organizational co-alignment processes work (Rocket and Schort 1989; Port 1986; Cvar 1986; Smith et al. 1989). The Center for Information Systems Research at the MIT Sloan School of Management in 1989 summarized these convergent studies when it stated that an organization's *ability to continuously improve its effectiveness in managing organizational interdependencies* was the critical element in successfully responding to the competitive forces of the 1990s (Rockert and Schort 1989). Effectiveness in managing organizational interdependencies refers to an organization's ability to achieve *co-*

alignment among its internal and external resources in a manner which is equal to or greater than existing world-class benchmarks for responding to environmental change.

Co-alignment is a unique form of organizational interdependence in which each of a firm's subunits clearly articulates its needs, concerns, and potential contributions to the organization's functioning in such a manner that management can forge an appropriate value-added configuration and linkage between units. An appropriate value-added configuration and linkage between units is one which integrates, coordinates, and controls each unit's needs, concerns, and contributions so that the outcome is mutually satisfying to the units involved and optimizing in value-added activities to the organizational functioning as a whole.

The transformation by high-speed management of traditional organizational communication processes

The task of management remains as it has always been "to make people capable of joint performance by giving them common goals, common values, the right structure, and the ongoing training and development they need to perform and respond to change" (Drucker 1988). However, this traditional role for management becomes complicated in a global organization by creating the need to rise above merely local differences in management style to develop a global management perspective and style. This involves the selection of a common language, goals, values, structures, and training that is at once neutral to national differences and adaptive to local issues (Cushman and King 1993).

In addition, the task of management requires still further modification in order to respond to its high-speed management capabilities of being innovative, adaptive, flexible, efficient, and rapid in response. Finally, all these modifications must be brought to bear on the primary organizational co-alignment processes, environmental scanning and value chain adjustment. It is in this process of joint action that the organizational concern for integration, coordination, and control meet and that communication and management become interdependent. It will therefore be the purpose of this section of our essay to analyze the transformations made by these demands to these processes.

First, we will explore the transformations made by high-speed management in the traditional organizational integrations processes.

Second, we will explore the transformations made by high-speed management in the traditional organizational coordination processes.

Third, we will explore the transformations made by high-speed management in the traditional organizational control processes.

Fourth, we will draw out the implications of these transformations for a theory of organizational communication processes.

The critical communication and management processes involved in organizational coalignment are an organization's integration, coordination, and control processes. *Organizational integration is achieved by three overlapping subprocesses—leadership, corporate climate, and teamwork.* Each has its unique function. Organizational leadership creates a focused set of goals for an organization. An appropriate corporate climate is achieved when an organization's various stakeholders——workers, investors, customers, suppliers, and governments—work together in such a manner as to make these goals achievable. Teamwork functions effectively when separate units, individuals within units, and systems across tasks, are co-aligned for goal attainment (Barrett 1987).

Organizational coordination is achieved through the sharing of information in such a manner as to optimize the value-added activities of each of an organization's subunits and environment. This normally involves linking customers, regulators, research and development, marketing, manufacturing, distribution, sales, and service in such a manner that the issues, concerns, and contributions of each link in the value chain can be optimized (Bower and Haut 1988).

Organizational control involves the planning, including the setting of targets for sales, productivity, and quality; monitoring progress towards those targets in real time; and the assessment after the fact of improvements which can be made in performance. These planning, monitoring, and assessment functions, if they are to be realistic, also involve co-alignment processes between environmental demands and the value chain which normally takes the form of specific targets or goals and the review of individual and group progress towards these goals which then forms the basis for the organization's recognition and reward system.

The co-alignment of each of these processes is the essential feature in time as an organizational basis for competitive advantage in the global economy.

The paradigm management tools for successful coalignment in the global economy are undergoing change today. Therefore it is necessary to explore what we are changing from and what we are changing to (see table 4.1).

Table 4.1. Fundamental Management Tools

Organizational Management Processes	Current Organizational Tools	New Organizational Tools
•Integration process	•Transformational leadership	•Global warrior leadership
	Matrix management	Global matrix management
•Coordination process	•MIS network Teamwork	•Telecommunication Continuous improvement
•Control process	•Goals, semiannual and annual reviews	•Stretch goals and targets Weekly review

The transformation in organizational integration processes

The co-alignment of organizational management processes in the global economy are currently rooted in several rather specific management tools. *Organizational integration processes are shifting from an emphasis on transformational leadership and matrix management to an emphasis on global warrior leadership and global matrix management.* Whereas transformational leaders employ their anticipatory, visioning, value congruence, empowerment, and self-understanding skills to present and implement successive visions for changing a corporation in response to environmental change, a global warrior develops and implements a single innovative, adaptive, flexible, efficient, and rapid response organizational framework which allows the organization to rationalize its response to change in a manner coherent to workers, investors, suppliers, customers, and regulators.

Whereas matrix management takes the various units in an organization's value chain and subjects them to the supervision of multiple managers with multiple interests—normally a product division manager and a market location manager—global matrix management changes the management team to a local market manager, a product team manager, and an international synergy manager.

The transformation in organizational coordination processes

Organizational coordination processes are also in the process of change. Centralized and decentralized MIS systems and the extensive use of teamwork systems are giving way to interactive telecommunication and continuous improvement systems. Whereas centralized and decentralized MIS systems require fixed entry, rigid frameworks for rapid information exchange, interactive telecommunication allows for multiple entry, flexible memory frameworks which can more adequately meet the need to coordinate individual differences as well as commonalities.

Whereas cross-functional, self-managed, and social-technical teamwork was instrumental in increasing quality, productivity, and profits, more permanent continuous improvement systems allow for individual as well as team responsibility in constantly improving these processes.

The transformation in organizational control processes

Organizational control processes are also involved in a radical change process. Whereas organizations used to set yearly performance targets or goals and conduct semiannual or annual reviews of individuals and unit contributions to those goals, responding to a volatile environment has forced organizations to employ stretch goals, namely those adjusted to quarterly fluctuations and weekly performance reviews in an effort to more rapidly adjust to increases and decreases in environmental change.

Each of these changes is an attempt to achieve more rapid, accurate, and continuous adjustment of organizational co-alignment aimed at optimizing the value-added activity of each organizational unit. All of these changes has moved the global corporation deeper and deeper into high-speed management systems.

What then are the unique contributions of communication to each of these shifts in a global organization's integration, coordination, and control processes? Do we have clear examples of how each shift works in a global context?

Implications for organizational communication processes

The shift from transformational leadership and matrix management to global warrior leadership and global matrix management involves two changes. *First,* the global warrior as leader seeks to develop a single organizational framework of goals and values which allows for the successful rationalization of organizational change in regard to workers, investors, customers, and regulators. This can be done only when the organizational framework consists of goals and values which each stakeholder in the organization can buy into and which considers each group's interests, concerns, and contributions to organizational effectiveness. When such a framework is constructed appropriately, a successful rationalization of organizational activity can be made through an appropriate appeal to these interests, concerns, and contributions. This process of constructing such an integrative framework and utilization of the rationalization of organizational activities is uniquely and primarily a co-alignment communication activity.

A prime example of such a global warrior framework is the articulation of the four goals for General Electric by Jack Welsh, the CEO of the General Electric Corporation.

The first goal is to become the most competitive corporation in the world. This goal is currently operationalized to mean invest only in business with high growth potential where GE can become number one or two in market shares; divest low-growth businesses; decentralize power and responsibility to become more rapid and flexible in response to market forces; develop low-cost, high-quality, easily serviced products; monitor carefully the ability of each business to meet productivity, quality, and financial targets; and intervene when necessary to make each business a "win-aholic."

The second goal is to become the nation's most valuable corporation. This goal is currently operationalized to mean the most valuable in terms of market capitalization. To do this GE, now worth $58.4 billion, would have to leapfrog IBM with $74 billion, Exxon Corporation worth $68 billion, and Philip Morris worth $62 billion. This goal is operationalized to mean keep sales and profits rising at 10 to 15 percent per year, stock appreciation at 15 percent, shift earning mix to high growth areas, keep production rising at 10 percent, keep exports at 50 percent, and maintain management's reputation as entrepreneurial, agile, knowledgeable, aggressive, and effective as competitors.

The third goal is to develop a skilled, self-actualizing, productive, and aggressive work force. This goal is currently operationalized to mean GE wants to create an environment which will be a challenging place to work and which will significantly enhance workers' skills so that they can find another job if the company no longer needs them— a place where employees are ready to go but eager to stay, to develop employees' awareness that the only road to job security is increasing market shares, to hold employees responsible for meeting productivity, quality, and fixed goals while upgrading their own skills.

The fourth goal is to develop open communication based on candor and trust. This goal is operationalized to mean sharing corporation objectives, facts, and vision with all employees; opening each employee up to discussion regarding his or her strengths, weaknesses, and the possibility for change; and to motivate employees to become happier, more self-confident, and energized workers.

This organizational framework allowed Jack Welsh to rationalize the selling of over $11 billion in businesses, to acquire over $9 billion in other businesses, to cut 130,500 employees, undertake a $1 billion stock buyback program, invest billions in modernizations, close 73 plants, and reduce 100 businesses to 14. Over a five-year period, revenues increased 27 percent, earnings 42 percent, stockholder equity 43 percent, with an average annual growth in earnings at 10 percent per share. GE's market value went from $12 billion (11th in the nation) to $58 billion (2nd in the nation).

Second, the shift from matrix management to global matrix management subjected units in an organizational value chain to three manager/supervisors rather than two. This can be effectively implemented only when each manager is aware of each of the other manager's demands upon those units and integrates his or her demands accordingly. When such a structure is created, it only works when the interests, concerns, and contributions of each manager are integrated in such a manner as to yield consistent action. This process is uniquely and primarily a co-alignment communication activity.

A prime example of the effective use of global matrix management is Asea Brown Boveri (ABB). ABB's CEO Percy Barnevik detailed the unique features of this global matrix in an interview (Taylor 1990). The organizing logic of ABB's global matrix is as follows. At the bottom, ABB consists of some 1,100 local businesses averaging 200 employees in size. The manager of each local unit is responsible to the leaders of some fifty business areas worldwide and to a country manager. The fifty business managers and over eighty country managers are grouped into eight business areas and four geographic regions which are responsible to the thirteen member executive committee and the CEO. The business areas are global in focus and make product strategy and performance decisions irrespective of national or regional boundaries. The geographic region and country managers focus on regional and local issues in product design and mix. The local managers focus on the running of their local units. All managers interact at the management level in English and at the local level in their appropriate local language.

Last year ABB had sales of $21 billion and profits of $589 million with 85,000 employees who, due to the organizational integration processes of global matrix management, were able to think globally and act locally, to be big and small, to be centralized and decentralized, and to be fast and slow through communication.

The shift from MIS networks and teamwork to telecommunication networks and continuous change involves two significant changes. *First,* the shift from MIS networks to telecommunication networks involves a shift from pure information systems which are rigid and focused on the consensual use of data, to telecommunication networks which are flexible, multichannel, and allow for both system commonalities and individual differences in perspective and messages. This encourages the co-alignment of both similarities and differences through human interaction.

An excellent sample of this telecommunication networking is the Ford Motor Company. Ford platforms research and development and manufacturing from four specialization centers throughout the world one located in Europe, one in the United States, one in Latin America, and one in Australia. The products from each of these centers are then shipped to and combined with products from the other centers at the point of distribution and sales. In order to coordinate this effort, Ford has a telecommunication capability in each office and factory around the world. Audio, visual, and data interaction are possible among all units. This coordination effort has allowed the co-alignment of commonalities and diversities globally.

Second, teamwork has given way to continuous improvement processes around the world. Continuous improvement processes may involve either individuals, groups, or teams and allow for short- or long-term focus. Several recent studies have demonstrated that teamwork is not the only way to get organizational improvement and not necessarily the best way for most problems (Lefton and Buzzota 1987). What separates continuous improvement processes from teamwork is the communicative co-alignment of worker and task whether it be by individuals, groups, or teams.

One example of such a continuous improvement process is GE's workout program. Each week the managers of various units meet with workers to discuss problems within the organization. Then workers and managers decide upon the best structure for solving the problems be they individual training, group, or teamwork processes. Responsibility is delegated for solving the problems and a timeframe established. Each week this process is repeated. Over the first two years of its operation at GE Plastics, it is estimated that over $3 million dollars in savings occurred from this workout process (Paul 1991).

The shift from long term goals and annual and semiannual reviews to quarterly stretch goals and weekly reviews involves two changes. First, a recognition that in a volatile economic climate, long-term goals and annual reviews are necessarily vague and shifting, and second, that short-term goals and weekly monitoring allow the adjustment of both goals and performance to change in a predictable manner. The communication of changes in stretch goals and weekly performance evaluation is another instance of organizational coalignment in setting and meeting realistic targets.

One example of the effective use of such a control process is the Cypress Corporation and its CEO T. J. Rodgers' implementation of four overlapping software programs aimed at channeling interaction and work within tightly specified boundaries in order to minimize errors (Rodgers 1990). Cypress is a semiconductor manufacturer within the volatile computer chip market. Rodgers believes that effective organizational management can be broken down into four subprocesses—hiring, setting and meeting goals, resource allocation, and performance appraisal. For each of these processes, his firm has an interactive computer program which monitors each system carefully and gives instant feedback. For example, in the case of manufacturing, its "killer software" shuts down the system if any critical rules and procedures of the system are violated.

Let us explore in detail one of these software processes. Each week, each manager is encouraged to set challenging organizational goals and stipulate a time frame, preferably a week or less, for meeting these goals. These decisions are entered into a database. By Tuesday morning, each manager's manager reviews these goals for possible conflicts, challenges, and time problems, and talks with the individuals involved. By Friday, each manager is expected to complete the goal or indicate the problem and the new time frame. For individuals, it is expected that they will complete 75 percent of their goals within a week, for groups 70 percent. Managers can track subordinates and groups of subordinates on a weekly basis, and take corrective action when necessary. Once a week each vice president checks each division under him or her and takes corrective action if necessary.

The result is that goals are met 75 percent of the time and the organizational targets can be accurately adjusted on a quarterly basis. At Cypress, completed goal reports trigger a mini-performance review which is used to update performance evaluations more easily and make setting achievable stretch goals equally easily. Early diagnosis of goal or performance problems leads to rapid response in correcting problems. Setting manageable goals leads to the better allocation of individual and group resources and the more predictable co-alignment of organizational activities.

At the center of each of these changes in organizational co-alignment is the need for interactive communication in an open and frank manner and equally significant the appropriate inclusion of individual interests, concerns, and contributions into the organizational outcomes. When organizational integration, coordination, and control processes function in this manner, value-added activities and organizational adaptations achieved at one point in the value chain add to those obtained in other parts of the value chain in such a way as to create a sustainable competitive advantage.

Summary and Conclusions

What then has our rather long inquiry into communication and management within the global economy taught us about communication and management processes in the latter half of the twentieth century?

First, let us consider management. Here Drucker's definition of the process remains constant. However, the strategies and tools involved in order to respond to a new larger and more volatile environment have changed. A new form of leadership has emerged—the global warrior—leaders with a global perspective who will scan the globe for needed resources, who will establish portions of the value chain for their organization wherever they can generate value-added activities, and who monitor diverse markets for product opportunities while providing an organizational framework of goals and values capable of rationalizing innovative, flexible, efficient, and rapid responses to customers and competitor activities. Such a leader employs global matrix management, telecommunication networks, and continuous improvement programs, setting short-term achievable stretch goals which can accurately be monitored on a weekly basis in order to reorient the value chain rapidly to environmental change.

Second, let us consider communication. Here again, Cushman and King's definition of the process remains constant. Effective communication follows a strategy of co-alignment of diverse interests, concerns, and contributions through the use of an open flexible communication system which allows for the co-alignment of both similarities and differences into an innovative, flexible, efficient, and rapid response system. Co-alignment is made more complex by including within a single organizational structure, culturally and linguistically diverse people who want and demand a recognition of their differences as a prerequisite to the formations of communities that allow for the effective integration, coordination, and control of organizational activities.

It is clear from our analysis, that *communication and management are interdependent.*

Note

Portions of this essay are adapted from D. P. Cushman and S. S. King "High-Speed Management," in Stanley Deetz (ed.), *Communication Yearbook* 16 (1993), Sage Publications; S. S. King and D. P. Cushman, "Communication and Management in the Global Economy," a paper presented to the Conference on Communication and Culture in the Global Economy in Paris, France, May 1991; D. P. Cushman and S. S. King, "High-Speed Management and Continuous Improvement Programs," paper presented to the Conference on Corporate Communication, Fairleigh Dickinson University, May 1992; and D. P. Cushman and S. S. King, "High-speed Management: A Revolution in Organizational Communication in the 1990's," chapter 2 in *A Reader in High-Speed Management: A Revolution in Organizational Communication in the 1990's* (1994), SUNY Press.

References

Baig, E. 1989. Where is the global economy going? *Fortune,* 13 July, 71–88.

Barrett, F. D. 1987. Teamwork—How to expand its power and punch. *Business Only* 24–31.

Balant, D., R. Browning, and G. Foster. 1990. How Hewlett-Packard gets numbers it can trust. *Harvard Business Review* (January/February): 178–82.

Borrus, A. 1990. Japanese streak ahead in Asia. *Business Week,* 7 May, 54–55.

Bower, J. L., and T. M. Hout. 1988. Fast cycle capability for competitive power. *Harvard Business Review* (November/December):110–18.

Castells, M. 1986. High-technology, world development and the structured transformation: The trends and debate. *Alternatives* 11:297–342.

Cushman, D. P., and S. S. King. 1987. The role of communication in high technology organizations: The emergence of high-speed management. In *Human Communication as a Field of Study,* ed. S. S. King. Albany, NY: SUNY Press.

———. High-speed management. In Communication Yearbook 16 (1993). Sage Publications, pp. 209–237.

————. 1994. *High-speed management: Organizational communication in the 1990's.* Albany: SUNY Press.

————. 1992. High-speed management and continuous improvement programs. Paper presented to the Conference on Corporate Communication, Fairleigh Dickinson University, May 1992.

Cvar, M. 1986. Case studies in global competition patterns of success and failure. In *Competition in Global Industry,* ed. M. Porter. Boston: Harvard Business School Press.

Dumaine, B. 1989. How managers can succeed through speed. *Fortune,* 13 February, 54–59.

Drucker, P. F. 1988. Management and the world's work. *Harvard Business Review 66 (September/October): 65–76.*

Feigenbaum, E., P. McCorduck, and P. Nii. 1988. *The rise of the expert company.* New York: Times Books.

Fraker, S. 1984. High-speed management for the high tech age, *Fortune,* 13 February, 34–60.

King, S. S., and D. P. Cushman. 1991. Communication and management in the global economy. Paper presented to the conference on Communication and Culture in the Global Economy, Paris, France, May 1991.

Lefton, R. E., and V. R. Buzzota. 1987. Teams and teamwork: A study of executive level teams. *National Productivity Review* 7 (Winter): 7–19.

Main, J. 1989. How to go global and why. *Fortune* 119 (28 August): 70–76.

Paul, T. 1991. Human relations management at GE Plastics: A high-speed management analysis. M.A. thesis, SUNY–Albany.

Pepper, C. B. 1989. Fast forward. *Business Month,* February, 25–30.

Port, O. 1986. High tech to the rescue. *Business Week,* 16 June, 100–108.

Rockart, J., and J. Schort. 1989. IT in the 1990's: Managing organizational interdependencies. *Sloan Management Review* 30 (Winter): 7–17.

Rodgers, T. J. 1990. No excuses management. *Harvard Business Review* 19 (July/August): 84–98.

Ruffin, W. 1990. Wired for speed. *Business Month,* January, 56–58.

Russell, E., A. Adams, and B. Boundy. 1986. High-technology test marketing Campbell Soup Company. *The Journal of Consumer Marketing* 3(Winter): 71–80.

Smith, K. G., C. M. Grimm, M. J. Chen, and M. J. Gannon. 1989. Predictors of response time to competitive strategic action: Preliminary theory and evidence. *Journal of Business Research* 19:245–58.

Stalk, Jr., G. 1988. Time—The next source of competitive advantage. *Harvard Business Review* (July/August): 41–51.

Taylor, W. 1991. The logic of global business: An interview with ABB's Percy Barnevik, *Harvard Business Review*, 69 (March/April): 91–105.

Tichy, N., and R. Charzon. 1989. Speed, simplicity, self-confidence: An interview with Jack Welch. *Harvard Business Review* 14 August, 112–120

Treece, J., and J. Howr. 1989. Shaking up. *Business Week*, 14 August, 24–80.

Wall Street Journal. 1990. The global giants. 27 September, R27.

Walton, J. 1985. The IMF riot. Paper delivered at the I.S.A. Conference on the Urban Impact of the New International Division of Labor, Hong Kong.

Young, J. 1990. An American giant rethinks globalization. *Information Strategy*, Spring, 6:5–10.

AUGUST T. HORVATH
JANET FULK

5 Information Technology and the Prospects for Organizational Transformation

A flood of works over the past decade have linked the widespread adoption of computerized information and communication technologies to radical organizational change. The technologies for which these claims are made run the gamut from the humble, familiar word-processor to advanced decision support systems and virtual meeting facilities now only in the prototype stages. The effects posited for these technologies range through the domains of organizational structure and performance, including more streamlined organizations, less hierarchical organizations, more satisfying organizations, and more productive organizations.

Taken as a whole, this literature presents a bewildering array of arguments, including some ill-defined and contradictory claims. For example, information technology has been expected to centralize (Smith 1989), decentralize (Nilles 1982), or reinforce (Dutton and Kraemer 1982) existing power structures. Even the reader determined to cut through the fashionable jargon to expose the basic positions being elaborated must conclude that information technologies are implicated in at least several different arguments about organizational change.

This chapter integrates many of these diverse viewpoints under a single rubric. Our synthetic premise is that much previous research implicating information technologies in organizational transformation implicitly or explicitly posits that information technology alters the information environments within and between organizations. The most salient feature of these information environments is commonly assumed to be the cost of handling and communicating information of various kinds. We argue that most accounts of information technology and organizational change can be understood in terms of information-processing costs and the implications of these costs for communication and organizational structures and performance.

Despite its ubiquity, we find the information-processing-cost perspective inadequate for understanding the causes and consequences of organizational media use. This chapter summarizes theory and research findings on other aspects of information technologies and organizations—including their social, symbolic, and cultural dynamics—to defend our position that information-technological intervention based on the information-environment perspective can have unsatisfactory and sometimes disastrous consequences.

Recent theory and research that do not fit into information-processing models of organizations open a new dimension to the study of organizational technology. They evidence a concern, not merely with mechanistic communication and decision processes, but with socially negotiated outcomes and the subjectivity of interpretation in organizations. For researchers, these perspectives argue against generalized pronouncements on the nature and impact of information-technological innovation that ignore the unique features and specific conditions of the adopting organization. They suggest also that organizational practitioners should be wary of dramatic claims for technological intervention, considering carefully the implications of new media for their organizations' prevailing modes of interaction. In short, consideration of the broader social texture of organizations and technologies can help to explain the widely varying, and often disappointing, results achieved by information technologies in organizations.

Beginning with a discussion of the implications of information technology for the structural transformation of organizations facing turbulent environments, we focus on how the information-costs approach is variously employed to predict technology-supported organizational transformations. We suggest an alternative view that stresses the social and cultural aspects of organizations, illustrating how this more textured perspective can enhance our understanding of the relationship of information technology to organizational transformation.

Information technologies and the transforming organization

The 1990s find organizations more actively considering sweeping structural change than at any time since the rise of Taylorism. Environmental pressure from a variety of sources presently impels executives and managers to seek routes to organizational change (Kanter 1983). The economic climate in which commercial organizations operate is globalizing; the pace of economic life is quickening, with product development cycles dramatically shortened and competition accordingly intensified. Recent works on the subject of information technology and organizations have often pronounced the current business environment "turbulent" and predicted that it will likely remain so for the foreseeable future (e.g., Scott Morton 1991).

Prediction can be a dangerous exercise, especially in economics, but the forecast of continuing business turbulence is relatively safe. Less certain is the implied premise that organizational environments previously have been serene—a characterization that would be acceptable to few managers at any time since the Industrial Revolution. Turbulence is built into the definition of a market economy, especially those definitions that include technical and social change as an integrated component, as Schumpeter's (1934) did. Schumpeter recognized that developments such as the expansion of markets through new suppliers, new customers, new competitors, or the acceleration of production through technology periodically generate tumultuous economic conditions of "creative destruction." Innovative new firms spring up to take advantage of, and contribute to, the new possibilities offered by technical and other parameters. The resulting increase in general productivity brings about the demise of laggard firms, as well as a good many of the innovating firms (Pfeffer and Salancik 1978; Schumpeter 1934).

The knowledge that waves of innovation-generated turbulence are systemic and periodic does not lessen the gravity of these periods from the standpoint of the individual firm. Increased productivity becomes a necessity of survival in such an environment. Moreover, the required productivity is often of a new kind, for some of the innovations behind the shakeout involve more than the traditional increase in production as a function of capital and labor inputs. The relevant outputs, in present economic circumstances, are not simply gross quantities produced, but also the quality of the product, the customization associated with just-in-time manufacturing, the speed with which the product can be brought from conception to production, and its adaptability both to different cultures across geographic space and to modification and improvement over time. Many of these suddenly necessary achievements are not easily measurable by traditional performance indicators (Strassman 1985).

The difficulty of coping with the mounting demands of the business environment seems compounded by indications that employees demand more meaningful participation in organizational processes. In this context, organizations find it unattractive to seek greater efficiency through further centralization and work segmentation. Organizational designers instead consider whether arrangements involving broader distributions of power, responsibility, and satisfaction can outperform hierarchical approaches, even in the categories long assumed to be the unique strengths of centralized organization. Increasingly, information and communications technologies are heavily implicated in the desired organizational transformations, often being cited as the means by which the desired alterations may be achieved.

Computer technology and its associated "information revolution" are sometimes held to be not only the means, but the ultimate cause of radical organizational change. Information-technological determinism has a long, if not always auspicious, history in communication science. Although the history of information and communication technology is studded with as many spectacular failures as revolutionary successes, the basic technology-push argument is still explicitly called upon to account for the introduction and widespread use of information devices in organizations (e.g., by Venkatraman 1991). Theorists of information technology and organizations have built convincing arguments that information and communication technology deserve special consideration, apart from technology more generally, as possible determinants of organizational structure. While widely varying forms of organization are admittedly compatible with a given production technology, information technology structures organizational activities of cooperation, coordination and control—elements whose arrangements are taken to define the very nature of the organization (Scott Morton 1991, 9–10). To some researchers, these characteristics of computer-based information and communication technologies differentiate them sufficiently from production or "process" technologies to warrant their designation simply as "new" technologies (e.g., Pennings and Buitendam 1987).

The conclusions of empirical investigations of information technology as a catalyst for organizational restructuring are less dramatic than these theoretical expectations. When the relationships between large, multifaceted concepts like "information technology" and "organizational structure" are investigated in social science, the conclusions are almost always ambivalent and conditional. The complexity of the technological and organizational conditions on which the relationship has proven contingent, and the small variance explained in structural variables when a relationship was found, has helped ensure that no comprehensive and definitive conception of the technology-structure relationship has been produced.

From these uncertain results, a more cautious view has emerged. Abandoning strictly determinist language, scholars now speak of information technology "enabling" new "possibilities" in organizations (Rockart and Short 1991; Allen and Hauptman 1987). Early conclusions that information technology would wreak such extreme decentralization as to virtually destroy the solidarity that holds organizations together (Nilles 1982) have been replaced with the more moderate position that new arrangements are possible within existing organizational frameworks (e.g., Bikson, Eveland, and Gutek, 1989; Keen 1990).

Information costs, information environments, and organizational transformation

Any argument linking information technology to structural change inevitably rests upon implicit or explicit assumptions about how information processing is implicated in the generation and maintenance of organizational structure. A key factor in most of these explanations is the cost of information exchange and processing. Implicitly, a communication-cost logic is the basis of a body of organizational theories arguing that, under norms of rationality, cost-efficient structural arrangements are produced by co-locating individuals and units whose interdependence is driven by needs for extensive and rapid information exchange (Galbraith 1977; Tushman and Nadler 1978). A second approach more explicitly refers to communication costs in formulating a view of organizations using principles from economic theory. In this perspective, organizational structures are seen as alternatives to markets for the information-processing function in economic activity. This model highlights most strongly the role that information costs have played in predictions of organizational transformation in the so-called "information age," drawing the notion of information costs more visibly into the analysis.

The neoclassical economic determination that markets are the most efficient way of allocating economic resources assumes "perfect information" as one of the simplifications of actual economic activity necessary to elucidate fundamental phenomena. Under this assumption, learning about suppliers and buyers, setting prices, and coordinating activity are assumed to require zero time and zero cost. Political economists had long noted that the assumption of perfect information is rarely approximated in actual markets, but the systematic pursuit of the organizational implications of imperfect information awaited the "transaction-cost" theories of the 1970s (e.g., Williamson 1975).

Transaction-cost theories concur with classical economics that markets are optimal structures for allocating resources when communication is free (or at least inexpensive). The market may be seen as an extremely decentralized information technology in which information is so thoroughly distributed that no concentrations of information processing exist. Every individual economic unit, such as a household or firm, solves its own small piece of the economic equation using only the information relevant to it—its needs and the prices of goods that meet those needs. In a system of many buyers and sellers, the overall outcome of these calculations is quantitatively optimal by certain utilitarian criteria. But, transaction-cost theories proposed, when transaction and coordination costs are high, hierarchical organizations that internalize transactions, creating internal monopolies with prices set by decree, can allocate resources more efficiently than markets (Williamson 1975). In such a hierarchy, the decreased information costs of surveillance and bargaining (i.e., the minimization of expensive communication) more than compensate for the inefficiencies of making price decisions more arbitrarily. Under these models, changes in the cost of information gathering, storage, processing, and transmission have clear implications for the relative efficacy of hierarchical as opposed to distributed, or even marketlike, transactions within organizations: high transaction costs favor hierarchies, while low transaction costs favor markets.

Information technology, in many current theories, causes or assists organizational transformation primarily through its effect on one type of transaction cost. Economists have traditionally defined "technology" as precisely the quantitative ratio or function of the productive outputs achievable to the corresponding inputs required to produce them; a change in this function is "technological change," whether or not new hardware or processes are used. By this strictly economic definition, "information technology" would be precisely a change (normally, one hopes, a reduction) in per-unit information-processing costs. Starting, often tacitly, from these premises, the typical argument for new organizational media runs as follows: To the extent that information technology restores the viability of the assumption of perfect information, it may not only reduce transaction costs enough to make less hierarchical structures competitive, but may allow for the development of decentralized forms of organization whose allocative efficiency is superior to that of hierarchical forms (Malone, Yates, and Benjamin 1987).

The decentralized organizational forms suggested by communication-cost theories may not have the totally uncoordinated character of markets, but can replace limited, carefully planned communication channels with much more numerous and flexible channels, both laterally and vertically. In one popular view, information flows can be dictated "adhocratically" by needs at any given moment (Malone and Rockart 1991). Inasmuch as the structure of an organization is defined by communication links, this structure itself will thus be subject to change as projects or circumstances warrant. At the same time, it is recognized that markets are the most decentralized decision-making forms, so a move from hierarchy toward more distributed arrangements should also satisfy employee demand for greater individual autonomy and responsibility.

Many accounts of information technology and organization fit a pattern in which organizational change is created or enabled by information technologies through alterations in their prevailing information costs. While some authors make specific reference to transaction-cost analysis in formulating their theories (Francis 1986), others employ new jargon referring to lower information costs or the more densely linked networks they are expected to create: "connectivity" (Hiltz 1984; Madnick 1991), "interrelatedness," (Rotemberg and Saloner 1991), and "increased information accessibility" (Huber 1990).

Buitendam's (1987) vision of the restructured organization is among the more carefully crafted illustrations of the role of new technology in the transformed organization. Buitendam emphasizes the horizontal dimension of organizational communication, suggesting that decentralization can be achieved through the creation of semi-autonomous, specialized work teams that cooperate in interdependent decision-making. Borrowing a concept form social exchange theory, Buitendam emphasizes that team units should be arranged so as to have relatively equal (or "symmetrical") dependencies on each other, an arrangement that promotes stability and cooperation rather than dominance and conflict. These groups are to be integrated by means of information technology, creating an overall coordination that would be rendered impossible in a large, pre-electronic organization by high communication costs.

Another relatively well-developed conception of the new firm is the "networked" organization (Rockart and Short 1991). Again predicated on the reduction of information costs toward zero with information technology, the networked organization seeks to be "communication-rich." The potentially high interconnectedness of members of the networked organization can allow a large organization to retain some of the desirable characteristics of small organizations, such as flexibility and responsiveness to clients and changing conditions. Networking allows the distribution of information, expertise, cooperative work, reward, and responsibility throughout the organization. The loose and dynamic connections, heavy lateral interaction, and task-oriented nature of this system prompt Malone and Rockart (1991) to liken the networked organization to Toffler's (1971) notion of "adhocracy."

Even more radical internal organizational forms are proposed by some theorists. One straightforward interpretation of the transaction-cost perspective is that, if lower or near-zero information costs favor markets, many of the internal activities of a firm could take on a marketlike character. In the extreme case, this could lead to a disintegration of the firm into smaller units having only temporary, contractual relations with each other. An intriguing intermediate possibility is that market institutions like competitive bidding could occur within firms. Thus, if a specialized product or service is needed and several individuals or units within the organization are capable of providing it, bids can be solicited and competitive prices quoted based on those units' skill, track record, availability, and competitive drive. Unlike the distributed or network models, in which the transformed organization remains recognizable as a distinct unit, the concept of organizations-as-markets threatens to blur the distinction between organizations and the outside world.

Finally, several authors make no detailed claims for information technology as catalyst for organizational transformation, but stress its positive effects on performance variables, chiefly "productivity." Almost invariably, lower information costs (expressed as faster, cheaper, and more accurate information) are offered as the source of these productivity gains. These writers typically stress the present economy's status as an "information economy," in which most workers are involved in the "production" of information rather than material goods (Rice and Bair 1984). When augmented by programs of organizational redesign to optimize the benefits of information technology, the potential productivity gains from the new media technology seem dramatic, and an impressive array of research findings have substantiated some of these gains (Rice and Bair 1984). These results are controversial, however, when contrasted with the numerous documented failures of organizational information technology (Panko 1984) and the lack of any perceptible general increase in economic productivity during the period of widespread computer adoption (Forester 1989).

Inter-organizational communication

Theoretical positions about the evolving nature of interorganizational economic relations often start from the same transaction-cost perspective as do theories of intra-organizational change. In the most direct application of transaction-cost theory to the market level of analysis, the widespread use of information technologies within and between organizations is presumed to portend a dramatic drop in information and coordination costs. Instant and free access to all relevant market information and the rapid negotiation of prices and contracts would remove much of the transaction-cost justification for incorporating peripheral activities within organizational hierarchies. Therefore, firms will shed these activities, and many processes presently organized hierarchically will come to be controlled by market mechanisms, through a gradual dissolution from hierarchy to a networked organization, a "biased" market, and finally to a fully decentralized market (Malone, Yates, and Benjamin 1987).

Theories of hierarchy-to-market transition seem superficially unproblematic, but empirically, they defy the general direction of change in economic organization. Influential economic commentators (notably Galbraith 1967, preceded by Schumpeter 1943) have noted a trend toward concentration and planning in economic activity, associated with the scale of industry, the need to anticipate long-term developments, and the resources required for research-intensive innovation. The increasing centralization of developed economies suggests that there must be additional economic benefits, overlooked by transaction-cost theory, accruing from concentration and centralized control. For example, the attractiveness of centralization may be enhanced by the geographic expansion and heightened competitiveness of the modern economy. A transaction-cost-driven tendency toward market mechanisms is thus more likely to produce a tension between market and hierarchical forms of economic organization at macro levels than a wholesale swing toward markets.

Less radical theories of information technology and inter-organizational relations consider the evolution of the market form, rather than with the replacement of hierarchies by classical markets. Although concurring with transaction-cost theorists that rapid and substantially free information transfer enhances the effectiveness of market mechanisms, these perspectives question the perpetuity of the marketplace of independent, individuated firms. In a concept closely akin to the intra-organizational notion of connectivity, Rotemberg and Saloner (1991, 95) hypothesize that information technology creates "'interrelatedness' among firms, markets, and products." Two general effects of this interrelatedness are: (1) cooperation among competitors in interconnected market environments by means of networks, manifested in such universal information-technological services as automatic bank teller machines and airline reservation systems, to share in gains that none could have realized individually; and (2) cooperation among firms making compatible products, as an attractive alternative to vertical integration (buying or merging with other firms). Extremely low information costs are held to enable more horizontal cooperation between firms, without the loss of autonomy created by vertical integration.

A summary such as we have presented necessarily overlooks many modifications and elaborations of the central information-cost hypothesis in the theories discussed. These theories are meaningfully differentiated in many respects, including the specific consequences of enhanced information processing for appropriate managerial action and the particular media that are held to be most effective at altering information costs. Our summary's purpose is to demonstrate the ubiquity of models based on a single, crucial aspect of information technology: its capability to lower the cost of information processing, conceptualizing costs broadly to include labor, time, and inaccuracy. In the remainder of this chapter, we draw attention to other aspects of information technology, overlooked or considered only superficially in much of the organizational literature.

Social aspects of information technologies and organizations

Recent years have seen the growth in organizational studies of theories of technology that seek to explain dependent variables other than organizational efficiency or formal structure. In these theories, the factors determining the efficacy of information-technological intervention are not the need to reduce information costs or the ability to enhance the productivity of information workers. Attention is focused instead on the perceptions, images, and feelings of organization members with respect to their organization and the available communication media; the implications of various forms of technological mediation for the dynamics of interpersonal interaction and decision-making; and the prior social characteristics of individuals and groups within organizations. These perspectives can be ranked loosely in order of the importance they assign to social factors in explaining technological outcomes. They range from rationalist perspectives, only briefly considering social factors within a framework generally compatible with the communication-cost models discussed above, to approaches that depict information technologies as symbolic or political interventions whose effect on organizational dynamics is not primarily based on the formal structure of information processing.

Rationalist perspectives

Huber's (1990) theory of information technology effects exemplifies the rational approach by explicitly assuming that competitive environments will force organizations, in time, to adopt the most rational use of technology in their information processing activities, and that social dynamics will not seriously impede such rational use in the long run. Huber's faith in market forces and the political utility of rational action provides the basis for several specific propositions about the effects of computer-mediated decisions systems and communication technologies. Some of these are structural in nature and are generally consistent with the networked-organization pattern; the implications for information processing outcomes are invariably positive. Computerized decision and communication technologies should lead to faster and more accurate identification of problems, faster and better intelligence about those problems, faster and better decisions, and faster action (Huber 1990). A similarly operational view of the benefits of organizational media is provided by Rice and Bair (1984), who offer an extensive survey of predicted and obtained benefits of computerized communication in organizations, but without the general theoretical propositions offered by Huber, or any acknowledgment that a social and political context is being overlooked. McKersie and Walton (1991) also consider the decision to implement information technologies from a rational perspective, assigning matters of organizational "climate" to the operational considerations of human resource strategies and implementation management. They concede that a specific information technology is compatible only with some organizations, and that political factors play a role in this compatibility. These political factors are depicted as manipulable through strategic initiatives by managers, either before, during, or after an information-technological intervention.

Hiltz (1984), in a case study of a computer conferencing system among scientists, took a stance slightly more oriented to social variables. Hiltz defined *a priori* a large number of individual and organizational variables potentially related to use of computer-mediated communication, including personal and work-group social factors. In a limited way, Hiltz thus examined how the social dynamics of groups determine the outcomes of technological intervention. Hiltz's approach to information technology is fundamentally deterministic, but in its consideration of the broad social characteristics of work groups, it demonstrates how far removed are the characteristics and context of real-world media use from the rationality suggested by many theorists.

King and Kraemer (1985) and Danziger and Kraemer (1986) have conducted extensive studies of computerization in a specific type of complex organization: local government. Their approach is similar to that of Hiltz in that they acknowledge the organizational, technological, and individual context of computer use, incorporating it in the form of *a priori* inputs to their model, but without making it central to the analysis (Danziger and Kraemer 1986, 9).

Sociotechnical perspectives

A second cluster of theorists and researchers views computer systems as simultaneously social and technical. In contrast to the generally positive assessments of information technology arising from more rationalist perspectives, these researchers are either more tentatively optimistic about the possibilities of computing or are much more unwilling to make general pronouncements about organizational media effects. Kling and Iacono (1988, 1989) stress the close connection of computerization and organizational-social reform by referring to such programs as "movements" or "interventions." They posit that the consequences of computer implementation in an organization are underdetermined by technical characteristics and even by prior individual, organizational, and task characteristics. The decisive variables are the strategic choices made in the process of the intervention itself (Kling and Iacono 1989, 340–41).

The Kling-Iacono analysis resembles sociotechnical systems research in its view of computerization as the simultaneous restructuring of people and artifacts. The sociotechnical tradition takes a dualistic view of organizations as interacting, parallel systems of interrelated individuals on the one hand, and technological arrangements on the other (de Greene 1973). Despite this assumption, sociotechnical systems research typically understates the importance of social factors compared to analysts such as Kling and Iacono. Rooted in the early examinations of automated physical technologies, sociotechnical researchers assume that "the most direct impact of technology is upon organizational productivity" and that effects on the psychological and social conditions of workers are more indirect, higher-order phenomena (Pasmore, Francis, Haldeman, and Shani 1982, 1184). Recent writers on sociotechnical systems have continued to stress the technical dimension of sociotechnical systems over the social dimension (e.g, Schultheiss 1988), emphasizing the positive aspects of structural and technological reorganization and discounting the constraints imposed by social conditions not subject to easy manipulation.

Many theorists emphasizing the social dimension of technological development predict (and often find, Kling and Iacono 1989) that the organizational consequences of information-technological intervention are far less certain and generally less positive than more rational perspectives suppose (e.g., Zuboff 1988). They stress that careful attention must be paid to the *meaning* of a technological intervention for work-organization, not just as an aspect of implementation or human-resources strategy, but throughout the intervention process. Writers such as Zuboff also stress the managerial choice aspect, arguing that effects are undermined by the technology alone. Managers, in choosing system configurations and implementation characteristics, may control the types of effects produced.

Culture perspectives

An alternative view of organizations and technologies stresses their social dimensions over their formal and physical structures. Organizational studies has seen the rapid rise of a cluster of organizational theories—some venture to call it a new "paradigm"—collectively termed the "culture perspective" on organizations.

Researchers working from a conception of organizations as cultures regard what appear to be strictly functional organizational artifacts, procedures, and relations as symbol-laden entities expressing implicit assumptions about the social foundation of the organization. Studies in this cultural-anthropology–influenced tradition focus on language, metaphor, and artifacts in a variety of manifestations from building architecture to illustrations in corporate annual reports, but they have identified computers and computer systems as often carrying particularly important symbolic connotations (Ciborra and Lanzara 1991; Ott 1989, 22–23; Scholz 1991). Computers can come to represent organizational change initiatives (popular or unpopular); Ott (1989) describes the case of an unused microcomputer, kept in a conspicuous place with garbage strewn upon it, to symbolize the organization's victory over a failed attempt at organizational change. The importance of communication media as cultural symbols is not surprising, as information technologies can become the central behavioral and symbolic features of information processing in an organization—what Scholz (1991) calls its "information culture." Or, they can strongly contradict the information and general culture of the organization, and face an uphill battle toward acceptance and the realization of organizational-structural or performance outcomes.

Unlike sociotechnical systems researchers, organizational-culture scholars in the anthropological tradition are skeptical of the facility with which the tacit barriers to technological intervention can be overcome from the top by applying standard formulas to organizational transformation. Just as "Hitler did not create Nazi Germany by himself" (Meek 1988, 463), senior managers cannot create networked organizations at will. The emphasis, instead, should be on designing or selecting organizational information technologies compatible with existing organizational cultures (Scholz 1991, 234).

Communication-quality perspectives

A very different mode of considering the role of social variables in organizational information technologies examines the social characteristics, not of the technology itself, but of the communication that is possible when using the technology. These perspectives can be considered an extension of the information-processing view of information technology, with two important augmentations. First, they recognize that the information environment of an organization affects not merely the structural organization and control of work, but also the social conditions implicated in collective activities such as decision-making and intra-organizational relationships. Second, the salient features of the information environment include not merely the quantity of information that can be handled or communicated at a given cost, but qualitative distinctions in the types of information that can be shared. Information is not a homogenous substance, but comes in differentially valuable forms. Information having particularly desirable characteristics, such as the ability to carry social context cues, may justify higher information costs in particular instances where such characteristics are demanded by the social use of the information.

Short, Williams, and Christie (1976) initiated the study of what they termed "social presence," or the user's perception of the inherent ability of a communication medium to carry important nonverbal information that supplies the social context of the communication (Short, Williams, and Christie 1976, 65). In experimental research, they measured perceived social presence through semantic-differential

scales associated with how personal, warm, or sensitive different media were, resulting in a hierarchical arrangement of media with face-
to-face communication at the top, followed by video, audio-only, and
finally print communication. Social presence was conceptually related
by these writers to the "intimacy" (capacity to foster attraction) and
"immediacy" (potential for personal closeness) of communication relationships, thus being identified as a more desirable media attribute in
some situations than in others. Occasions of potential emotional contact and conflict and those needing interpersonal feedback were singled
out as requiring the use of high-social-presence media.

Apparently independently, Daft and Lengel (1984, 1986) formulated the closely related concept of "media richness." Starting from a
conception of organizations as information-processing systems, these
authors noted that the two variables of uncertainty (lack of knowledge
about a situation) and equivocality (lack of agreement on interpretations of a situation) had been associated in organizational science with
higher frequencies of communication. Daft and Lengel (1986) hypothesized that particular configurations of uncertainty and equivocality
result in different organizational requirements not only for quantities,
but also for qualities of information. Rich information, they posited, is
especially useful for overcoming equivocal situations.

Daft and Lengel (1986, 560) identified four features of media that
describe their ability to convey rich information: "the medium's capacity for immediate feedback, the number of cues and channels utilized, personalization, and language variety." In this scheme, richness
is as much a characteristic of the information technology (or medium)
being used for transmission as of the information itself. Accordingly,
Daft and Lengel focus much of their subsequent attention on richness
differences among organizational media.

Although Daft and Lengel's definition of media richness is more
comprehensive than the social presence of Short and colleagues, the resulting hierarchical ranking of media, declining from face-to-face
through video, audio, and print, is substantially the same. Unlike Short
and colleagues, however, Daft and Lengel have adopted a view of media
richness as an objective, rather than subjective, attribute of a medium.
Notwithstanding their "symbolic interactionist" (Trevino, Daft, and
Lengel 1990) conception of situation equivocality, they array organizational media on a invariant richness continuum, supported by early studies, and do not allow for the possibility, suggested by Short and
colleagues, that either the richness of media or the equivocality of a given
situation is redefined in each organizational instance. For example, in a
study of managers' abilities to match appropriate media to differentially

equivocal situations, Daft, Lengel, and Trevino (1987) determined *a priori* both the richness of each medium and the equivocality of each message, and hence the appropriate matches. Any alternative representation of appropriateness on the part of managers was designated by the researchers as the managers' incompetence at selecting media.

Fulk, Schmitz, and Steinfield (1990) have sought to address this departure from social constructivism by returning to the argument that richness is perceived by the user, instead of being given by technical parameters. Fulk, Schmitz, and Steinfield (1990) argue that social context variables—preeminently the evaluations of co-workers—determine users' media richness perceptions, and Schmitz and Fulk (1991) have found modest empirical evidence to this effect.

In the hands of Daft and Lengel and Fulk and colleagues, the social presence concept of Short, Williams, and Christie has undergone considerable refinement, being defined with increasing precision in terms of specific, perceived media attributes. These researchers have also moved the study of these organizational media characteristics out of the laboratory and into naturalistic organizational settings. The dependent variables of interest for most information-richness research have been individual-level media choice and managerial performance, but recent work (Ryu and Fulk 1991; Fulk 1993) explores the empirical connection between media richness and group-level variables, including cohesion, conformity, and compliance.

Media-richness findings may be useful in interpreting the results of less theoretically oriented small-group research in computer-mediated meetings and problem solving. Kiesler, Siegel, and colleagues have conducted an extensive program of experimental research examining differences in the performance and behavior of groups undertaking decision tasks under face-to-face and various computer-mediated conditions. Having first opposed computer-mediated to more traditional forms of group interaction, these researchers found that computer-mediated groups took longer to reach decisions, but that mediated interaction was more equitable, more passionate, and contained more ideas (Siegel, Dubrovsky, Kiesler, and McGuire 1986). To clarify the causal forces possibly at work, Kiesler, Siegel, and McGuire (1984) found it necessary to vary the characteristics of the media used in their experiments, in accordance with hypotheses that contain elements of social presence and media richness variables. The experimental results of these researchers are apparently consistent with media richness explanations, although Walther (1992) criticizes them as inconsistent with naturalistic field studies and explicable by the researchers' choices of experimental situations and variables.

The various individual- and small-group-level research programs, emphasizing the importance of social cues and multiple information channels in mediated communication, raise additional social issues typically overlooked by optimistic overviews of information technology and organizational transformation. The transformed organization is commonly seen as one in which rigid, restricted, and vertical channels of command are replaced by lateral, flexible, and numerous connections (made possible by the information-cheapness of new technology) through which organization members negotiate action by more participative and democratic means. But if the information technology supplying the connections has such poor social information transmission capacity as to be abhorrent to users, the actual level of connectivity may confound the dense structure technically in place. Further, even if individuals enjoy the system and use it to negotiate organizational action, the social nature of a computer-mediated as opposed to physical negotiation setting may have detrimental consequences for organizational decision-making.

Poole, Holmes, and DeSanctis' (1991) research speaks to this issue. Working from an application of structuration theory (Giddens 1979) to group processes via group decision support system (GDSS) technology (Poole and DeSanctis 1990), they found that group processes and communication technology determine each other. Group norms and activities determine what features of the GDSS are actually used by the group, which in turn effects group processes and structure. Although this research has been confined to the group level and the use of a single technology, broader application of Giddens' theory of social action shows promise. One possible model is evident in the results of Barley's (1986, 1990) structurational study of the integration of medical imaging technology into the occupational, organizational, and social structure of a medical services delivery organization. A second model is Contractor and Seibold's (1993) application of self-organizing systems theory to organization communication technology interventions.

Social variables and organizational transformation

Dramatic general claims that new organizational media will radically transform organizational structure and productivity through increased connectivity and low communication costs are not well supported, either by considering economic sectors in the aggregate (Franke 1987) or at the level of specific cases (Kling and Iacono 1989; Ott 1989). Many successful implementations of new information technologies in organizations have been achieved, but the lack of uniform success indicated that more comprehensive social theories of media and organizations are needed to explain, predict, and guide practitioners toward the effective deployment of communication technologies in the service of organizational goals. Most programs of organizational technology research that seek a sophisticated view of the complex social circumstances surrounding organizational technology are young, yet they have already produced important conclusions and useful practical guidance.

Organizations are information-processing systems. They gather, manipulate, combine, copy, and communicate information relevant to their other purposes, both within and across their own boundaries. Technology that alters the economics of these information operations, allowing for faster processing, cheaper communication, and the handling of previously unwieldy types of information can thus decisively influence the activities that comprise a major preoccupation of modern organizations.

But organizations are much more than information-processing systems, and information and communication technologies are much more than devices for lowering information costs and increasing "connectivity." Organizations are complex social systems containing personal interaction, status and legitimacy, social power, ideology, and something akin to "culture." These features of organizational life are embodied in both the behaviors of organizational members and the physical arrangement and content of their surroundings. The information technologies used in an organization—whether they be paper and pencils, bureaucratic procedures, or computers—interact with the dimensions of organizations as social systems. In addition, as Weick (1990) notes, communication technologies structure interaction within the organization by their roles as the media of discourse and negotiation. They affect the kinds of information that can be shared, and have differing levels of privacy and permanence. Their use is associated with normative expectations about communication that are unique to a particular setting (Kling and Iacono 1989). These social dimensions of information technologies have important implications for organizational researchers and managers.

Implications for theory and research

Organizational theories must recognize that numerous characteristics of organizations, including their size, goals, past structures, the educational and other characteristics of their members, and ingrained modes of interpersonal interaction significantly affect the likelihood that the introduction of new media will have the desired results (Hiltz 1984; King and Kraemer 1986). Explanation of many of these relationships are still essentially intuitive or post hoc, but they provide a basis for future theory and for projecting the likelihood of benefits from technological intervention in specific instances.

Theories of communication technology in organizations are quickly recognizing the importance of social factors in the implementation and success of technological initiatives. Up to a point, existing approaches based on information-cost theories can be augmented by the additional considerations of social variables (Hiltz 1984), by categorizing the various factors in our models as either "technical" or "social" (Kling and Iacono 1988), or by qualifying deterministic statements of relationships by the users' differing views of technologies and organizational reality (as Schmitz and Fulk {1991} have done with the media richness concept of Daft and Lengel {1987}). But we may easily become dissatisfied with the results obtainable from grafting social-variable appendages onto essentially rationalist theories.

As researchers come to appreciate the role of interpretation and symbolism, not only in the perception of technologies and tasks, but in the fundamental definition of one's organization and oneself, they face the often unfamiliar premises of relativism, with its epistemological hostility to any focus on the "objective" constructs of productivity and transaction cost. To gain the insights provided by the culturist investigators (Scholz 1991), researchers may need to suspend their belief in these traditional categories, at least momentarily conceding the entire range of organizational existence as open to social negotiation. Within communication studies, this epistemological gulf was confronted by the discipline of mass communication research a decade ago, spurring numerous, variably successful attempts to fashion theories incorporating the insights of both positivist and constructivist traditions. Organizational communication may now be poised for such ferment, with studies of communication technology emerging as a possible site of this interaction.

Implications for management

The most important practical implication of recent research into organizational technologies is that the introduction of a new information technology should be understood as not merely the installation of tools to make the job of interaction easier and cheaper, but a social intervention into the basic processes of the organization (Kling and Iacono

1988). This understanding underscores the need, often appreciated by less theoretically inclined observers (Bowen 1986), for the redesign of modes of work and interaction as an accompaniment to new technology. It may be suspected that the reorganization, rather than the technology, is the key to many organizational media success stories.

The manager must also consider that putting forward a new technology is itself a communication—a symbolic prescription about appropriate practice in the organization (Horvath 1991). This prescription may not always be comprehended or accepted by organizational members, who are embedded in a culture-like web of norms and representations with which some information technology initiatives may be incompatible (Ott 1989). Executives who do not carefully consider the meaning of the message they are putting forward by means of technological intervention, or at least seek ways of integrating new media into prevailing perceptions of organizational roles, risk counterproductive and sometimes extreme resistance to their efforts.

Finally, we must consider the new forms of social interaction implied by heavy reliance on computerized information technology, and consider whether—even with the falling cost of transmitting more and more social information—low-tech solutions such as personal meetings are not still the most effective means to many decision-making ends (Fulk, Schmitz, and Steinfield 1990). We must ask whether our organizations should maintain the ritualistic human contact associated with chance encounters in hallways and with that most ubiquitous of group support systems, the water cooler or coffee pot. These are issues that speak to the central elements of organizational cultures and of personal relations with work and co-workers. As Kraut, Galegher, and Egido (1990) found, information technology often can only capture a fraction of the quality of information essential to harness the creative capabilities of collaborative efforts in organizations.

References

Allen, T. J. and O. Hauptman. 1987. The influence of communication technologies on organizational structure. *Communication Research* 14: 575–87.

Barley, S. R. 1986. Technology as an occasion for structuring: Evidence from observations of CT scanners and the social order of radiology departments. *Administrative Science Quarterly* 31:78–108.

———. 1990. The alignment of technology and structure through roles and networks. *Administrative Science Quarterly* 35:61–103.

Bikson, T. K., J. D. Eveland, and B. A. Gutek. 1989. Flexible interactive technologies and multi-person tasks: Current problems and future prospects. In *Technological support for work group collaboration*, ed. M. Olson. Englewood Cliffs, NJ: Erlbaum.

Bowen, W. 1989. The puny payoff from office computers. In *Computers in the human context*, ed. T. Forester. Cambridge, MA: MIT Press.

Buitendam, A. 1987. The horizontal perspective of organization design and new technology. In *New technology as organizational innovation*, ed. J. M. Pennings and A. Buitendam. Cambridge, MA: Ballinger.

Ciborra, C. U., and G. F. Lanzara. 1991. Designing dynamic artifacts: Computer systems as formative contexts. In *Symbols and artifacts: Views of the corporate landscape*, ed. P. Gagliardi. Berlin: de Gruyter.

Contractor, N. and D. Seibold. 1993. Theoretical frameworks for the study of structuring processes in group decision support systems: Adaptive structuration theory and self-organizing system theory. *Human Communication Research*, 19:528–63.

Daft, R. L., and R. H. Lengel. 1984. Information richness: A new approach to managerial behavior and organization design. In *Research in organizational behavior*, vol. 6, ed. L. L. Cummings and B. M. Straw. Greenwich, CT: JAI Press.

———. 1986. Organizational information requirements, media richness and structural design. *Management Science* 32:554–71.

Daft, R. L., R. H. Lengel, and L. K. Trevino. 1987. Message equivocality, media selection, and manager performance: Implications for information systems. *MIS Quarterly* 11:355–66.

Danziger, J. N., and K. L. Kraemer. 1986. *People and computers: The impacts of computing on end users in organizations*. New York: Columbia University Press.

Davis, S. M. 1984. *Managing corporate culture*. Cambridge, MA: Ballinger.

de Greene, K. B. 1973. *Sociotechnical systems: Factors in analysis, design, and management*. Englewood Cliffs, NJ: Prentice Hall.

Dutton, W. H., and K. L. Kraemer. 1982. The management of computer applications in local government. *Public Administration Review* 42:234–43.

Forester, T. (ed.). 1989. *Computers in the human context*. Cambridge, MA: MIT Press.

Francis, A. 1986. *New technology at work*. Oxford: Clarendon Press.

Franke, R. H. 1987. Technological revolution and productivity decline: Computer introduction in the financial industry. *Technological Forecasting and Social Change* 31:143–54.

Fulk, J. 1993. Social construction of communication technology. *Academy of Management Journal,* 36:921–50.

Fulk, J., J. A. Schmitz, and C. W. Steinfield. 1990. A social influence model of technology use. In *Organizations and communication technology,* ed. J. Fulk and C. W. Steinfield. Newbury Park, CA: Sage.

Galbraith, J. 1977. *Organizational design.* Reading, MA: Addison-Wesley.

Galbraith, J. K. 1967. *The new industrial state.* New York: Houghton Mifflin.

Giddens, A. 1979. *Central problems in social theory.* Berkeley: University of California Press.

Hiltz, S. R. 1984. *Online communities: A case study of the office of the future.* Norwood, NJ: Ablex.

Horvath, A. T. 1991. A communication perspective on technological systems. Paper presented at the annual meeting of the American Sociological Association, Cincinnati, OH.

Huber, G. P. 1990. A theory of the effects of advanced information technologies on organizational design, intelligence, and decision making. In *Organizations and communication technology,* ed. J. Fulk and C. W. Steinfield. Newbury Park, CA: Sage.

Kanter, R. M. 1983. *The change masters.* New York: Simon and Schuster.

Keen, P. G. W. 1990. Telecommunications and organizational choice. In *Organizations and communication technology,* ed. J. Fulk and C. Steinfield. Newbury Park, CA: Sage.

Kiesler, S., J. Siegel, and T. W. McGuire. 1984. Social psychological aspects of computer-mediated communication. *American Psychologist* 39:1123–34.

King, J. L., and K. L. Kraemer. 1985. *The dynamics of computing.* New York: Columbia University Press.

Kling, R., and S. Iacono. 1988. The mobilization of support for computing: The role of computerization movements. *Social Problems* 35:226–43.

———. 1989. Desktop computerization and the organization of work. In *Computers and the human context,* ed. T. Forester. Cambridge, MA: MIT Press.

Kraut, R., J. Galegher, and C. Edigo. 1990. Patterns of contact and communication. In *Intellectual teamwork: Social and technological foundations of cooperative work,* eds. J. Galegher, R. Kraut, and C. Egido. Hillsdale, NJ: LEA.

Madnick, S. E. 1991. The information technology platform. In *The corporation of the 1990s: Information technology and organizational transformation,* ed. M. S. Scott Morton. New York: Oxford University Press.

Malone, T. W., and J. F. Rockart. 1991. Computers, networks and the corporation. *Scientific American,* September, 92–99.

Malone, T. W., J. Yates, and R. I. Benjamin. 1987. Electronic markets and electronic hierarchies. *Communications of the ACM* 30:484–97.

McKersie, R. B., and R. E. Walton. 1991. Organizational change. In *The corporation of the 1990s: Information technology and organizational transformation,* ed. M. S. Scott Morton. New York: Oxford University Press.

Meek, V. L. 1988. Organizational culture: Origins and weaknesses. *Organizational Studies* 9:453–73.

Nilles, J. M. 1982. *Exploring the world of the personal computer.* Englewood Cliffs, NJ: Prentice Hall.

Noble, D. F. 1985. Social choice in machine design: The case of automatically controlled machine tools. In *The social shaping of technology,* ed. D. MacKenzie and J. Wajcman. Philadelphia: Open University Press.

Ott, J. S. 1989. *The organizational culture perspective.* Chicago: Dorsey.

Panko, R. 1984. Electronic mail: The alternatives. *Office Administration and Automation* 45:37–43.

Pasmore, W., C. E. Francis, J. Haldeman, and A. Shani. 1982. Sociotechnical systems: A North American reflection on the empirical studies on the '70's. *Human Relations* 35:1179–1204.

Pennings, J. M., and A. Buitendam. 1987. In *New technology as organizational innovation,* ed. J. M. Pennings and A. Buitendam. Cambridge, MA: Ballinger.

Pfeffer, J., and G. R. Salancik. 1978. *The external control of organizations: A resource dependency perspective.* New York: Harper & Row.

Poole, M. S., and G. DeSanctis. 1990. Understanding the use of group decision support systems: The theory of adaptive structuration. In *Organizations and communication technology,* ed. J. Fulk and C. W. Steinfield. Newbury Park, CA: Sage.

Poole, M. S., M. Holmes, and G. DeSanctis. 1991. Conflict management in a computer-supported meeting environment. *Management Science* 11:1–36.

Rice, R. E., and J. H. Bair. 1984. New organizational media and productivity. In *The new media: Communication, research, and technology,* ed. R. E. Rice et al. Beverly Hills: Sage.

Rockart, J. F., and J. E. Short. 1991. The networked organization and the management of interdependence. In *The corporation of the 1990s: Information technology and organizational transformation,* ed. M. S. Scott Morton. New York: Oxford University Press.

Rotemberg, J. J., and G. Saloner. 1991. Interfirm competition and collaboration. In *The corporation of the 1990s: Information technology and organizational transformation,* ed. M. S. Scott Morton. New York: Oxford University Press.

Ryu, D., and J. Fulk. 1991. Group cohesiveness and perceptions of media richness in the workplace. Paper presented at the annual meeting of the International Communication Association, Chicago.

Schmitz, J. A., and J. Fulk. 1991. Organizational colleagues, media richness, and electronic mail: A test of the social influence model of technology use. *Communication Research* 18:487–523.

Scholz, C. 1991. The symbolic value of computerized information systems. *Symbols and artifacts: Views of the corporate landscape,* ed. P. Gagliardi. Berlin: de Gruyter.

Schultheiss, E. E. 1988. *Optimizing the organization: How to link people and technology.* Cambridge, MA: Ballinger.

Schumpeter, J. A. 1934. *The theory of economic development.* Cambridge, MA: Harvard University Press.

———. 1943. *Capitalism, socialism, and democracy.* New York: Harper & Row.

Scott Morton, M. S. 1991. Introduction. In *The corporation of the 1990s: Information technology and organizational transformation,* ed. M. S. Scott Morton. New York: Oxford University Press.

Short, J., E. Williams, and B. Christie. 1976. *The social psychology of telecommunications.* London: Wiley.

Siegel, J., V. Dubrovsky, S. Kiesler, and T. W. McGuire. 1986. Group processes in computer-mediated communication. *Organizational Behavior and Human Decision Processes* 37:157–87.

Smith, S. 1989. Information technology in banks: Taylorization or human-centered systems? In *Computers in the human context,* ed. T. Forester. Cambridge, MA: MIT Press.

Strassman, P. A. 1985. *Information payoff.* New York: Free Press.

Taylor, F. W. 1911. *Principles of scientific management.* New York: Harper & Row.

Toffler, A. 1971. *Future shock.* New York: Bantam.

Trevino, L. K., D. L. Daft, and R. H. Lengel. 1990. Understanding managers' media choices: A symbolic interactionist perspective. In *Organizations and communication technology,* ed. J. Fulk and C. Steinfield. Newbury Park, CA: Sage.

Tushman, M. L., and D. A. Nadler. 1978. Information processing as an integrating concept in organizational design. *Academy of Management Review* 3:613–24.

Venkatraman, N. 1991. IT-induced business reconfiguration. In *The corporation of the 1990s: Information technology and organizational transformation,* ed. M. S. Scott Morton. New York: Oxford University Press.

Walther, J. B. 1992. Interpersonal effects in computer-mediated communication: A relational perspective. *Communication Research* 19:52–90.

Weick, K. E. 1990. Technology as equivoque: Sense making in new technologies. In *Technology and organizations*, ed. P. S. Goodman et al. San Francisco: Jossey-Bass.

Williamson, O. E. 1975. *Markets and hierarchies: Analysis and antitrust implications*. New York: Free Press.

Zuboff, S. 1988. *In the age of the smart machine: The future of work and power*. New York: Basic Books.

DAVID R. SEIBOLD
MARK A. HELLER
NOSHIR S. CONTRACTOR

6 Group Decision Support Systems (GDSS): Review, Taxonomy, and Research Agenda

Collaborative decision-making is an integral part of organizational life (Bradford 1976; Fisher and Ellis 1990; Zander 1989). Meetings often are used to facilitate decision-making processes because all parties can be involved and pertinent issues can be addressed collectively in a single setting (Maier 1980). *The Wall Street Journal* (Hymowitz 1988) reported that managers spend from 25 to 50 percent of their total work time in group meetings. While immediate, collective intelligence can improve decision-making (Shaw 1981), meetings often are inefficient—failing to resolve issues, to complete decisions, and to handle problems effectively (Huber 1990; Mintzberg 1973).

New technologies, including the personal computer, are being reconfigured to enhance the efficiency of such meetings. With their information-processing capabilities (information retrieval, retention, processing, graphic display, etc.), as well as new developments in computer networking and software sharing programs (Johansen 1988; Saffo 1991; Shrage 1990), the *group*-friendly computer is possible. Hardware and software have been designed for work groups not only to share the information generated by computers, but to edit it together in real time, with immediate results. Developing the potential of the *impersonal computer* is the rationale behind computer hardware and software for increasing the effectiveness and efficiency of the daily meeting (DeSanctis and Gallupe 1987; Kraemer and Pinsonneault 1990).

143

However, the technological advances and increased capabilities of personal computers do not completely explain why collaborative technologies are being introduced into organizational meetings. The larger trend toward collaborative work and collaborative technologies in U.S. organizations offers additional insight into the role and results of the computer's introduction into meeting support. For example, Schrage (1990) argues that organizations today increasingly hire and train members to become specialists in order to deal with the daily plethora of specific problems and opportunities. Ideally, this diversity in specialization should provide better meetings and meeting outcomes. Yet, Shrage (1990) argues, sharing unique information between the specialists is not sufficient to harvest that diversity. Organizations need to focus more on collaboration (mutual creation between at least two people) than simply on information sharing. Successful meetings should include the active integration of those insights and thinking processes in order to create superior collaborative efforts. The computer, with its continually improving abilities to process, track, organize, incorporate, and analyze information, becomes a powerful tool in shaping a more *collaborative* organizational culture.

Group Decision Support Systems (GDSSs) are a recent innovation in communication technology with direct implications for collaborative group work. GDSSs are interactive computer-based systems that combine communication, computer, and decision technologies to support groups' formulation and solution of unstructured problems (De-Sanctis and Gallupe 1987; Jessup, Connolly, and Galegher 1990; Kraemer and Pinsonneault 1990). As coordination tools designed to improve group performance, GDSSs vary in their capability to support meetings (Huber 1984; Kraemer and King 1988; Kraemer and Pinsonneault 1990). However, the emphasis is on giving "access to the positive aspects of coordination—not just preventing collisions" among group members (Greif 1988, 9). Some GDSSs offer simple communication support—sometimes called Group Communication Support Systems (GCSS) (Kraemer and Pinsonneault 1990), Level 1 GDSS (De-Sanctis and Gallupe 1987), or "display" level support (Seibold and Contractor 1991)—and are intended primarily to support interaction processes among members. This simplest type of GDSS is designed to reduce communication barriers in groups by providing tools such as a third communication channel (text based) which can, for example, support anonymous contributions. Some GDSSs "poll" users by asking them to rank order alternatives (cf. Hiltz, Johnson, and Turoff 1987). Others allow for brainstorming and idea organizing by having users type ideas for display in a common viewing area and then linking them together verbally (e.g., Stefik, Foster, Boborow, Kahn, Lanning, and Suchan 1987; Stefik and Brown 1989). Other GDSSs provide more complex support such as the capability to structure meetings; run complicated tasks like PERT and strategic planning; provide mathematical forecasting; and utilize Robert's Rules of Order among many possibilities (Dennis, George, Jessup, Nunamaker, and Vogel 1988; DeSanctis and Gallupe 1987; Poole and DeSanctis 1990; Seibold and Contractor 1991). Still other types of GDSSs augment group interaction by providing expert support systems (Malone, Grant, Lai, Rao, and Rosenblitt 1989).

The increase in the number of GDSSs and in their capabilities is well documented. Since the seminal work by Steeb and Johnson (1981), recent bibliographies by DeSanctis (1989) and the 3M Corporation (1991) indicate that between 200 and 300 papers directly related to GDSS were available by 1991. Although only a small portion of these are empirical studies of GDSS use and effects, research facilities increasingly are being established in a variety of academic institutions for the purpose of conducting systematic research on GDSS. Recent reviews (Kraemer and King 1988; Kraemer and Pinsonneault 1990; Seibold and Contractor 1991; Vogel and Nunamaker 1990) point to twelve different U.S. universities that have GDSS social research facilities. Additionally, at least seven major corporations including IBM, Marriot, and Dell Computer Corporation have invested from fifty to two hundred thousand dollars installing GDSS facilities at company locations (Bulkely 1992). Finally, a number of corporate research sites specifically designed to develop this collaborative technology's potential have emerged (Johansen 1988; Kraemer and King 1988).

In the remainder of this essay we undertake three tasks. First, we review recent research on GDSSs with primary attention to major reviews in the area. Inconsistent findings concerning GDSS effects, as well as recent theoretical development, lead us, second, to propose a taxonomy of contextual contingencies for interpreting and anticipating GDSS effects—a framework that represents a philosophical, theoretical, and empirical departure from previous classificatory schemes. Finally, new perspectives and promising directions for the future of GDSS research are discussed. Both the framework provided and the perspectives discussed are couched within the emergent perspective (Pfeffer 1982) on organizational action and, as we demonstrate in the conclusion, are consistent with how this metatheoretical approach has been applied to information technologies' use and effects in organizations (Markus and Robey 1988; Contractor and Eisenberg 1990).

Review

The majority of GDSS research has focused on exploring new options and designing prototypes (for reviews see Greif 1988; Dhar and Olson 1989). There have been fewer studies which have hypothesized specific individual or organizational *outcomes* of GDSS. Most of the hypotheses proposed are based on the assumption that computer-mediated communication has specific unchanging attributes. For instance, computer-mediated communication is said to have a lower degree of social presence (Short, Williams, and Christie 1976) and media richness (Daft and Lengel 1986) than face-to-face communication. Therefore, for example, computer-mediated communication is hypothesized to be well suited for those tasks which do not require the social presence and media richness offered by face-to-face communication.

Within the domain of GDSS effects research, several reviews of the literature have appeared. These summaries can be differentiated based on the taxonomic categories employed in each. Some reviews organize the GDSS effects literature in terms of technological sophistication, or capabilities of the GDSS, and the level of decision-making support that the system provides (DeSanctis and Gallupe 1987; Kraemer and Pinsonneault 1990; Seibold and Contractor 1991). Other reviews have assayed studies in terms of physical arrangements or attributes of GDSS systems such as whether GDSS users are dispersed or face-to-face; or whether communication support is synchronous or asynchronous (Dennis et al. 1988; Smith and Vanacheck 1989; Kraemer and King 1988; Kraemer and Pinsonneault 1990; Smith and Vanechek 1989). Third, some reviewers have argued that experimental design manipulations and operational definitions of process and outcome variables need to be mapped more precisely (George 1989; Kraemer and Pinsonneault 1990; Kudsi 1991; Seibold and Contractor 1991). Finally, others have attempted to illustrate task differences in terms of the complexity, characteristics, completion time, and type of task existing between studies (DeSanctis and Gallupe 1987; Gallupe, DeSanctis and Dickson 1988; McGrath and Hollingshead 1991a) as well as how different system support environments most appropriately "fit" with certain tasks (DeSanctis and Gallupe 1987; Gallupe and DeSanctis 1988; Huber 1984; Jarvenpaa, Rao, and Laase 1988). These approaches, and specific reviews typical of each, are described next. Any single review that we highlight as typical of one approach may also encompass some of the other taxonomic approaches mentioned above, but this is unusual. Importantly, even if a particular literature review evidences several of the approaches mentioned, we will emphasize whichever aspect seems to offer the greatest insight into the GDSS literature. Even then, as will be evident, there are many other contingencies that affect GDSS interactions and outcomes which these schemes fail to incorporate. Those contingencies will be the focus of the subsequent section.

Three reviews are representative of those taxonomies that seek to categorize GDSSs in terms of their *technological sophistication, capabilities, and level of decision-making support.* DeSanctis and Gallupe (1987) differentiate GDSSs by the three levels of support they can be designed to provide. They argue that as these GDSSs increase in sophistication, they will have differential effects on interaction dynamics. Seibold and Contractor (1991) inventoried seventeen GDSS studies and grouped them according to five hierarchical levels of support. Pinsonneault and Kraemer (1990) divided thirty-three GDSS studies into two types of GDSS: Group Decision Support Systems and Group Communication Support Systems. Seibold and Contractor (1991) and Pinsonneault and Kraemer (1990) used their classification scheme to search for patterns of effects; both failed to find any uniform pattern with their classification schemes. Pinsonneault and Kraemer (1990) provided three possible explanations for their findings: developmental stage differences in groups between studies, failure of the GDSS to meet user expectations, and differences in task focus between studies—all contextual variables beyond the focus of their classification schemes.

A second class of reviews has been concerned with discriminating how the *physical arrangement or specific attributes of a GDSS system might effect outcomes.* Dennis et al (1988) inventoried studies of computer supported groups versus noncomputer supported groups. Because of the vast configuration differences in their review, they separated these comparisons by type of GDSS arrangement: those which utilized local area decision networks and those which used decision rooms. Decision rooms typically are designed to function with all group members present in the same room. Local area decision networks are not necessarily designed to host all participants in the same room (users may be in different rooms, floors, or even different buildings depending on the nature of work and decision-making task). Kraemer and King (1988) classified thirteen different collaborative decision-making technologies by six types of computer-support arrangements (electronic boardroom, group network, decision conference, collaboration laboratory, teleconference facility, and information center). Each of the six systems had very different physical arrangements and support characteristics. For instance, an electronic boardroom takes the form of computer " 'storyboards' or computer controlled audiovisuals (e.g., slide projectors, video projectors, movie projectors) used for presentations" (Kraemer and King 1988, 119). On the other hand, a collaboration laboratory consists of workstations that are build into a conference table to permit face-to-face communication as well as sharing an electronic chalkboard and interactive document-editing software. A decision room had a similar physical arrangement to a collaboration laboratory—but it usually utilizes different types of software (e.g., decision-tree modeling, strategic planning, etc.). These differences serve to illustrate the point that different GDSS attributes and arrangements augment collaborative decision-making in different ways. Kraemer and King (1988) assert that these various systems have been indiscriminately thrust under the definition of GDSS.

Operational definitions of process and outcome variables as well as experimental design manipulations distinguish yet another class of GDSS reviews. For example, George (1989) scrutinized just four GDSS studies and noted several reasons why they may be inappropriate for comparison. He illuminated several elements of the research designs that could create inconsistencies in effects, such as channel selection (face-to-face only, computer only, or both), number of subjects, and treatments. Seibold and Contractor (1991) surveyed the most prevalent group outcomes associated with GDSS use and refined them in six categories. However, Kudsi (1991) re-reviewed each process and outcome variable in those studies and argued that those operational definitions varied considerably between studies.

At least two reviews have *classified GDSS studies in terms of task differences.* McGrath and Hollingshead (1991a) surveyed several GDSS studies and differentiated them according to the task type, complexity, and the time involved in the completion of each. DeSanctis and Gallupe (1987) applied McGrath's (1984) circumplex model of task differences to classify GDSS research by the way a particular system serves to support the needs associated with different types of tasks.

A final class of taxonomic reviews has attempted to classify how *different GDSS environments most appropriately "fit" with certain types of tasks.* DeSanctis and Gallupe (1987) integrated task, level of GDSS, and group size within their classificatory table. They argued that classifying GDSS studies in terms of these three factors helps to define the environmental contingency for an appropriate fit. Huber (1984) and Jarvenpaa and colleagues (1988) also discussed the importance of different environmental contingencies and how they might fit with the task at hand. This notion of "fit" is consistent with the central thesis of this paper. Current attempts to organize the GDSS effects literature have been limited in explanatory power because they force a multitude of acknowledged differences into simple categorical differentiations—causing *any* decipherable patterns of effects to be interpreted as "isolated islands within a sea of ambiguity" (McGrath and Hollingshead 1991b).

As is evident from even this cursory review, generalizations about the effects of GDSS on group decision-making have been plagued by inconsistencies between study findings. For example, while a number of investigations have found that member satisfaction and group consensus were enhanced in GDSS groups, other studies revealed no differences beyond chance expectation. Further, although some studies have reported significant decreases in members' participation rates in GDSS groups, others have found that participation was significantly higher in GDSS supported groups. Indeed, one review of GDSS research concluded that "the most obvious generalization that can be made . . . is that the results from these studies are inconsistent" (Dennis et al. 1988, 600). For the most part these reviews all follow from a similar assumption: in order to illuminate the troubling inconsistencies in study by study comparisons, something must be done to organize the variety of studies, manipulations, systems, and environments that constitute GDSS research. Accordingly, each offers a singular, often narrow framework for classifying and accounting for GDSS effects. Most reviewers also acknowledge that theirs is by no means the only way to classify previous research. These reviews typically conclude that more research needs to be done illustrating the multitude of important contextual contingencies that are associated with the variety of studies. Two issues are apparent from these problems, and they serve as the bases for the two sections which follow.

First, as *descriptive* devices for categorizing potential factors upon which GDSS effects are contingent, these taxonomies may be too narrow and simplistic. None has addressed the *multiple* combination of factors that may affect GDSS use and, therefore, outcomes. The aforementioned approaches focus attention almost exclusively on their respective classifications for understanding GDSS effects. Rather than arguing that one taxonomy should be adopted over others, it is possible that all are correct to some degree. The assessment of multiple approaches *in combination*—the special attention to how the contextual contingencies might be functioning hierarchically in any one study— may provide researchers with increased explanatory power. The GDSS effect literature has yet to adopt a comprehensive framework for understanding all of the potential contingencies operating within any one study. Utilizing simple taxonomies or hierarchies of singular characteristic differences may inhibit researchers' abilities to be attuned to the

full range of potential differences operating in association with reported outcomes. The following sections offer an alternative, more
comprehensive and more synthetic framework classifying *contextual
factors on which GDSS effects may be contingent.* Second, as *explanatory* devices for accounting for differences reported in GDSS effects studies, these taxonomies—like many of the individual studies
they review—are rooted in the premise that the impact of GDSS technology ought to be consistent across groups using it. In the final section of this essay we question that assumption and identify nascent
theories of GDSS effects which are grounded in assumptions antithetical to this one. Importantly, these are perspectives that also incorporate or permit incorporation of the multiple contextual contingencies
identified next.

GDSS contextual contingencies

Given the inconsistencies and limitations noted in the previous review,
this section proposes a synthesis of important characteristics differen-
tiating GDSS research. Conclusions from previous reviews suggest *that
effects should be viewed in terms of a combination of contextual contingencies* (Contractor and Seibold, 1993; Drazin and Van de Ven
1985; Gutek 1990; Poole and DeSanctis 1990). We propose that the
most appropriate framework for conceptualizing these contingencies
can be found in three global categories of GDSS: (1) *system characteristics,* (2) *use characteristics,* and (3) *user characteristics.* These categories have several subcategories that clarify the boundaries of the
constructs. The subcategories are not meant to be exhaustive, but are
illustrative of contextual variables mentioned in the literature and believed to have possible effects on outcomes. As demonstrated in ten
short years since Steeb and Johnson's (1981) work, innovations in
GDSS are occurring faster than research studies. This suggests that as
this collaborative technology continues to develop, the contextual contingencies must also be modified to reflect current environmental developments. For example, with advances in laptop computers, real-time
processing, graphics capabilities, and user friendliness, communication
through computers as a medium is developing in terms of its ability to
retain richness (Daft and Lengel 1986; Johansen 1988). Combinations
such as these exist in every situation where a GDSS might be studied,
and any classification system must be elastic enough to incorporate
these changes. Three global categories and their subcategories are ex-

plicated next as aids to categorizing combinations of such contextual contingencies (see table 6.1).

GDSS systems, and by extension research on them, can be differentiated according to *system characteristics,* those technological attributes associated with a particular GDSS and the character of support they provide (see table 6.1). First, the system's *physical configuration* will be apparent. Any GDSS can be characterized in terms of the number of computers associated with the system, the complexity of arrangement in a decision room, the system's speed of operation, whether it provides sophisticated decision-making support, its synchronous or asynchronous communication capabilities, and the number of support tasks it is designed to fulfill. The physical configuration subcategory also includes the spatial arrangement (Bradford 1976) of computers in a network (e.g., whether they are dispersed across the country, in the same building or in the same room, and how much the computers impede natural interaction). A very important consideration is that the physical configuration of a GDSS can be designed to completely support communication or merely augment it. This distinction can be manifested in terms of interaction impedance, spatial arrangement, modules of support, and the implicit rules about that use that exist in the design of the particular support module. Finally, a system's capability to enable anonymity is included in the physical configuration construct (Connolly, Jessup, and Valacich 1990; Jessup, Connolly, and Galegher 1990; Vogel and Nunamaker 1990).

The second system characteristic along which any GDSS may be differentiated is the *system's adaptability of appropriateness of support.* Two predominant systems in the GDSS research literature reveal important differences in this respect. The PlexCenter at the University of Arizona is designed for a multitude of tasks and is located within a single site to which managers can be flown. There are two different large meeting rooms supporting 16 and 24 workstations respectively. Several smaller conference rooms surround the two larger decision rooms, each of which can host computers to run smaller meetings or have larger ones broken into subgroups. SAMM, at the University of Minnesota, is designed on the other hand to be easily programmed as needed for different groups that require unique tasks. SAMM is a scaled down or more portable package than the PlexCenter. SAMM can be reconfigured, whereas the PlexCenter meeting room is a massive moduled system that is not mobile and is designed to host a multitude of different meeting types and complex tasks. SAMM is currently limited to hosting 3 to 16 users, whereas the PlexCenter can host up to 65. The important point in the distinction between these

Global Level

System Characteristics

TABLE 6.1

	Parameters	Sub Categories
1	Which Category of System does it fall under? (e.g., LAN, E-Mail, Decision Room, EMS, CSS, Linking, etc.) (Dennis, et al., 1988)	Physical Configuration
2	Number of Computers (Johansen, 1988)	
3	Degree of Interaction Impedence (Rice & Love, 1984; Kiesler, 1990)	
4	Spatial Arrangement (Bradford, 1976; Shaw, 1981; Fisher & Ellis, 1991)	
5	Dispersed/Face-To-Face (Dennis, et al., 1988)	
6	Degree of Complexity of System Setup (George, 1989; DeSanctis & Gallupe, 1987; Seibold & Contractor, 1990)	
7	The System's Speed of Operation (Johansen, 1989; Seigel et al., 1984)	
8	Capacity for Anonymous Support (Jessup, Connolly, &Tansik, 1990)	System Adaptability or Appropriateness of Support
9	Synchronous/Asynchronous (Poole & DeSanctis, 1990; Seibold & Contractor, 1990; Dennis et al., 1988)	
10	Degree of Mobility of the System (Vogel & Nunamaker, 1990)	
11	Degree of Specialization in Support (Johansen, 1989)	
12	Programmability (Adaptable to Changing needs of groups) (Huber, 1984)	
13	Degree of Capability in support of Multitude of Tasks (Vogel & Nunamaker, 1990; Johansen, 1989)	
14	Rigid/Flexible in Design of Procedures for Use (Easton et al., 1989; Vogel & Nunamaker, 1990)	Level of User Friendliness
15	Easy/Difficult to Learn (George, 1989; Poole & DeSanctis, 1990)	
16	Easy/Difficult to Use (George, 1989; Poole & DeSanctis, 1990)	
17	Degree to which System is Chauffeur/User/or Facilitator Driven (George, 1989; Poole & DeSanctis, 1990)	Who Drives the System?

Global Level
Use Characteristics

#	Parameters	Sub Categories
1	Design/Research Question (s) (e.g., factorial, time series, independent/dependent variable(s) etc.) (Campbell & Stanley, 1978; Lipsey, 1990; Hare, 1976; Shaw, 1981)	Experimental Manipulations and Designs
2	Manipulation (e.g., Anonymity, Proximity, Task, Confederate, Climate, etc.) (Hare, 1976; Shaw, 1981)	
3	GDSS vs. FTF or LAN vs. GDSS or GDSS vs. Structured FTF (Dennis et al., 1988; George, 1989)	
4	Clear operational definitions of outcome variables (Seibold & Contractor, 1990; Kiesl, 1991)	
5	Operant rules about reaching final decision (e.g., Consensus: mode of decision making) (Davis, 1973)	
6	Task Type (McGrath, 1984; Desanctis & Gallupe, 1987; Poole & Doelger,1986)	Task Differences
7	Task Complexity (McGrath, 1984;Desanctis and Gallupe,1987; Poole & Doelger, 1986)	
8	Degree of Realism or Salience (McGrath, 1984)	
9	Degree of Uncertainty (McGrath, 1984)	
10	Degree to which deadline was imposed (Gersik, 1989; McGrath & Hollingshead, 1991a)	Time Constraints
11	Accomplished in one meeting or several (Zigurs et al.,1988; McGrath & Hollingshead, 1991a)	
12	Degree to which computer is encouraged to be the dominant channel (George, 1989)	Channel Selection
13	Degree to which face-to-face is encouraged to be the dominant channel (George, 1989)	
14	The degree to which freedom of user choice is allowed(e.g., no explicit rules for interaction-George, 1989)	
15	Type of training (e.g., demonstration, walk through) (George, 1989; Poole & Desanctis, 1990)	Training
16	Extent of training (e.g., 20 minutes, twice a week etc.) (Poole & DeSanctis, 1990)	
17	Thoroughness of training (e.g., "Subjects were trained until everyone could use the system") (George, 1989; Poole & Desanctis,1990)	

153

TABLE 6.1 cont.

Global Level
User Characteristics

#	Parameters	Sub Categories
1	Class, major, age, history during time of experiment – undergraduates (Campbell & Stanley, 1978; Dennis et al., 1988; Shaw, 1981; Bormann, 1970)	Sample Differences
2	Profession ,age, years of experience, tenure, type of job, etc. (Hare,1976)	Sample Differences
3	Total number of members per group (Shaw, 1981)	Group Size
4	Degree to which there is a hierarchy in the group (Fisher & Ellis, 1990; Bikson & Eveland, 1990; Shaw, 1981)	Group Structure
5	Extent of History (e.g., Time) (Bormann, 1970; Hall & Williams, 1972)	History of Interacting Together
6	Degree of familiarity among members (Shaw, 1981)	History of Interacting Together
7	Nature of history (e.g. workgroup, production team) (Hare, 1961)	History of Interacting Together
8	Level of comfort with training (Poole & Desanctis, 1990)	Training
9	Level of motivation toward training (Kiesler, 1990; Poole & Desanctis, 1990)	Training
10	Appropriateness of training (DeSanctis, Donofrio, Sambamurthy & Poole, 1989; Daft & Lengle, 1986; Poole & DeSanctis, 1990)	Training
11	Degree of comfort with using this technology (Poole & DeSanctis, 1990)	Attitude/Degree of Respect toward use of New Technologies
12	Expectations of the technology's performance/capabilities (Poole & DeSanctis, 1990)	Attitude/Degree of Respect toward use of New Technologies
13	Degree of consensus about use of this technology(Poole & DeSanctis, 1990)	Attitude/Degree of Respect toward use of New Technologies
14	Level of computer knowledge (Poole & DeSanctis, 1990;Barley, 1986)	Level of Computer Expertise
15	Peer evaluation of technology (Contractor & Eisenberg, 1990)	Level of Computer Expertise
16	Amount of exposure to new technologies(uncertainty/equivocality)(Daft & Lengle,1986)	Level of Computer Expertise
17	Time/ History with using computers (Poole & DeSanctis, 1990; McGrath, 1990)	Past Experience Adapting .o New Technologies
18	Number of new technologies actually using/incorporated/ adopted (Fulk et al. , 1990)	Past Experience Adapting .o New Technologies
19	Perceptions of personal adaptability to new technology (Poole & Desanctis, 1990; Fulk & Stienfield, 1990)	Past Experience Adapting .o New Technologies

systems is not merely in their environments, but in their respective abilities to handle specific tasks. Furthermore, the PlexCenter is permanent, expensive, and not easily programmed, having fixed and massive capabilities that usually require a facilitator to run, while SAMM is quite easily set up and programmed at any location for owners to run and specialize. Finally, level of adaptability or appropriateness of the system for a given type of collaborative work may affect interaction, and differently so (Jarvenpaa et al. 1987).

A third system parameter related to any GDSS is the matter of *who drives the system*. Some decision room systems reported in the GDSS literature are *chauffeur driven*, requiring a technical person who has expertise and the knowledge necessary to run complex GDSS systems, but users typically direct which modules to run and in which order they should appear. Other systems are *facilitator driven*, wherein the facilitator directs, structures, makes suggestions, and aids in technical problems. The facilitator is trained to run a specific type of meeting and assumes the role of both technical advisor and chauffeur. The facilitator's presence is always known and can have additional dynamic effects on the group. Finally, a GDSS may be *user driven*, wherein users drive the system themselves. For this form of support, a facilitator need only be present at first to train users on the system. Different norms may develop depending on how a GDSS is driven, and these norms may differentiate the groups depending on the degree of control groups have over how they will use the GDSS (e.g, Poole and DeSanctis 1990).

Level of user friendliness is a final system characteristic important for interpreting GDSS use and effects. While reviewers (Gallupe and DeSanctis 1987; Kraemer and King 1988; Seibold and Contractor 1991) have categorized GDSS systems variously, none has attempted to assess *how easy the systems are for subjects to use*. Although the concept of textual computer conferencing (simple message exchange between subjects) seems easy enough, it may not be for some users. Lack of user friendliness may heighten frustration and hinder successful decision-making (e.g., Hiltz, Johnson, and Turoff 1986; Kiesler et al. 1984; Siegel, Dubrovsky, Kiesler, and McGuire 1986). Some people may have difficulty typing (Suchan, Bui, and Dolk 1987), and others may have difficulty with interpreting procedures (Hiltz, Johnson, and Turoff 1987; Siegel et al. 1986).

The second category of parameters within which GDSS studies and findings may vary involves *use characteristics* of GDSS (see table 6.1). Use characteristics can be defined as conditions, manipulations, and constraints associated with the use of a particular GDSS in a particular setting for a particular task. To the extent that variations exist within and across these categories, all these factors have the potential to differentially affect the outcome of GDSS studies.

First, the multitude of *experimental manipulations* in GDSS research can confound attempts to organize effects. Some researchers have manipulated physical proximity (Hiltz et al. 1986; Siegel et al. 1986), while others have manipulated proximity in a factorial design combined with anonymity (Jessup et al. 1990). Although many studies have claimed to study similar decision-making outcomes, interstudy variation and few replications make drawing valid conclusions problematic.

Similarly, *clear and consistent operationalizations of outcome variables have proved troublesome.* Several variables such as "satisfaction" have received much attention in the GDSS literature. However, a review of fifteen GDSS experiments revealed inconsistent operational definitions in many of these constructs (Kudsi 1991). While multi-operational approaches are sometimes desirable, they do not always measure the same aspects of a construct, and therefore should not be inventoried as the same global variable when conducting meta-analytic classifications. For example, many studies have investigated "participation," variously defined as distribution of influence behavior (Zigurs, Poole, and DeSanctis 1987), total computer participation (Jessup et al. 1990), number of ideas generated (Nunamaker, Applegate, and Kosinsky 1987), time spent typing during a meeting (Kiesler 1990), time spent using GDSS during the meeting (Poole and DeSanctis, 1990), and total number of comments generated in a meeting (Siegel et al. 1986). All have been categorized under the rubric of "participation" despite clear differences in which aspect of group process they reveal. Lumping these definitions together can confound attempts to assess patterns of findings because they are measuring different aspects of participation (e.g., verbal participation, typed participation, time of meeting devoted to computer input, etc.).

Furthermore, *variations in the modalities afforded by the GDSS must be considered when interpreting findings.* For instance, decision rooms are different from dispersed Local Area Networks, but often are grouped under the rubric of GDSS (Dennis et al. 1988). Some experiments looked at the difference between face-to-face communication and GDSS "decision rooms" (Zigurs et al. 1987; Nunamaker et al. 1987) while others looked at the difference among two to three types of meeting support (Ellis, Rein, and Jarvenpaa 1989; Jarvenpaa et al. 1988). Others have looked at the difference between GDSS and paper and pencil versions of that support package (Watson, DeSanctis, and Poole 1988).

Task differences arguably have always been a concern for researchers when generalizing and organizing effects and when task differences are associated with different group outcomes (McGrath 1984). The first element that can separate studies is task *type*. Some researchers have studied idea generation (Nunamaker et al. 1987), others have included stakeholder identification (Easton, Vogel, and Nunamaker 1989). The *complexity* of a given task also can confound attempts to organize outcomes (Gallupe, DeSanctis, and Dickson 1988). Some tasks may involve many phases and material support before a decision is reached (Billingsley 1991; McGrath and Hollingshead 1991a), whereas others may only involve number of ideas generated (Nunamaker et al. 1987). If outcomes are measured in terms of satisfaction and participation distribution, the complexity of the task is at least as important as the technological support that the system provides. For example, Shaw (1981) argues that the complexity of a particular task may influence participation. Third, the *realism* or *salience* of a task is also important for interpreting dependent variables such as participation (McGrath 1984). Fourth, the *degree of uncertainty* associated with a task can have an effect on outcomes. Some GDSS studies have utilized risky shift tasks (McGuire, Kiesler, and Siegel 1986) in which the outcomes of given recommendations are uncertain for subjects. Other GDSS researchers have used more simplistic decision tasks for which an optimal answer can be determined (Steeb et al. 1981). Gallupe and DeSanctis (1988) directly tested the difference between a brainstorming task and a resource allocation task. The two tasks proved to differentially effect outcomes (Gallupe and DeSanctis 1988).

Time is an important variable in the study of groups in general (McGrath and Hollingshead 1991b; Gersick 1989), and certainly should be in GDSS studies as well. *Time constraint* is included as a use characteristic category in table 6.1 because the limits imposed on users for the completion of their tasks often varies between studies. Some of the GDSS research involves tasks that are completed within a maximum twenty minute period (Siegel et al. 1986), while others are allowed to run to completion (Watson et al. 1988). Some tasks in the literature were stretched over several meetings (Zigurs, DeSanctis, and Billingsley 1989), others were completed in one (Hiltz, Johnson, and Turoff 1986).

Another use characteristic parameter is *channel selection*. Interpreting GDSS effects is contingent upon the rules functioning during the meeting with regard to channel selection (George 1989). Some experiments have instructed subjects to communicate through the computer only (Hiltz, Johnson, and Turoff 1986; Siegel et al. 1986). Other investigations (especially those conducted in decision rooms where subjects are face-to-face) have not been explicit about the rules operating with regards to channel selection. Some GDSS may only be used to aggregate numeric data (Johansen 1988). In the users' training, or even across study conditions, did implicit rules operate that required subjects only to use the computers for certain tasks?

The final use characteristic in table 6.1 follows from the last point. Does the *training that the experiments provide* about use of the GDSS have a subsequent effect on outcomes? Were subjects given a demonstration? Were they allowed to walk through a practice meeting? What rules about use are inherent in the type of training? Answers to these questions are fuzzy in the literature.

The final global category of contextual contingencies, within which aspects of GDSS studies can be arrayed and compared, we term *user characteristics* (see table 6.1). User characteristics can be defined as the various attributes that individual members or groups bring to GDSS meetings that have implications for how the GDSS might be used. Eight categories combine to define and differentiate user characteristics: (1) sample differences, (2) group size, (3) group structure, (4) members' history of interacting together, (5) user training, (6) attitudes about use of technology, (7) computer expertise, and (8) experience adapting to new technologies. These categories represent attributes of GDSS users which may contribute to different GDSS outcomes.

First, *sample differences* refers to the variety of participants used in each study in the literature. GDSS studies have included business teams (Ellis et al. 1989), technical researchers (Steeb and Johnson 1981), undergraduate business majors (Jessup et al. 1990), and military personnel, among others. Second, *group size* is an important variable related to outcomes in the group literature such as distribution of participation (Fisher and Ellis 1990; Shaw 1981) and should be no less important in GDSS research. GDSS studies vary from three in a group to as many as twenty-two (cf. Pinsonneault and Kraemer 1990). Third, *group structure* can mediate and affect outcomes (Fisher and Ellis 1990; Shaw 1981; Poole, Seibold, and McPhee 1985). An active hierarchy operating in a group may influence participation or satisfaction differently than that of a leaderless group. There is some evidence that a leader can influence how the group uses the GDSS (Poole and DeSanctis 1990). Fourth, *a history of interacting together* can potentially affect the process and outcomes of meetings (Hall and Williams 1966; Torrance 1957). A group with a shared history together may orient to new technologies differently because of their collective experience with uncertain situations. Fifth, *subject attitude* toward the type, extent, and thoroughness of training provided prior to using a GDSS has differed throughout the literature (George 1989), resulting in potentially important differences in users' skills with the particular GDSS studied. Sixth, *attitude about using new technologies* for problem-solving can affect outcomes (Barley 1986; Poole and DeSanctis 1990). Seventh, users' general *level of computer expertise* may influence how they act during meetings where they are encouraged to use one (Kiesler 1990). Too, peer evaluation of a task and technology can mediate perception outcomes (Contractor and Eisenberg 1990; O'Reilly and Caldwell 1985). Eighth, *past experience* (adapting to new technologies) can influence how people use and are effected by it (Barley 1986; Fulk, Schmitz, and Steinfield 1990; Monge 1990).

The three global categories above provide a general framework within which other investigators can add theoretically relevant subcategories for examining *combinations* of factors on which GDSS outcomes are contingent. It is not meant to be an exhaustive taxonomy, merely a descriptive framework to illustrate the world of *contextual* differences between and within many GDSS studies. Attention to the combination of factors present in individual studies as well as across studies can add qualitative insight into the assessment of empirical findings. In addition, this descriptive framework provides researchers with a sensitizing device that documents key environmental considerations present in GDSS research. Finally, this approach provides an agenda for theory building in that contextual variables have been noted as crucial domain specifications for assessing outcomes (e.g., Contractor and Seibold, in press; Poole and DeSanctis 1990).

To summarize, we have surveyed the previous review literature on GDSS effects. A common observation in this literature is that there needs to be some way to organize the conclusions across the many variables that differentiate studies. A review of major reviews in the area revealed the need for a comprehensive descriptive framework for identifying contingencies. These contingencies can be arrayed and organized hierarchically by researchers to better interpret detected effects, as well as as a means to better "fit" their research into the literature. Incorporating environmental contingencies which differentially affect GDSS outcomes has been an important basis for taxonomic classification, but the GDSS literature is limited to singular contingencies which ignore influences occurring *in combination*. A conceptual framework was introduced in an attempt to incorporate the most important contextual contingencies explicitly addressed or alluded to in the GDSS literature. These distinctions were summarized within three global categories: system, use, and user characteristics.

Conclusion

Many of the GDSS studies, and GDSS reviews discussed throughout this essay, demonstrate that group process and outcome effects have not been systematically associated with the system, use, and user characteristics potentially present in GDSS use. In several cases, studies conducted at the same level of computer intervention have reported positive, negative, *and* no effects on key processes and outcomes. Perhaps the most significant implication of the essay is to reconsider the *assumption* surrounding previous work: that uniform effects should obtain within and across studies. As Malone (1985) points out, the majority of research on the social organization of work is based on the premise that the impact of a technology is consistent across adopting groups. However, this tradition of organizational research has repeatedly been confronted with the "dual effects hypothesis": communication technologies can have *opposite* impacts simultaneously and in spite of one another (Mesthene 1981). The introduction of telephones fostered both decentralization (the growth of the suburbs) and centralization (the growth of the skyscraper) at the same time (Pool, Decker, Dizard, Isreal, Rubin, and Weinstein 1981). After providing a comprehensive review of 251 articles, Johansen (1977) failed to arrive at unequivocal conclusions linking various configurations of organizational teleconferencing to specific communication tasks. Short, Williams, and Christie's (1976) series of carefully controlled experiments failed to demonstrate that telecommunication media characteristics (such as social presence) systematically influenced organizational communication tasks.

It seems increasingly evident that the tradition of research based on the technological imperative—including much of GDSS research—has failed repeatedly to provide an adequate understanding of mediated communication processes in the workplace. We propose that the study of technologies in organizations is better served by what Pfeffer (1982) called the "emergent perspective" on action in organizations. On this view, "the uses and consequences of information technology emerge unpredictably from complex social interactions" (Markus and Robey 1988, 588). In terms of the present review, adopting an emergent perspective would require a closer examination of the pragmatics and norms surrounding the use of GDSS in groups and the organizations in which they are embedded, considering at once the reciprocal relationships among goals, technology, and interactions that constitute emergent patterns and effects (Contractor and Eisenberg 1990).

Research of the sort we encourage has already proved fruitful in the study of other technologies. Johnson and Rice (1987) documented norms that evolved about the use of word-processing. Rice and Contractor (Fulk, Schmitz, and Steinfield 1990) showed that the introduction of integrated office information systems significantly alter the users' conceptualization of what constitutes effective communication. Steinfield and Fulk (1990) reported that users of a recently implemented electronic mail system used the medium to censure certain forms of communication (such as "flaming"). Steinfield and Fulk also described how the medium was used to structure users' perceptions of "message discipline" including the frequency of checking electronic mail, and the acceptable turnaround time for responses. Blomberg (1988) described how a computer-based design environment altered the social organization of the design process; equally significant was her finding that the evolution and meaning of the technology was influenced by the reallocation of tasks among designers and software engineers.

Similarly, we propose that the recursive interplay between goals, technologies and actors is an adaptive process by each group of GDSS users, thus allowing for widely divergent outcomes using the same level of GDSS in similar settings. Outside GDSS research an excellent example of research based on this premise is Barley's (1986) description of the introduction of the same technology in two radiology units. Barley's (1986) analysis revealed that the introduction of computerized tomography (CT scanners) occasioned similar dynamics but led to very different structural outcomes in the two units studied. Within the GDSS domain, Poole and DeSanctis (1990) have conceptualized GDSS use and effects as a process of adaptive structuration, and considerable empirical research has emerged within this perspective (e.g., DeSanctis, D'Onofrio, Sambamurthy, and Poole 1989; DeSanctis and Poole, 1990, 1991; DeSanctis, Poole, Dickson, and Jackson, in press; Holmes and Poole 1991; Poole and DeSanctis 1989, 1992; Poole, DeSanctis, Kirsch, and Jackson 1991; Poole, Holmes, and DeSanctis 1991; Poole, Holmes, Watson, and DeSanctis 1990). Contractor (this volume) explicates a self-organizing system perspective which we have formally contrasted with Poole and DeSanctis' adaptive structuration theory (Contractor and Seibold, 1993). Both theoretical approaches acknowledge that there are various contextual contingencies that mediate how GDSSs are used (e.g, Poole and DeSanctis propose a "double contingency" model). The comprehensive assessment of the various combinations of contextual contingencies we have provided (see table 6.1) not only expands and illuminates the first contingency in the Poole and DeSanctis model but hopefully provides an important starting point for enhancing our understanding of the *recursive* interplay between the various systems, uses, and users of GDSSs.

References

Barley, S. R. 1986. Technology as an occasion for structuring: Evidence from observation of CT scanners and the social ordering of radiology departments. *Administrative Science Quarterly* 31:78–108.

Bikson, T. K., and J. D. Eveland. 1990. The interplay of work group structures and computer support. In *Intellectual teamwork: Social and technological foundations of cooperative work,* ed. J. Galegher et al. Hillsdale, NJ: Erlbaum.

Billingsley, J. M. 1991. *Longitudinal or over time analysis in a GDSS environment: Discussion and directions.* Paper presented at the annual conference of the Speech Communication Association, Chicago, November 1991.

Blomberg, J. L. 1988. The variable impact of computer technologies on the organization of work activities. In *Computer-supported cooperative work: A book of readings,* ed. I. Grief. San Mateo, CA: Morgan Kaufmann.

Bormann, E. G. 1970. The paradox and promise of small group research. *Communication Monographs* 37:211–17.

Bradford, L. 1976. *Making meetings work: A guide for leaders and group members.* San Diego, CA: University Associates.

Bulkeley, W. M. 1992. "Computerizing" dull meetings is touted as an antidote to the mouth that bored. *Wall Street Journal,* 28 January.

Campbell, D. T., and J. C. Stanley. 1978. *Experimental and quasi-experimental designs for research.* Boston: Houghton Mifflin.

Connolly, T. M., L. M. Jessup, and J. S. Valacich. 1990. Effects of anonymity and evaluative tone on idea generation in computer-mediated groups. *Management Science* 36:689–703.

Contractor, N., and E. M. Eisenberg. 1990. Communication networks and new media in organizations. In *Organizations and communication technology,* ed. C. Steinfield and J. Fulk. Newbury Park, CA: Sage.

Contractor, N., and D. R. Seibold. 1991. *Theoretical frameworks for the study of structuring processes in group decision support systems: Comparison of adaptive structuration theory and self-organizing systems theory.* Paper presented at the annual convention of the International Communication Association, Chicago, May 1991.

———. 1993. Theoretical frameworks for the study of structuring processes in group decision support systems: Comparison of adaptive structuration theory and self-organizing systems theory. *Human Communication Research* 19:528–63.

Daft, R., and R. Lengel. 1986. Organizational information requirements, media richness, and structural design. *Management Science* 32:554–71.

Davis, J. H. 1973. Group decision and social interaction: A theory of social decision schemes. *Psychological Review* 80:97–125.

Dennis, A. R., J. F. George, L. M. Jessup, J. F. Nunamaker, and D. R. Vogel. 1988. Information technology to support electronic meetings. *Management Information Systems Quarterly* 12:591–624.

DeSanctis, G. 1989. *Bibliography #1 for the group decision support systems research project.* Unpublished manuscript.

DeSanctis, G., M. D'Onofrio, V. Sambamurthy, and M. S. Poole. 1989. Comprehensiveness and restriction in group decision heuristics: Effects of computer support on consensus decision making. *Proceedings of the Tenth International Conference on Information Systems.* Boston.

DeSanctis, G. and B. Gallupe. 1987. A foundation for the study of group decision support systems. *Management Science* 33:589–609.

DeSanctis, G., and M. S. Poole. 1991. Understanding the differences in collaborative system use through appropriation analysis. In *Proceedings of the Twenty-Fourth International Conference on System Sciences* 3:547–53, Los Alamitos, CA: IEEE Computer Society Press.

DeSanctis, G., M. S. Poole, G. Desharnais, and H. Lewis. 1992. Using computing to facilitate the quality improvement process: The IRS-Minnesota project. *Interfaces* 21:23–36.

DeSanctis, G., M. S. Poole, G. W. Dickson, and B. M. Jackson. In press. An interpretive analysis of team use of group technologies. *Journal of Organizational Computing.*

Dhar, V., and M. H. Olson. 1989. Assumptions underlying systems that support work group collaboration. In *Technological support for work group collaboration,* ed. M. H. Olson. Erlbaum.

Drazin, R., and A. Van de Ven. 1985. Alternative forms of fit in contingency theory. *Administrative Science Quarterly* 30:514–39.

Easton, A. C., D. R. Vogel, and J. F. Nunamaker. 1989. Stakeholder identification and assumption surfacing in small groups: An experimental study. *Proceedings of the Twenty-Second Annual Hawaii International Conference on System Sciences* 3:344–52.

Ellis, C. A., G. L. Rein, S. L. Jarvenpaa. 1989. Nick experimentation: Some selected results. *Proceedings of the Twenty-Second Annual Hawaii International Conference on System Sciences* 3:359–69.

Fisher, B. A., and D. G. Ellis. 1990. *Small group decision-making: communication and the group process.* 3rd ed. New York: McGraw-Hill.

Fulk, J., J. Schmitz, and C. Steinfield. 1990. Social influence model of technology use. In *Organizations and communication technology,* ed. C. Steinfield and J. Fulk. Newbury Park, CA: Sage.

Gallupe, R. B., DeSanctis, G. and Dickson, G. W. 1988. Computer-based support for group problem finding: An experimental investigation. *MIS Quarterly* 12:277–98.

George, J. F. 1989. A comparison of four recent GDSS experiments. *Proceedings of the Twenty-Second Annual Hawaii International Conference on System Sciences* 3:397–402.

Gersick, C. J. 1988. Time and transition in work teams: Toward a new model of group development, *Academy of Management Journal* 31:9–41.

Greif, I. 1988. Overview. In *Computer-supported cooperative work: A book of readings,* ed. I. Grief. San Mateo, CA: Morgan Kaufmann.

Gutek, B. A. 1990. Work group structure and information technology: A structural contingency approach. In *Intellectual teamwork: Social and technological foundations of cooperative work,* ed. J. Galegher, R. Kraut, and C. Egido. Hillsdale, NJ: Erlbaum.

Hall, J., and M. S. Williams. 1966. A comparison of decision-making performances in established and ad hoc groups. *Journal of Personality and Social Psychology* 3:214–22.

Hare, A. P. 1976. *Handbook of small group research.* New York: Free Press.

Hiltz, S. R., K. Johnson, M. Turoff. 1986. Experiments in group decision-making: Communication process and outcome in face-to-face versus computerized conferences. *Human Communication Research* 3:225–52.

———. 1987. Experiments in group decision-making 2: The effects of designated human leaders and statistical feedback in computerized conferences. Unpublished manuscript.

Holmes, M., and M. S. Poole. 1991. The longitudinal analysis of interaction. In *Studying interpersonal interaction,* ed. B. Montgomery and S. Duck. New York: Guilford.

Huber, G. P. 1984. Issues in the design of group decision support systems. *Management Information Systems Quarterly* 8: 195–204.

Huber, G. P. 1990. A theory of the effects of advanced information technologies on organizational design, intelligence and decision making. *Academy of Management Review* 15:47–71.

Hymowitz, C. 1988. A survival guide to the office meeting. *Wall Street Journal* 35, 21 June.

Jarvenpaa, S. L., V. S. Rao, and T. D. Laase. 1988. Computer support for meetings of groups working on unstructured problems: A field experiment. *Management Information Systems Quarterly* 12:645–66.

Jessup, L. M., T. Connolly, and J. Galegher. 1990. The effects of anonymity on GDSS group process in an idea-generating task. *Management Information Systems Quarterly* 14:312–21.

Jessup, L. M., and J. S. Valacich. In press. *Group support systems: New perspectives.* New York: Macmillan.

Jessup, L. M., and T. M. Connolly. 1990. Toward a theory of automated group work: The deindividuating effects of anonymity. *Small Group Research* 21:333–48.

Johansen, R. 1988. *Groupware: Computer support for business teams.* New York: Free Press.

Johansen, R. 1977. Social evaluations of teleconferencing. *Telecommunications Policy* 1:395–419.

Johnson, B., and R. E. Rice. 1987. *Managing organizational innovation: The evolution from word processing to office information systems.* New York: Columbia University Press.

Kiesler, S. 1990. *Group decision making and communication technology.* Unpublished manuscript.

Kiesler, S., J. Siegel, and T. W. McGuire. 1984. Social psychological aspects of computer-mediated communication. *American Psychologist* 39:1123–34.

Kraemer, K. L., and J. L. King. 1988. Computer-based systems for cooperative work. *Computing Surveys* 20:115–46.

Kraemer, K., and A. Pinsonneault. 1990. In *Intellectual teamwork: social and technological foundations of cooperative work,* ed. J. Galegher, R. Kraut, and C. Egido. Hillsdale, NJ: Erlbaum.

Kudsi, S. 1991. A review of group decision support system research. Unpublished manuscript.

Lipsey, M. W. 1990. *Design sensitivity: Statistical power for experimental research.* Newbury Park, CA: Sage.

Maier, N. R. F. 1980. Assets and liabilities in group problem solving: The need for an integrative function. In *Intercom: Readings in organizational communication,* ed. S. Ferguson. Newark, NJ: Hayden.

Malone, T. W. 1985. Designing organizational interfaces. *Proceedings of the ACM Conference on Computer-Human Interaction.* New York: Association for Computing Machinery.

Malone, T. W., K. R. Grant, K. Lai, R. Rao, and D. A. Rosenblitt. 1989. The information lens: An intelligent system for information sharing and coordination. In *Technological support for work group collaboration,* ed. M. H. Olson. Hillsdale, NJ: Erlbaum.

Markus, M. L., and D. Robey, 1988. Information technology and organizational change: Causal structure in theory and research. *Management Science,* 34:583–598.

McGrath, J. E. 1984. *Groups: Interaction and performance.* Englewood Cliffs, NJ: Prentice Hall.

McGrath, J. E., and A. Hollingshead. 1991a. *Putting the "G" back in "GSS": Some theoretical issues about dynamic processes in groups with technological enhancements.* Paper submitted for publication.

———. 1991b. *Interaction and performance in computer-assisted work groups.* Paper presented at Conference on Team Decision-making in Organizations, January 1991.

McGuire, T. W., S. Kiesler, and J. Siegel. 1987. Group and computer-mediated discussion effects in risk decision making. *Journal of Personality and Social Psychology* 52:917–30.

Mesthene, E. G. 1981. The role of technology in society. In *Technology and man's future,* ed. A. H. Teich. New York: St. Martin's Press.

Mintzberg, H. 1973. *The nature of managerial work.* New York: Harper & Row.

Monge, P. R. 1990. Theoretical and analytical issues in studying organizational processes. *Organizational Science* 1:406–31.

Nunamaker, J. F., L. M. Applegate, and B. R. Kosynski. 1987. Facilitating group creativity: Experience with a group decision support system. *Proceedings of the Twentieth Annual Hawaii International Conference on System Sciences* 1:422–30.

O'Reilly, C. A., and D. F. Caldwell. 1985. The impact of normative social influence and cohesiveness on task perceptions and attitudes: A social information processing approach. *Journal of Occupational Psychology* 58:193–206.

Pfeffer, J. 1982. *Organizations and organization theory.* Marshfield, MA: Pitman.

Pinsonneault, A., and K. L. Kraemer. 1990. The effects of electronic meetings on group processes and outcomes: An assessment of the empirical research. *European Journal of Operational Research* 46:143–61.

Pool, I. S., C. Decker, S. Dizard, S. Israel, P. Rubin, and B. Weinstein. 1981. Foresight and hindsight: The case of the telephone. In I. S. Pool (Ed)., *Social impacts of the telephone* (pp. 127–157). Cambridge: MIT Press.

Poole, M. S., and G. DeSanctis. 1989. Use of group decision support systems as an appropriation process. *Proceedings of the Twenty-first Annual Hawaiian International Conference on Social System* 4:149–57.

———. 1990. Understanding the use of group decision support systems: the theory of adaptive structuration. In *Organizations and communication technology,* ed. C. Steinfield and J. Fulk. Newbury Park, CA: Sage.

———. 1992. Microlevel structuration in computer-supported group decision making. *Human Communication Research* 19:5–49.

Poole, M. S., and J. Doelger. 1986. Developmental processes in group decision-making. In *Communication and group decision-making,* ed. R. Hirokawa and M. S. Poole. Newbury Park, CA: Sage.

Poole, M. S., M. Holmes, and G. DeSanctis. 1991. Conflict management in a computer-supported meeting environment. *Management Science* 37:926–53.

Poole, M.S., D. R. Seibold, and R. D. McPhee. 1985. Group decision-making as a structurational process. *Quarterly Journal of Speech* 71:74–102.

Poole, M. S., G. DeSanctis, L. J. Kirsch, and M. Jackson. 1991. An observational study of everyday use of a group decision support system. Paper presented at the Twenty-Fourth Annual Hawaii International Conference on Systems Sciences, Kuaui.

Poole, M. S., M. Holmes, R. Watson, and G. DeSanctis. 1990. Group decision support system and group communication: A comparison of decision making processes in computer-supported and nonsupported groups. Unpublished manuscript, University of Minnesota, Department of Speech Communication.

Rice, R. E., and G. Love. 1987. Electronic emotion: Socio-emotional content in a computer-mediated network. *Communication Research* 14:85–108.

Saffo, P. 1991. Future Conference Room Furniture: Personal Workstations. *InfoWorld* 13 (17): 50–51.

Seibold, D. R., and N. Contractor. 1991. EVALUATING GROUP DECISION SUPPORT SYSTEMS: TAXONOMY, RESEARCH REVIEW, AND EFFECTS. Paper presented at the Annual Convention of the International Communication Association, Chicago, May 1991.

Shaw, M. E. 1981. *Group dynamics: The psychology of small group behavior.* 3rd ed. New York: McGraw-Hill.

Short, J., E. Williams, and B. Christie. 1976. *The social psychology of telecommunications.* London: Wiley.

Schrage, M. 1990. *Shared minds: The new technologies of collaboration.* New York: Random House.

Siegel, J., V. Dubrovsky, S. Kiesler, and T. W. McGuire. 1986. Group processes in computer-mediated communication. *Organizational Behavior and Human Decision Processes* 37:157–87.

Smith, J., M. T. Vanechek. 1989. A nonsimultaneous computer conference as a component of group decision support systems. *Proceedings of the Twenty-Second Annual Hawaii International Conference on System Sciences* 3:370–77.

Steeb, R., and S. C. Johnston. 1981. A computer-based interactive system for group decision making. *IEEE Transactions on Systems, Man, and Cybernetics* 11:544–52.

Stefik, M., G. Foster, D. Boborow, K. Kahn, S. Lanning, and L. Suchan. 1987. Beyond the chalkboard: Using computers to support collaboration and problem solving in meeting. *Communications of the ACM* 30:32–47.

Stefik, M., and J. S. Brown. 1989. Toward portable ideas. In *Technological support for work group collaboration,* ed. M. H. Olson. Hillsdale, NJ: Erlbaum.

Steinfield, C., and J. Fulk. 1990. The theory imperative. In *Organizations and communication technology,* ed. C. Steinfield and J. Fulk. Newbury Park, CA: Sage.

Suchan, J., T. Bui, and D. Dolk. 1987. GDSS effectiveness: Identifying organizational opportunities. *Proceeding of the Twentieth Annual Hawaii International Conference on System Sciences* 1:441–49.

3M Corporation. 1991. Electronic bibliography of computer mediated meeting support. Unpublished electronic bibliography.

Torrance, E. P. 1957. Group decision-making and disagreement. *Social Forces* 35:314–18.

Vogel, D., and J. Nunamaker. 1990. Group decision support system impact: Multi-methodological exploration: In *Intellectual teamwork: Social and technological foundations of cooperative work,* ed. J. Galegher, R. Kraut, and C. Egido. Hillsdale, NJ: Erlbaum.

Watson, R. T., G. DeSanctis, and M. S. Poole. 1988. Using a GDSS to facilitate group consensus: Some intended and unintended consequences. *Management Information Systems Quarterly* 2:462–77.

Zander, A. 1987. *Making groups effective.* London: Jossey-Bass.

Zigurs, I., M. S. Poole, and G. DeSanctis. 1987. A study of influence in computer-mediated communication. *Management Information Systems Quarterly* 12 : 625–44.

Zigurs, I., G. DeSanctis, and J. Billingsley. 1989. Exploring attitudinal development in computer-supported groups. *Proceedings of the Twenty-Second Annual Hawaii International Conference on System Sciences* 3:353–58.

DAYNA FINET

7 Interest Advocacy and the Transformation in Organizational Communication

The last several decades of American social history have been characterized, perhaps as much as any feature, by normative conflict and transformation involving a variety of social "movements": environmentalism, feminism, consumerism, civil rights, animal rights, Native American rights, gay and lesbian rights, older persons' rights, AIDS activism, antinuclear activism, gun control, abortion, and more. The changes initiated by these normative shifts, along with the social and political backlash often generated by them, have, arguably, permanently altered some of the principles which govern individual and collective social arrangements and relationships.

None of these normative transformations "just happened." Instead, organized collectivities have used communication strategically—if not always skillfully or effectively—in order, depending on organizations' interests and their members' visions of the good society, to attempt to accomplish or block these changes. This is organizational communication with effects of great substance, affecting fundamentally the nature and quality of our society. When analyzing the societal impact of these normative shifts, it is important to address a most significant question: how can social scientists explain why some of these movements succeed—success conceptualized as a movement's ability to transform itself from special interest to mainstream social concern—and why others fail? This chapter argues that the study of interest advocacy, informed by an organizational communication perspective, is uniquely qualified to handle this important question.

At one level, it is possible to view interest advocacy as just another communicative tactic of political groups with specific agendas of relatively narrow scope. But to do so risks that the more important substantial implications of this phenomenon for organizational communication scholarship will be overlooked. Instead, interest advocacy can be more productively conceptualized as an index of the social normative shifts characteristic of the contemporary sociopolitical world.

This view of interest advocacy represents a stance philosophically new within the field of organizational communication. Certainly the field has witnessed an expansion of interest—though relatively modest—in the investigation of relations between organizations and their external environments. This work is characterized, however, by an orientation which centralizes focal organizations and conceptualizes environments as the location of variables which affect organizational outcomes in causal ways.

The philosophical perspective advocated in this chapter reverses this arrangement of conceptual and research priorities. This new perspective begins with a more explicit concern for understanding the interdependencies between organizations and environments, and argues that the societal consequences of organizational action are at least as important as the organizational consequences of environmental variables. This view of interest advocacy implies that organizations must no longer be viewed as independent social agents, but as constituent elements of the larger society, both affecting and affected by their external environments. In that society will exist often competing views of what is socially good and appropriate—certainly sometimes driven by self-interest, acknowledged or not, but also sometimes guided by a true commitment to achieve a better world. Due to interest advocacy and the social normative shifts related to it, organizations which had grown accustomed to consider self-interest the only criterion for decision-making and action must now seriously and responsibly deal with competing sociopolitical points of view.

More important though, the perspective outlined here is philosophically new because it focuses centrally on societal analysis, on the ways in which the interest advocacy practices of organizations, acting cooperatively or as adversaries, influence the normative and institutional character of our social world. In other words, this new perspective emphasizes the utility of the investigation of interest advocacy, grounded in an organizational communication orientation, for the development of our understanding of our own particular sociopolitical normative arrangements.

New theoretical and methodological approaches correspond to the new philosophy implied in this approach to the study of interest advocacy. The bulk of this chapter is devoted to the development of these new theoretical and methodological strategies, which are briefly summarized in this introduction.

The perspective articulated in this paper is theoretically new partly in its emphasis on "macro" political and sociological features of organizational communication, a focus which has traditionally been relatively underrepresented in the organizational communication literature. Because these normative transformations in essence involve changes in the relationships between organizations and social actors in these organizations' sociopolitical environments, the chapter outlines theoretical work on the topic of organizational environments, focusing on institutional theory (Meyer and Rowan 1977; Meyer and Scott 1983; Zucker 1988) which offers the most substantive analysis, within the field of organizational theory, of organizations' relations with their sociopolitical environments.

More significant, however, is the new theoretical emphasis on organizational communication practices—in other words, interest advocacy—as central to processes of sociopolitical normative change. Although some institutional theorists have recently begun to correct the oversights of early institutional formulations by examining the question of agency (DiMaggio 1988) and organizational resistance (Oliver 1991) in institutional processes, they have still failed to comprehend the interactional dynamics—again, the interest advocacy—which institutionalization involves.

To make interest advocacy a central analytical component of institutional processes requires a particular focus on the communication practices of organizations involved in the dynamics of sociopolitical normative change. This chapter classifies organizations directly involved in institutional processes as "change advocates" or "change targets," and focuses most specifically on analysis of the strategically "opportunistic" or "oppositional" character of the communication practices of these advocate and target organizations.

The new philosophical and theoretical imperatives of the perspective advocated throughout this chapter are particularly elusive to the methodological techniques traditionally employed by organizational communication researchers, making innovative research strategies useful, and necessary, for investigation of the consequences of interest advocacy, as organizational communication, in the context of widespread sociopolitical normative transformation. This methodological approach emphasizes an explicitly exploratory approach to seldom-used alternative sources of data, primarily archival, such as published histories of sociopolitical normative movements and popular cultural artifacts: radio and television call-in and talk shows and prime-time network and syndicated current-affairs programs. The chapter also describes ways of dealing with the assessment of normative consensus, an issue obviously crucial in understanding relations between interest advocacy and sociopolitical normative arrangements.

The communicative practices of interest advocacy

The theoretical perspective advanced in this chapter starts with a basic presumption that sociopolitical change and stability are both social accomplishments, which occur only through the predominantly communicative actions of organized social and political interests. This premise logically demands that theoretical explanations of normative processes—whether these result in the maintenance of an existing sociopolitical "status quo" or in dramatic sociopolitical transformation—require a grounding in the perspective of organizational communication.

Organizational theories which focus on interaction between organizations and their external environments offer the most extensively articulated approach useful in the analysis of relationships between organized interest advocacy and the sociopolitical norms which characterize a society. The explication of the organizational communication practices involved in relations between organizations and external environments remains, however, relatively undeveloped. This section of the chapter first discusses the scholarly literature dealing with the topic of organizational environments, particularly emphasizing institutionalization theory, which most specifically focuses on organizations' sociopolitical environments. An elaboration of the role of communication in institutional processes follows. This discussion emphasizes the oppositional and opportunistic characteristics of the communication practices of organizations directly involved, as change advocates or change targets, in sociopolitical normative processes.

Organizations and sociopolitical environments

To assert that organizations cannot be fully understood without some reference to their relationships with social agents beyond their own boundaries may seem obvious, and it is curious that relatively little of the organizational communication literature addresses topics concerning organizational environments. The importance of relationships between organizations and their external environments has been expressed in various ways for decades, perhaps most fundamentally in the work of various systems theorists (Parsons 1956; Scott 1987a; Thompson 1967). The ideas of these analysts are still important because of their basic shared premise that organizational processes cannot be adequately understood if explanation is restricted to internal interaction alone, and that organizations' external relations, which can have significant organizational consequences, must also be studied. The open systems perspective also established two conceptual themes still relevant to the analysis of organizations' environmental interaction: (*a*) that turbulence or instability originating in the external environment represents a significant threat to organizations' success and perhaps, survival; and (*b*) that effective organizations act in ways to manage this turbulence, either through accommodation to external demands or through attempts to manipulate or alter those demands. The first theorists to investigate these ideas focused on organizations' market and technological environments (Burns and Stalker 1961; Emery and Trist, 1965; Lawrence and Lorsch 1967), but these themes are also apparent in the literature which deals to some extent with organizations' social and political environments, such as resource dependence theory (Pfeffer and Salancik 1978) and, especially, institutional theory (Meyer and Rowan 1977; Meyer and Scott 1983; Zucker 1988).

> Institutional theorists . . . reflect and advance a growing awareness that no organization is just a technical system and that many organizations are not primarily technical systems. All social systems— hence, all organizations—exist in an institutional environment that defines and delimits social reality. And just as with technical environments, institutional environments are multiple, enormously diverse, and variable over time. To neglect their presence and power is to ignore significant causal factors shaping organizational structures and practices: to overlook these variables is to misspecify our causal models. (Scott 1987b, 507–8)

The strength of institutional theory is its emphasis on the external social and political factors which affect organizations. Organizational "legitimacy," first defined by Parsons (1956) as the perception on the part of influential external actors that organizations' philosophies and practices are socially and politically appropriate, represents the institutional approach's central concept. Legitimate organizations enjoy a diminished level of turbulence in their sociopolitical environments, giving them freedom to operate in relatively unrestricted ways. But when external social norms change—fueled, often, by the advocacy efforts of interest groups—expectations of what constitute appropriate organizational behavior may change too. Organizations which fail to adapt to new normative demands—or which cannot establish normative alternatives more consistent with their interests—may lose legitimacy and experience external criticism, challenge, and opposition.

In the past, institutional theory has described such phenomena as "decoupling" (Meyer and Rowan 1977; Meyer and Scott 1983), the "logic of confidence" (Meyer and Rowan 1977; Meyer and Scott 1983), and institutional "isomorphism" (DiMaggio and Powell 1983) as relatively passive structurally adaptive responses to legitimacy challenges. Consequently the theory tended to overlook the importance of human agency, the active participation, including their communicative participation, of actual people, in institutional processes (DiMaggio 1988; Oliver 1991; Perrow 1985; Powell 1985). More recent work within the institutional framework has remedied this problem (Oliver 1991), describing a range of communicative strategies and tactics which organizations use in dealing with institutional pressures brought about by interest group advocacy. Oliver's work expands importantly upon the conceptualizations of organizational response articulated by earlier institutional theorists: her five categories of strategic response to institutional pressure—acquiescence, compromise, avoidance, defiance, and manipulation—include the passive responses which dominate prior institutional literature, but also incorporate several types of resistance-oriented response.

Organizational communication and social transformation

The ideas of several recent institutional theorists (DiMaggio 1988; Oliver 1991; Perrow 1985; Powell 1985) have made valuable contributions in their recognition of the necessity of organizational agency in institutional processes and of the potential for organizational resistance, as well as adaptation, in response to normative pressures originating in organizations' institutional environments. However, these analyses are inadequate for two primary reasons.

First, institutional theory—like other approaches to the study of relations between organizations and environments—prioritizes the perspective of focal organizations, concentrating almost exclusively on the causal effects of environmental variables on organizational structure and process. Similarly—and also like other theories of organizational environments—the institutionalization perspective neglects any exploration of the interdependencies of organizations and the larger social world, and in particular, the societal consequences of organizational involvement in institutional processes.

Second, the institutional literature has not considered that specific communicative practices may represent the predominant forms of organizations' institutional agency. Neither has work in the institutional tradition explored the communicative behaviors of organizations which advocate normative change as well as those which defend the normative status quo, or the systemic interactional processes within which institutional processes are embedded.

To address these two important issues is to arrive at the investigation of interest advocacy as a unique and significant form of organizational communication, with the possibility of capturing the most intellectually and socially significant features of normative stability and change. Three aspects of this conceptualization of interest advocacy as organizational communication are most significant.

First, interest advocacy essentially involves an organizationally grounded struggle over dominant social meanings. These meanings are highly significant for organizations, because they form the basis for assessments of organizational legitimacy which in turn, can substantially affect the health and survival of established organizations or those in the process of emergence. The stakes in this struggle are high, too, because the contest over meaning most commonly is defined as a zero-sum game in which one side wins, one loses, and the coexistence of multiple meanings becomes impossible.

Second, an interest advocacy framework is fundamentally dynamic in character. Normative change is commonly uneven, nonsequential, incomplete, and fragmentary. Yet, an understanding of the organizational and social consequences of interest advocacy must begin with the effort to specify the stages of sociopolitical normative evolution—the growth, the persistence, and the decline of social meanings evident in "emerging" (where conflict between norms is still visibly apparent), "mature" (situations of widespread social consensus favoring a new normative perspective), and "declining" (in which established new norms are challenged in turn) normative movements.

Finally, a concern with interest advocacy focalizes the central importance of "organizing" in the understanding of normative change. To accomplish normative transformation, or to block it, requires that comparatively independent social actors communicate to build organizational strength, forging alliances with similar agents who share common normative interests, and recruiting and motivating movement members, supporters, and allies. In other words, the strategic influencing of social norms only occurs through organizations' communicative action, or, in more dynamic terms, through continual, ongoing organizing.

The present discussion focuses on the communicative practices of two types of organizations with direct roles in processes of normative transformation: "change advocates" and "change targets."[1] Change advocate organizations attempt to encourage wider social acceptance of counter-normative positions which they represent; "political" in the widest sense of the term, these organizations are as likely to be conservative as progressive in their sociopolitical orientation (even though conventional wisdom generally describes as "special interest groups" those organizations—Greenpeace, PETA, NOW, NARAL—with progressive political views, conservative groups—NRA, WAR, Operation Rescue—fit the conceptual definition of change advocates equally well). Change targets are those organizations whose behavior, although consistent with prevailing normative views, change advocates wish to alter in a direction which parallels the ideals and objectives of the movement. Often business and trade groups, and in some situations government organizations and professional associations, serve as change targets. It is also important to note that change advocate organizations within the context of a given normative movement may be considered change targets in a different situation of normative advocacy.

The communication practices of both advocate and target groups can involve activities which might be termed "neutral," as well as those more directly focused on influencing their sociopolitical adversaries and the sociopolitical normative context. Such neutral communication practices as sociopolitical information scanning, for example, have been described in a variety of contexts, from the literature on organizational boundary spanning (Adams 1980), to contemporary research on corporate social responsibility and responsiveness (Sethi 1991) and, in the long term, must be included in the development of an overall explanatory model of institutional transformation.

However, this chapter focuses on those communication practices more directly involved in organizations' strategic efforts at normative influence, for these are the communicative acts which most centrally involve interest advocacy, and which most clearly reveal the dynamics of the organizational struggle over dominant social meanings. This chapter describes such communicative practices as "oppositional" or "opportunistic" in character. Each intentional and socially strategic, these forms of organizational advocacy communication are interesting because they represent organizations' efforts to simultaneously speak to, and influence, two primary external audiences—the opposing sociopolitical side and the larger normatively-structured community. Indeed, it is not possible to even comprehend the oppositional or opportunistic nature of advocacy communication unless that communication is viewed in terms of its relationship to sociopolitical adversaries and the normative climate. Oppositional advocacy exploits conflict and difference between the political positions of change advocates and change targets. Organizations using opportunistic advocacy seek accommodation with the competing normative priorities of their sociopolitical adversaries.

A brief case description of a contemporary social normative change movement, animal rights activism, demonstrates the continual conflict between normative perspectives and the oppositional and opportunistic communicative acts which characterize the efforts of change advocates and change targets to influence dominant normative views.

Oppositional and opportunistic communication in the animal rights movement

In recent years animal rights activism has grown more vocal and visible, in the process increasing the number of its supporters. Yet, at the time of this writing widespread normative approval of the goals and tactics of animal rights activists has yet to fully develop, with much of the public maintaining a negative stance toward the goals and tactics of the movement.

Advocates of animal rights are primarily recognized for their oppositional communicative acts: the destruction of research laboratories; the distribution of films detailing cruel and outrageous examples of deliberate animal abuse by laboratory personnel; physical attacks on fur-wearers; and bloody, graphic anti-fur advertising.

A membership recruitment brochure distributed by the prominent animal rights organization *People for the Ethical Treatment of Animals* illustrates the use of oppositional communicative strategies— underscoring the inhumanity of the methods employed by the primary targets of the animal rights movement—in animal rights advocacy efforts.

A graphic description of the technology of animal experimentation is intended to demonstrate the cruelty which pervades animal testing labs.

In poisoning tests, products are force-fed by mouth or tube and the results monitored. Typical symptoms include convulsions, vomiting, paralysis, and bleeding from the eyes, nose, and mouth; animals who survive the test are killed. In typical blinding tests, six to nine albino rabbits are strapped into stocks to stop them from rubbing their eyes with their paws. Their lower eyelids are pulled back to form small cups; the test substance is poured in and the eye then held closed. With caustic substances, the rabbits scream in pain. The eyes are examined over days or weeks for bleeding; ulcerated corneas and blindness, all common results. No treatment is given. (People for the Ethical Treatment of Animals)

The PETA brochure similarly portrays the bloody, brutal methods of fur harvesting.

[R]anchers kill the animals with the cheapest method. Electrocution, neck-breaking, poisoning with strychnine or hot unfiltered engine exhaust, and gassing are painful and common techniques. Animals caught in the notorious leghold traps also suffer. Some animals, especially those with dependent young, chew off their trapped limbs to escape, becoming vulnerable to gangrene, fever, blood loss and predators. If they remain caught and alive until the trapper returns they may be drowned, beaten, or stomped to death. (People for the Ethical Treatment of Animals)

Such graphic information about the practices of the targets of animal rights activism is oppositional communication in character and intent. Responses by these targets—the cosmetics, fur, and medical research industries—have been both opportunistic and oppositional in nature. Much of the cosmetics industry has reacted opportunistically to the demands of the animal rights movement by eliminating the use of animal testing and animal ingredients in cosmetics manufacturing and more important, by communicating this opportunism in advertising, promotion, and packaging strategies.

A promotional flyer for the *Origins* brand of cosmetics demonstrates one marketer's alignment with the intentions of animal rights activism (even addressing, at the same time, the concerns regarding human health and safety often voiced by critics of the animal rights movement):

Preservation of the animal. Origins uses absolutely no animal derived ingredients in any of our formulations or products—not even our brushes. In our mind, there is simply no need to use animal-derived ingredients when there is a wealth of plant materials available that deliver the same or similar benefits. In addition, Origins does *no* testing on animals. Using today's technology, we've found alternate means of providing for your safety, comfort, and peace of mind. (Origins)

Adoption of the opportunistic strategy illustrated by the Origins flyer has been widespread throughout the cosmetics industry, as a response to external criticism of the use of animal products and animal experimentation.

But the fur industry, which cannot very easily substitute nonanimal alternatives for the real thing (and still remain in the same business), has countered animal rights activism with oppositional communication of its own. Advocacy advertising placed by the fur industry illustrates this oppositional stance, posing individual freedom of choice as a cherished normative value threatened by the agenda of the animal rights movement. An exemplary ad placed by Saga Fox features a full-page photograph of smiling, wholesome woman and child, the woman wrapped in fur, with one sentence of copy intended to appeal to one of the most significant concerns of those opposed to the animal rights movement:

Some people are opposed to a very basic luxury: your freedom of choice. (Saga Fox)

Medical research organizations also have met the oppositional communicative practices of the animal rights activists with oppositional strategies of their own. This sophisticated oppositional approach portrays the saving of animal lives and the saving of human lives as fundamentally incompatible normative priorities, and promotes this normative message through industry-sponsored "grassroots" front groups such as the Americans for Medical Progress Educational Foundation. Headlined "How Many More Will Die Before You Say 'No?' to the Animal Rights Movement?," advocacy advertising sponsored by this group provides an example of the oppositional techniques used by opponents of the animal rights movement:

The cure for AIDS will come like every cure before it, through animal research. And yet, there is a growing movement of animal rights activists who oppose any use of animals in biomedical research. . . . Although a tiny minority in our society, the animal rights movement will stop at nothing to achieve its aims. Their methods range from disinformation, to intimidation, to outright terror. Their efforts must be stopped, or all medical research may one day come to a dead halt. (Americans for Medical Progress Educational Foundation)

Strategies for researching interest advocacy

Even those scholars who use institutional theory as their own conceptual framework have noted problems with the focus and specificity of institutional research (Zucker 1987); the relatively high level of abstraction characteristic of the institutional perspective can render it elusive to empirical investigation. Examining the actual communicative practices of change advocate and change target organizations begins to address this problem; it is especially important that the most immediate research in this area be approached with an exploratory attitude appropriate to the state of existing knowledge about the role of organizational communication in general, and interest advocacy in particular, in the institutional processes of normative transformation.

An earlier section of this chapter outlined in conceptual terms the three most important features which characterize the communicative phenomenon of interest advocacy—the struggle to influence dominant sociopolitical normative meanings, the continuously dynamic nature of interest advocacy, and the centrality of organizing in the accomplishment of social normative influence. Each of these features makes the study of interest advocacy a cumbersome topic for the traditional social scientific methods most commonly used in organizational communication research.

Organizational communication researchers, of course, have long been well-acquainted with methodological techniques capable of investigating subjective phenomena, over-time social interactive processes, and patterned communicative relations, which correspond to the main conceptual features of interest advocacy. Researchers interested in investigating and analyzing these features simultaneously can, with some effort, do so, through the strategy of triangulation. And, as knowledge of interest advocacy processes and effects becomes more detailed and sophisticated, researchers may find it useful to focus more directly on issues of meaning, process, or organizing alone. In these cases, specific methodological choices will naturally correspond to the more specific interests of researchers.

This paper instead recommends the collection and analysis of archival data as a methodological alternative which most comprehensively meets the conceptual requirements for immediate research on the topic of interest advocacy and its organizational and societal consequences. Archival data which directly and indirectly describes the empirical communicative practices of change advocate and change target organizations is, of course, abundantly available. In the case of the animal rights movement such relevant archival data might include, for example, advocacy advertising (such as that sponsored by fur and medical research organizations, described earlier), or, as another example, specialized publications aimed at recruiting and motivating movement members (such as the animal rights magazine *The Animals' Agenda* and the consumer guide *Save the Animals*). Though valuable as artifactual evidence of the communicative acts of change advocate and change target organizations, these forms of archival data still do not fully represent issues of meaning, process, and organizing central to interest advocacy as organizational communication practice.

The use of published histories is rare within the field of organizational communication, despite the availability of exemplars such as Martin and Siehl's (1983) analysis of countercultural pressures at General Motors, based on two existing (and competing) historical narratives of the organization. Yet, the published histories of sociopolitical normative movements provide ideal, if nontraditional, archival means of investigating and analyzing the central characteristics of interest advocacy—as evident in Belasco's (1989) history of the transformation of the natural food movement from the preoccupation of a fringe group of "health food nuts" to an everyday concern of average American consumers. These movement histories serve not as "case studies," but instead represent a detailed, rich source of raw data which comes close to representing the actual empirical phenomena of interest advocacy communication and sociopolitical influence—particularly if analysis includes histories written from competing normative positions.

The assessment of sociopolitical consensus

This chapter has focused on specific communicative practices of change advocate and change target organizations, and it has not been the intent here to comprehensively model the role of communication in institutional processes. Nevertheless, the particular communicative acts involved in interest advocacy matter because of their presumed relationship to shifting perceptions of the sociopolitical legitimacy of change advocate and change target organizations, and legitimacy is based on social normative consensus. The assessment of normative consensus matters even more, perhaps, in terms of the philosophical position which informs this work and which prioritizes understanding of the societal consequences of organizational interest advocacy. Traditional methodology, such as survey research, clearly offers one acceptable alternative for assessing social normative consensus; this type of investigation might, for example, generate data dealing with evaluative perceptions of change advocate and change target groups, or the extent of philosophical agreement with the rhetorical themes of advocate and target organizations, or individuals' personal identification with them, or respondents' reports of personal or political behavior consistent with the normative agenda of a social movement.

The use of popular cultural sources of archival data, like the use of published histories as data, is unusual in organizational communication scholarship; perhaps such data has been largely irrelevant to a field which has seldom dealt with relationships between organizations and their larger societal context. Popular cultural artifacts of many types—movies, television, popular fiction, comic strips, product advertising, and so on—obviously provide data reflective of the normative status of a culture. Among the many available sources of popular cultural data, however, radio and television call-in and talk shows and prime time network and syndicated current affairs programs are, even to the intuitive eye, noticeably likely to reflect shifting mainstream social knowledge and evaluation of sociopolitical normative trends.

Interest advocacy and the institutional character of society

Although social movement advocates often may be frustrated with the extent or the rate of sociopolitical reform, change does happen, with meaningful consequences for individuals and collectives. The academic disciplines of political and organizational sociology, both focused to a significant extent on issues of social stability and change, have found an institutionally based analytic framework especially productive (March and Olsen 1984; Zucker 1987). Indeed, understanding the consequences for organizations of social reforms of the 1960s was a primary motive for at least some important institutional theorists (Meyer and Rowan 1983)—though with an apparent, and troubling (Perrow 1985; Powell 1985) politically conservative bias.

For a number of reasons beyond the scope of this paper, the field of organizational communication has not traditionally demonstrated much interest in analyzing the ways in which organizational communication affects and is influenced by the larger social world. To suggest that our field develop in such a direction is the philosophical premise of this chapter, with corresponding theoretical and methodological implications which suggest than an organizational communication orientation to the question of social change, articulated in terms of interest advocacy, is particularly well-suited for solving the most serious deficiencies in the institutional approach to this topic. The practical implications of this approach extend to concerns not traditionally associated with the narrower priorities of *managerial* practice, but which instead involve broader questions of *social* practice and their consequences for the fundamental character of our "organizational society." This section of the chapter discusses the quality of the sociopolitical expression of collectives as one of the most significant of these consequences of the social practices of organizational interest advocacy. Though rarely analyzed in organizational communication scholarship, this topic is one to which the field of organizational communication might contribute some insight and understanding. The chapter concludes with brief comments on one other issue deserving of consideration: the entanglement of the topic of interest advocacy with the question of values in social research.

The sociopolitical expression of collectives

This chapter has argued that the oppositional-opportunistic character of change advocates' and change targets' communication is of central significance in understanding the sociopolitical implications of interest advocacy. The oppositional and opportunistic communication of change advocates and change targets is important for social practice because it influences societal normative consciousness, a widely-dispersed definition of what constitute appropriate and inappropriate organizational actions. External normative demands by definition suppress, if they do not oppress, the expression of unpopular social and political positions, and tend to favor social stability rather than social change. Yet change advocates do voice counternormative points of view, and this expression serves as an impetus for often important instances of social transformation. Thus the oppositional and opportunistic question essentially involves the issue of collective sociopolitical voice.

So far, this chapter has focused primarily on analytical purposes, without exploring in much detail the larger political implications of such inquiry. But the practical meaning of this analysis is largely political, and consideration of the question of collective sociopolitical voice underscores this point.

"Politics" is commonly intertwined with basic questions of social disparity, accounting for the existence of the socially privileged and the socially disadvantaged. In the case of interest advocacy the differences between change advocate groups and change target groups as organizational "haves" and "have-nots" is reflected in the ways in which these organizations use oppositional and opportunistic communication to accomplish their normative goals. The discussion presented in this chapter has argued that all sides of a given normative conflict will communicate strategically, employing oppositional or opportunistic approaches, whether exclusively, simultaneously, or sequentially, in order to influence the normative status of the larger social and political world. To argue that organizations with opposing social views communicate strategically does not, however, imply that the conflicting sides are evenly matched, and a more tenable position would suggest rather that the contest is an unequal one from the outset.

The inequality of organizations' capability for expressing normatively significant, collective social and political voice has its source in both the behavior of organizations directly involved in normative conflict, and in the normative prejudices of the larger social world. Particularly when they enjoy relatively widespread general normative support, organizations, both progressive and conservative, commonly aim to suppress expression of the perspectives of their normative adversaries. Existing normative priorities, frequently reflected in the messages of such indirect agents as news and entertainment media, also have encouraged the expression of normatively consistent sociopolitical views while discouraging normatively dissonant ones.

These organizational and societal normative pressures suggest that the sociopolitical voice of some organizations is awarded social priority based on normative conformity—not because these organizations are more deserving or because their views are right. By way of parallel, the options for expression of organizations with normatively unacceptable views are constrained regardless of merit. This apparent tendency toward constraint of collective sociopolitical voice is both analytically and socially significant.

Analytical approaches which have traditionally been used to explain "macro" organizational and political processes—such as pluralism (Dahl 1961), elite theory (Domhoff 1979, 1987; Mills 1956), or class analysis (Useem 1984)—cannot adequately account for both the inequalities of collective voice inherent in interest advocacy or for the strategic organizational interaction through which, however slowly or with whatever degree of opposition, social transformation does occur. Clegg's (1989) more current "circuits of power" perspective gives a better analytical fit to the phenomenon of organizational interest advocacy. Clegg's approach views power, as social disparity, as an inherent characteristic of organized social relationships. But power is a fluid and shifting thing, its form and shape determined by the strategic behaviors of organized interests pursuing political ends. Clegg's perspective can explain inequalities in opportunities for expression of collective sociopolitical voice as a reflection of differences in the social power of organized interests; his view can also account for normative transformation—emerging, mature, and declining movements—as the outcome of strategic collective communicative action.

The early pages of this chapter outlined an underlying philosophical conviction of the importance of inquiry into the social consequences of organizations' communicative practices, and this philosophical stance is directly relevant to the social significance of collective voice. Interest advocacy essentially involves organized social and political expression, influencing social outcomes. Any constraint on the free and unlimited exercise of collective voice will influence the shape of these societal effects, and philosophical consistency with the purposes of this chapter therefore requires exploration of the social implications of issues of collective voice.

To understand what the social and political expression of organized collectivities means to our society requires the making of judgments about its fundamental human significance. Despite recurring historical and contemporary threats to individual expression, much of the intellectual and cultural dogma of this society conceives of individual political voice as essential, regardless of its actual efficacy. Though the literature on individual voice in organizations is still minuscule (found, for example, in theory and research on indirectly related topics such as whistleblowing [Glazer and Glazer 1989; Miceli and Near 1992; Stewart 1980] and employee civil rights [Osigweh 1987, 1989; Werhane 1985]), it does provide some evidence of growing interest in this topic, with application to social contexts other than the political. The emergence, however slow, of this body of literature makes more plausible an argument that the motivation for expression is one of the essential elements which define human character and that organizational voice is no less socially significant than political voice.

The literature on individual voice in organizations aids recognition of the broader social significance of human expression. So far, though, the work in this area has not made equally clear the importance of collective, as well as individual, voice. Indeed, if anything, our limited thinking on the question of collective expression has been primarily characterized by a distrust of the social and political communication of groups reflected, for example, in the pejorative label "special interest groups."

The logic of this chapter asserts that collective sociopolitical voice, however much ignored or debased, is no less vital to our society than is individual expression. Earlier this chapter presented the fundamental reasoning which underlies its approach to the topic of interest advocacy, that normative change and stability both are possible only through the socially strategic behavior, primarily communicative, of organized social interests. In other words, individuals acting only as individuals have little, if any, significant, large-scale, social or political impact. So, while individual voice may satisfy an innate human motivation for self-expression, it has, in itself, few wider societal consequences. Collective sociopolitical expression—interest advocacy—is vital, therefore, because it represents the most plausible way for individuals to articulate their interests and affect the state of the social and political normative climate.

To view collective voice as a social good equal in importance to individual expression will require some social and political reassessment; as a society, we now have only the most primitive idea how the civil rights of organizations might conceivably look. Modification of existing perspectives on individual civil rights, where appropriate, represents one obvious starting point. The influential social thinker John Rawls (1971) proposes that justice requires, among other things, the widest possible array of civil rights, equally available to all members of society, and guaranteed protection of the rights of the socially weak. Extended so that they apply to questions of collective expression, Rawls' ideas first suggest that social policy make the equalization of expressive opportunities of all groups, no matter how socially legitimate, a political priority. But Rawlsian justice, made relevant to the context of organizations' political voice, goes farther, too, suggesting that as a society, we deliberately prioritize the expansion of sociopolitical expression of less legitimate organizations as a corrective to the normative tendency to suppress the voice of these organizations. Such a reconceptualization of the expressive rights of organizations focalizes the fundamental principle of collective communicative justice, that collective sociopolitical expression is so central in its societal significance that our social policies ought not only to protect, but actually to nurture it, when necessary.

A note on values and research

Analysts from divergent perspectives have for years offered their competing commentaries on the social obligations of organizational communication scholars. Such concerns are perhaps most central to the critical intellectual tradition (Deetz, 1992), grounded in the conviction that social inquiry ought to be conducted in the interest of positive social change. This perspective demands that researchers do the right thing by seeking to understand the social processes and arrangements which artificially privilege some social interests at the expense of others and by enlightening the oppressed about ways in which they might overcome the conditions of their existence, an approach reflected in the field of organizational communication by the exemplar of Mumby's (1988) participatory research project.

Different, of course, but certainly more widely accepted, are the ethical concerns of traditional social scientific researchers (Smith, 1988). This development in research thinking and practice focuses on important issues of deception, informed consent, confidentiality, anonymity, and access to results, but does not make the advancement of a particular moral agenda an explicit purpose or goal of research effort.

The investigation of interest advocacy involves moral and value questions in yet another way. As described in this chapter, the study of interest advocacy begins with a motivation to explain the influence of organizations' communication on the particular character of a normatively structured social world. The alignment of normative loyalties which characterizes a society will necessarily make winners and losers of competing social interests; in the zero-sum game of sociopolitical dispute, the advocates and opponents of, say, gun control or abortion or multiculturalism, cannot both have their way. Understanding the influence of interest advocacy on the normative priorities of a society means that researchers in this area possess a knowledge which can serve interests which these same researchers may find either most worthy or utterly despicable.

Organizational communication researchers (Finet and Harrison 1992) have portrayed the "pure research" model, according to which investigators refuse responsibility for the ways in which others use the findings of their work, as intellectually and morally nonviable. This approach cannot provide an adequate strategy for dealing with the political character of interest and advocacy research. Consistent with the spirit of tolerance and diversity currently vogue among communication scholars, this chapter suggests that both critical and traditional inquiry represent better alternatives to pure research.

A critical strategy provides a radical alternative, completely at odds with and much more credible than the ideology of pure research, for coping with the politics of knowledge involved in the study of interest advocacy. The researcher adopting this approach not only admits individual social and political preferences, but also allows these to drive and direct inquiry; the political loyalties of the researcher motivate the research. While an improvement on the false objectivity of pure research, critical inquiry into the subject of interest advocacy could also be strengthened by the development of appropriate evaluative standards.

Traditional researchers concerned with the study of interest advocacy can also improve upon the perspective of pure research. Contemporary issues of research ethics—deception, informed consent, confidentiality, anonymity, access to results—are certainly important to confront. However, these concerns deal with the actual conduct of research and do not address the personal political predispositions which, with the discrediting of "pure research," underlie the work of nearly every social scientist. Traditional researchers can do better by acknowledging their personal political convictions which might become entangled with the conduct of investigation into interest advocacy, an action not logically inconsistent with the maintenance of theoretical and methodological rigor (Finet and Harrison 1992).

As briefly outlined here, neither the critical nor the traditional approach to resolving the political complications of interest advocacy research is completely satisfying; each involves potential problems and constraints. To use either strategy does, however, demonstrate a recognition of the political and moral stakes involved in this research agenda, and a sense of the political and moral responsibility to confront them with intellectual honesty.

Note

1. A fully developed institutionally based comprehension of normative change, of course, also requires an examination of the communicative practices of social actors which play indirect roles—in other words, which do not act as either change advocates or change targets—in such change. Especially important is the role of mass media: journalism, [product] advertising, and popular cultural forms such as talk shows, music, and film. For purposes of this chapter, however, the communication of direct agents is the focus of analysis.

References

Adams, J. 1980. Interorganizational processes and organizational boundary activities. *Research in Organizational Behavior*, 2:321–55.

Americans for Medical Progress Education Foundation. Undated advertisement.

Belasco, W. 1989. *Appetite for change: How the counterculture took on the food industry, 1966–1988*. New York: Pantheon Books.

Burns T., and G. Stalker. 1991. *The management of innovation*. London: Tavistock Publications.

Clegg, S. 1989. *Frameworks of power*. Newbury Park, CA: Sage.

Dahl, R. 1961. *Who governs?* New Haven: Yale University Press.

Deetz, S. (1992). *Democracy in an age of corporate colonization*. Albany: State University of New York Press.

DiMaggio, P. 1988. Interest and agency in institutional theory. In *Institutional patterns and organizations: Culture and environment*, ed. L. Zucker. Cambridge, MA: Ballinger.

DiMaggio, P. & Powell, W. (1983). The iron cage revisited: institutional isomorphism are collective nationality in organizational fields. *American Sociological Review*, 48, 147–160.

Domhoff, G. 1979. *The powers that be: Processes of ruling class domination in America*. New York: Random House.

————. 1987. *Power elites and organizations*. Newbury Park, CA: Sage.

Emery, F., and E. Trist. 1965. The causal texture of organizational environments. *Human Relations* 18:21–32.

Finet, D., and T. Harrison. 1992. The social perspective in organizational communication. Paper presented at the annual meeting of the International Communication Association, Miami, May 1992.

Glazer, M., and P. Glazer. 1989. *The whistleblowers: Exposing corruption in government and industry*. New York: Basic Books.

Lawrence, P., and J. Lorsch. 1967. Differentiation and integration in complex organizations. *Administrative Science Quarterly* 12:1–47.

March, J., and J. Olsen. 1984. The new institutionalism: Organizational factors in political life. *American Political Science Review* 78:734–49.

Martin, J., and C. Siehl. 1983. Organizational culture and counterculture: An uneasy symbiosis. *Organizational Dynamics* 12:52–64.

Meyer, J., and B. Rowan. 1977. Institutionalized organizations: Formal structure as myth and ceremony. *American Journal of Sociology* 83:340–63.

Meyer, J., and W. Scott. 1983. *Organizational environments: Ritual and rationality*. Beverly Hills: Sage.

Miceli, M., and J. Near. 1992. *Blowing the whistle: The organizational and legal implications for companies and employees*. New York: Lexington Books.

Mills, C. 1956. *The power elite*. New York: Oxford University Press.

Mumby, D. 1988. *Communication and power in organizations: Discourse, ideology, and domination*. Norwood, NJ: Ablex.

Oliver, C. 1991. Strategic responses to institutional processes. *Academy of Management Review* 16:145–79.

Origins. Undated promotional flyer.

Osigweh, C. (ed.). 1987. *Communicating employee responsibilities and rights: A modern management mandate.* New York: Quorum Books.

————. (ed.) 1989. *Managing employee rights and responsibilities.* New York: Quorum Books.

Parsons, T. 1956. Suggestions for a sociological approach to the study of organizations. *Administrative Science Quarterly* 1:63–85, 225–39.

People for the Ethical Treatment of Animals. Undated membership brochure.

Perrow, C. 1985. Review essay: Overboard with myth and symbols. *American Journal of Sociology* 91:151–55.

Pfeffer, J., and G. Salancik. 1978. *The external control of organizations: A resource dependence perspective.* New York: Harper & Row.

Powell, W. 1985. The institutionalization of rational organizations. *Contemporary Sociology* 14:564–66.

Rawls, J. 1971. *A theory of justice.* Cambridge, MA: Harvard University Press.

Saga Fox. Undated advertisement.

Scott, W. 1987a. *Organizations: Rational, natural, and open systems.* 2nd ed. Englewood Cliffs, NJ: Prentice Hall.

————. 1987b. The adolescence of institutional theory. *Administrative Science Quarterly* 32:493–511.

Sethi, S. P. (1991). *Scaling the corporate wall: Readings in social issues of the nineties.* Englewood Cliffs, NJ: Prentice-Hall.

Smith, M. (1988). *Contemporary communication research methods.* Belmont, CA: Wadsworth.

Stewart, L. 1980. Whistleblowing: Implications for organizational communication. *Journal of Communication* 30 (4): 90–101.

Thompson, J. 1967. *Organizations in action.* New York: McGraw-Hill.

Useem, M. 1984. *The higher circles: The governing class in America.* New York: Random House.

Werhane, P. 1985. *Persons, rights, and corporations.* Englewood Cliffs, NJ: Prentice Hall.

Zucker, L. 1987. Institutional theories of organization. *Annual Review of Sociology* 13:443–64.

———— 1988. *Institutional patterns and organizations: Culture and environment.* Cambridge, MA: Ballinger.

MICHAEL HUSPEK

8 Critical and Nonfoundational Analyses: Are They Contradictory or Complementary?

Introduction[1]

It has long been recognized as something of a truism within critical scholarship that an inevitable contradiction exists within capitalist society between liberal democracy, on the one hand, and authoritarian organization and control of workplace institutions, on the other.[2] One strategy adopted by critical scholars as they attend to this issue has been a debunking one, marked by efforts to expose the untruths that undergird arguments of apologists for the contradictory alliance. This entails appealing to a more secure knowledge, based upon a foundationalist view of truth, which is leveled with certainty against ideology, mystification, or other forms of falsehood or deception. Thus, critics argue that the claim that capitalist ownership and control is consistent with the liberal right to hold private property (even workers, it is claimed by apologists, are owners of their own bodies), must be stripped of all validity once confronted by the *reality* of individuals within this arrangement being forced to relinquish ownership of their own bodies, control over their "right" to self-determination, as a requisite of survival. Or, to cite another example, critics point to how the reality of capital's penetration of all significant spheres of human activity makes utter mockery of the idealist claim that liberal principles function autonomously within the arena of political action.[3]

A more recent critical strategy has been deployed which is not only skeptical of any and all foundationalist claims to secure knowledge, but has voiced the concern also that any such claims carry with them the potential to generate tyrannical practices of social and political control. This more recent strategy purports to be nonfoundationalist, expressing rigorous neutrality with respect to questions of truth, and seeks not so much to debunk the sustaining myths or ideologies of the contradictory alliance between liberal democracy and capital, but rather to more positively treat such myths and ideologies as "truths" which, operating within discursive fields, produce numerous effects.[4] Those deploying this strategy,[5] for example, have focused upon varied and complex "truths" of subjectivity that are produced and reproduced within discourses that emanate from and sustain various contradictory alliances. This entails, in turn, investigating the "truths" of subjectivity that construct speakers as free, self-determining agents— in short, as participants in the liberal, democratic arena of politics— while also investigating the "truths" of subjectivity that construct speakers as subjects to systems and processes of capital over which they have little if any control. And rather than claiming either "truth" to be more real than the other, critics ask such questions as: In what ways do the "truths" of these different subjectivities impinge upon one another? Where and how are they most keenly felt? How do they get articulated over time? What overall effects do they produce?

The critical thrust of the nonfoundationalist strategy is located most specifically in the treatment of power and resistance, especially as the former is expressed in and through dominant discourses and the latter is expressed in discourses which are at once positioned by and oppositional to dominant discourses. The central claim here is not that oppositional discourses express a superior "truth" or reality, but that such discourses and the "truths" they express tend to be muffled or otherwise suppressed by the "truths" of dominant discourses. And for understandable reasons. For the "truths" of oppositional discourses are by their very nature antagonistic to power and thus inherently destabilizing. Once provided a sufficient hearing, these "truths" of oppositional discourses may find traction in speech communities where dominant discourses had previously succeeded in suppressing all potential rivals.[6]

It is in the analysis of the conjoined opposition between power and resistance in discourse that I believe a critical communication theory shows most promise. This for several reasons. First, at a descriptive level, emphasis on the oppositional other as expressed in discourses of resistance functions to define the limits of power. This may entail, for example, delineating the extent to which the "truths" of power succeed in creating subjects who must also be subjected before oppositional discourses emerge that express some degree of recognition of the contradiction. Second, beyond delineation of power's limits, such descriptions perform a significant critical function. For by revealing the "truths" of resistance that emerge in discourses of opposition, the analyst reveals a world of meaning and value that not only stands as otherness—now voiced—in relation to what power establishes as "truth" in its dominant discourse, but exists as an oppositional other which, by virtue of its existence, proves that power is something other than what its "truths" claim itself to be. In this sense, the critical operation is that of exposing the contradiction: here is what power is claimed to be; but its truth claims are contradicted by the "truths" generated by discourses of resistance.[7]

This critical function is not performed for its own sake—that is, it is not meant as simple negation—but seeks to invoke an "experience of discord"[8] which has ultimately a positive effect on those who are spoken by discourses of either power or resistance. For in undergoing this experience, the reader is also informed of the potentiality that inheres in oppositional otherness: not only does articulation of oppositional otherness expose the limits and contradictions of power, giving testimony as it does in the materiality of discourse to what power is not, but these oppositional discourses express meanings and values that point to potentially new forms of social and political life.[9] The critical communication theorist performs an especially valuable operation in this respect. Such meanings and values may not be fully apparent to those who are being spoken by either power or resistance. In explicating that which is only implied by oppositional otherness, the analyst goes beyond both description and critique and performs a transformative operation: power is not only revealed as what it is not, as evidenced by discourses of oppositional otherness, but those who are spoken by discourses of either power or resistance are incited to reflect upon normative alternatives which have previously not been pondered, let alone achieved, on account of the reign of power and its "truths."

There are those who remain unconvinced by this project, however. They charge that a contradiction inheres in any perspective that claims to be simultaneously both nonfoundationalist and critical, as the two concepts are antithetical. The analyst who subscribes to both is susceptible of the charge of engaging either in a logical or a performative contradiction. That is, in forfeiting any and all foundationalist claims, the analyst thus forfeits any and all justifications for mounting a critique: to deny this is to engage in a logical contradiction.[10] Or (and this appears to occur quite often), the analyst who claims to be both nonfoundationalist and critical is ultimately susceptible of the charge of smuggling in and tacitly appealing to the values or principles that inhere in oppositional discourses.[11] Beyond this amounting to a performative contradiction whereby one's practice contradicts one's words, it also amounts to a romanticizing of resistance that ultimately proves fallible when scrutinized in the face of empirical evidence; for even the most resolute romantic must ultimately acknowledge, when confronted with the facts, that resistance need not always hold up truths and values that, compared with those of power, are always worthy of acceptance or emulation. Resistance in fact may at times be manifested by such "truths" as racism or sexism—"truths" which even those who are most deeply inscribed by the "truths" of power may readily acknowledge as hardly being deserving of moral commendation.

In the remainder of this essay I want to defend the idea that analysis can be both critical and nonfoundationalist without becoming snarled in either logical or performative contradiction. My defense relies first upon a brief sketch of the concepts of power and resistance, the extent to which they are related, and the special significance their relationship has for critical analysis. I then turn to the specific objections raised above and argue that an analysis which is both critical and nonfoundationalist can overcome these objections once rigorous treatment is given to the dialectical workings of power and resistance. In support of my argument I offer empirical illustration that is meant to show how use of the concepts of power and resistance enhances our critical understanding of the contradiction between civic life in liberal society, on the one side, and subordination to the wage-capital relation, on the other. Finally, I conclude with a discussion of the significance of this form of critical analysis and its transformative potential.

Preliminary overview

An analysis which is both critical and nonfoundationalist emphasizes the significance of power and discourse. Power, on this view, is accorded enormous latitude, its reach being more extensive, its guises more varied, than what we have come to expect from theories predicated on foundationalist assumptions. An analysis that is critical and nonfoundationalist shows power to be everywhere, existing at all levels of society, and having multiple strategies, relations, programs, and techniques that are expressed in a wide array of human practices. Power constrains actors, but does so while also producing the very capacity to act: it is only on condition that actions are undertaken in and through power's modalities that they can be invested with meaning. Discourse is one of the chief modalities in and through which power institutes and legitimates itself. Power is able to constrain and enable actors, to transform actors into subjects whose subjectivity is made one in the same with subjection to power-infused practices, by enlisting the support of discourse, installing it with its own truth, and declaring a finite field of statements intelligible while ensuring that it is its own field which is made intelligible and none other as it suppresses any and all rival claims. Power does not thereby mask the operations of its truth by means of ideology, that is, distorted discourse, but rather constitutes "truth," "knowledge," "reality" as meaningful terms by investing them with materiality in their discursive forms.

Under the guise of prevailing discourses, power legitimates its own meanings by inscribing "otherness" which it both opposes and relies upon for support. By "other" I mean such meanings as "irrationality," "perversion," "immorality," which are affixed to subjects who, under power's discursive regime, are thereby inscribed as "irrational," "perverse," "immoral." "Otherness" stands in a contradictory relation with power. First, "otherness" is opposed by power—as "other"—and is frequently suppressed. This is manifested most visibly by institutionalizing the mad, shaming the perverse into silence, incarcerating the immoral for their transgressions. At the same time, however, "otherness" as power's creation also serves as power's support. Power thus depends upon the "otherness" it both creates and opposes. As power produces the prevailing meanings of reason, so also it produces irrationality as a limiting term; power as normalcy produces perversion; as morality it produces immorality. Without these discursively produced "others," existing as power's oppositional limits and supports, the "truths" of power would have nothing against which to exert themselves, and would immediately dissolve into nothingness.

Foremost among power's limits is that of resistance which operates as a counterforce to power. Resistance inheres in the meanings of "otherness" as produced by power, but it emerges as a dynamic force within the discursive practices of subjects who are inscribed by power as "other"—for example, as "irrational," "perverse," "immoral"— and speaks subjects in terms that are oppositional to the terms installed and legitimated in and through dominant discourses. Antilanguages are an exemplar case of oppositional discourses. The meanings generated by antilanguages are what they are by virtue of being the very opposite of what they are asserted to be under power's regime. While "immorality" in terms of power's dominant discourse has negative value, antilanguages may be used by those determined to be immoral to celebrate this "otherness" as a positive value ("We're bad!"), or they may reverse the positive value of morality, ascribing to it a negative value ("They're straight!").

The contradictory relation between power and resistance, as expressed by power's opposition to and dependence upon resistance, is evident also in the way resistance both needs and opposes the power which has produced it. On the one hand, oppositional discourses such as antilanguages are parasitic upon dominant discourses; for without power, resistance would have nothing to oppose, nor indeed would it have any cause to emerge in its form as opposition. But on the other hand, as opposition, discourses of resistance threaten to subvert the legitimacy of power's discursive regime, its truths, knowledge, reality. Discourses of resistance, that is, do not simply manifest "otherness" as discursively produced by power, but themselves produce countertruths which, in addition to being expressed by subjects who are dissatisfied with their subjugated status as the mad or perverted or uncivil, always carry the potential of usurping prevailing truths as expressed in and through dominant discourses. In this sense, oppositional discourses are always potentially revolutionary.

The existence of power and resistance, and the relations of opposition and dependence they form in discourse, pose conceptual-methodological problems for the critical analyst. One seemingly intractable difficulty is that of locating power. Although power is everywhere, it proves elusive by virtue of its being "hidden" in the meanings and practices that make up everyday reality. Power is truth; or at least truth cannot be separated from power. So too with knowledge, morality, reality. These concepts have a privileged status within dominant discourses by virtue of being infused with power. Yet they are presented within dominant discourses as objective, or as having intrinsic semantic properties. These concepts, moreover, operate as the semantic stuff which forms the basis of our perceptions of the world; and the analyst is not exempt from power and its dominant discourses. Analysis demands that a language be used, and that the analyst operate within the "true" if he or she expects to be credible. In this very basic sense, we all are power's products.

The crucial way in which the analyst who is critical and nonfoundationalist confronts the reality of operating within power's compass is to focus attention upon "otherness" as expressed in oppositional discourses. While in the embrace of a dominant discourse, the analyst listens for the rumblings of opposition; while pledging obeisance to the rules of rationality, the analyst also welcomes the counter assertions contained in the muted moans of those whose crime it is to have been irrational, different, or odd; and while feeling every exacting of moral discipline and control, the analyst also heeds the suppressed laughter of the immoral or the perverted, or the conniving of those who refuse to be controlled. Indeed, there is nothing that must preclude the analyst from partaking in these forms of "otherness," engaging in irrational acts or allowing his or her own laughter to intermingle with that of the immoral. And once having located these forms of "otherness," perhaps even partaken in them, the analyst's task is then to amplify their meanings and, especially, to reveal the ways in which these forms exist not in isolation but within a relationship with power. This operation enables the analyst to treat oppositional discourse as a vehicle of critique. For amplification of this resistant "other" points up the partial and contradictory nature of the "truth" of power and its production. Partial in that meanings inscribed by power fail to fully permeate this resistant "other." Contradictory in that the "truth" of resistance informs power and its attendant "truths" of what it, in fact, is not; and this, moreover, in the face of what the latter claims itself to be.

The "truth" of resistance, in this its critical capacity, operates as the antithesis of the "truth" of power: it exposes power for what it is, and what it is not, and the contradiction involved in both its being and nonbeing. The force of its critique, moreover, is strengthened by virtue of its position within a relationship with power. The "truth" of resistance signifies "otherness," to be sure; but this "otherness" is also "within". As "other within" it stands as power's own creation which exists as an integral member of a relationship within which it negates, as other, power's capacity to dominate. In this sense, oppositional discourses can not simply be dismissed as alien otherness that is different from dominant discourses. By the same token, the critical analyst who focuses on oppositional discourses is not simply introducing "otherness" as if it were some exotic, alien life form that might be entertained as a manifestation of cultural diversity. Discourses of resistance rather are intimately bound up with power, being power's product, support, and opposition within a relationship of co-constructed meanings. The critical analyst is thus holding up a mirror to power which exposes power's internal contradictions, that is, how it constructs "otherness" as a condition of its existence and then denies or otherwise suppresses this, its contrary "truth."

Objections and responses

With this brief sketch, two objections can be forwarded. The first voices skepticism concerning the critical analyst's purported nonfoundationalist position. How is it possible for the analyst to be disengaged from all normative ideals and values?[12] Is not the critical analyst in fact smuggling normative values of resistance into the analysis? If so, this calls for a justification that would ultimately contradict any nonfoundationalist position.

The second objection again directs itself to the critical analyst's purported nonfoundationalist stance. The charge is as follows: Surely the analyst must exercise some normative standards by which to assess power and resistance, for without any such standards there is no way of discriminating between either forms of power or forms of resistance. This would amount to a failure to distinguish between power and domination, on the one hand (e.g., liberalism based on consent vs. fascism based on force), and between resistance as liberation and terrorism, on the other (e.g., feminist movements vs. the Ku Klux Klan). This difficulty then prompts the question of why those who resist should even bother to resist; for all that can be hoped to be gained is another form of power which, from the analyst's espoused position, may be judged neither better or worse than what had preceded it.

Response to the first objection runs as follows: It is true that the analyst is introducing normative values into the analysis, but the values are not those of resistance, or at least not entirely those of resistance; rather, the values are predominantly those of power and are embedded within the very language code that any analyst must operate with in order to communicate with his or her audience. It is in fact with a conscious awareness of oneself operating in power's discursive domain of the "true" that the analyst is directed toward "otherness." This not because "otherness" represents an escape from power's domain—there is no escape—but that this "otherness," which is also "within" is a useful critical device for exposing the tyrannizing hold of the "truths" of power: "otherness" reveals the existence of alternative "truths" which carry the potential to gain traction not only among those who currently are spoken by oppositional discourse, but for analyst and reading audience as well.

The analyst can hardly avoid carrying the values suffused within his or her working language into the field of inquiry. But while this is done with an acknowledgment of the "truth" of the analyst's own discourse, it is also done with the aim of holding up the "truths" of this dominant discourse for critical reflection in light of the "countertruths" of oppositional discourse. This involves, as stated above, treating seriously the critical thrust of these "countertruths" and the transformative potentiality they represent. The aim here, moreover, is not to evaluate the "truths" of resistance in light of patronizing, idealized, or "nonideological" standards; but neither is it to uncritically accept the "countertruths" of resistance. Rather, the object of the analysis is to articulate the contours of the relationship between power and the "other within," to emphasize the contradictory nature of the relation, and to point out the transformative potentials that are implied by the contradictions.

This position—being bound up within the discursive regime of power while searching out and welcoming an "experience of discord"—does not contradict the nonfoundationalist position, but is in fact consistent with it. The nonfoundationalist position does not claim itself exempt from normative values; but neither does it seek to privilege one set of values over another. It can do this without being inconsistent. Its aim is to utilize critical techniques, facilitated by an articulation of the values of oppositional discourses, with the intent of showing the internal contradictions of power. This is what power claims itself to be, here are its alleged truths; yet here we are confronted by countertruths, and power's very own creations no less, which bring to view the partial and contradictory nature of the claim itself. This not with an appeal to higher truths, but to the very truths that are in currency within the relationship between power and its created opposition, resistance.

It should thus be clear how the analyst who is both critical and nonfoundationalist responds to the second objection. The analyst does bring into play normative standards, as such is an inescapable product of the analyst being a language-using animal. However, the analyst's normative standards may also provide license for developing modes of inquiry that are intended to reveal oppositional and potentially undermining values and norms. Once faced with oppositional norms, the analyst does not hold up one as superior to the other, but rather seeks to fully reveal their contradictory relationship, its effects, and its transformative potentials.

With this strategy the analyst is not so much concerned with distinguishing between power and domination but rather is concerned with how either produces "otherness" as opposition and the potentials for transformation such opposition carries. Similarly, the moral worth of oppositional words and meanings is not a direct concern. A central question raised by the critical analyst thus is not whether, say, the women's movement is normatively preferable to the KKK; nor even whether the women's movement offers a preferred normative alternative to male domination. Rather, the question asked by the critical analyst is directed toward power: How is it that such an alternative has emerged as opposition, and what does it tell us about the power that both incites its opposition and seeks to suppress it?

The analyst thus admits to operating with norms that are constitutive of his or her own moral universe, but then also endeavors to expose the internal contradictions of the dominant discourses that express and sustain that moral universe. And this, moreover, without aligning oneself with either power or resistance. This does not, however, render the analyst susceptible of the charge of being unable to discriminate between the values of power and those of resistance; nor does it suggest that the analyst is unable to address the question as to why anyone should even bother to resist.

The question, "Why resist?," when asked by those who are skeptical of analysis that claims to be critical and nonfoundationalist, is predicated on the assumptions (1) that any one form of power, if displaced, must be replaced by another form of power and (2) that the critical analyst must either betray his or her nonfoundationalism by supporting one form of power or another, or, in remaining neutral, must forfeit any claim to critique. Neither assumption is tenable, however. Regarding (1), resistance need not seek either to overthrow power with the intent of installing a successor, nor indeed need it seek to liberate itself from power's grasp (as if this were possible!). Rather, resistance may have as its goal the diminishment of power's current expanse. I believe much of the empirical literature shows the latter to be the case; that strategies of total overthrow are recognized by those who resist as either too dangerous or too unrealistic. But this concern might also be addressed on a more purely structural level. That is, in the event that resistance does overthrow power-1, it does thereby transform itself into power-2 which must then inevitably produce new forms of resistance. But the analyst who is critical and nonfoundationalist, on this view, is not concerned with evaluating the normative justifications of power-1 versus power-2, but rather is most determined to assess the dynamics of power and its oppositional "other within."

This still begs the question, informed by assumption (2), as to the normative stance taken by the analyst in relation to power and resistance. Here the response is as follows: If the analyst belongs to a culture in which there are no meanings for engaging in critique, then we could hardly conceive of the operations being described here. But assuming the analyst does belong to a culture that values critique, then it can be argued that the critical enterprise may be undertaken without the analyst taking up any principled position for or against power's supportive norms. The critical operation rather is one in the same with the analyst's amplification of the voice of resistance and the contradictions expressed by its opposition to power. And while the operation amplifies resistance, it does not either condemn or support its normative bases. Whether resistance is commendable or condemnable is not the analyst's concern. The concern rather is how resistance is produced within power's domain, how it exists as "otherness within" its relationship of opposition and support, and the transformative potentiality—"good" or "bad"—implied by the relationship. If this is to be considered a shortcoming (i.e., the analyst foregoing principled inquiry), so it goes. There is so much to be gained, however, because of this "shortcoming."

Before continuing this defense, I want to offer a brief analysis of power and resistance as expressed within a speech community comprised of male, unskilled, lumber industrial workers.[13] The analysis is meant to give general illustration to how power and resistance are discursively constituted but, more specifically, to demonstrate how power and resistance may be critically analyzed in ways that are consistent with the above defense.

Empirical illustration

The illustration first points to power both as it is located within a prevailing political discourse of liberalism and the ways it produces two forms of subjectivity: (1) subjects as citizens, free, self-constituting, and autonomous, and (2) subjects as wage earners who must alienate their labor, subjugate themselves to the wage-capital relationship, as a condition of survival. In producing both instances of subjectivity—free agency and subjugation—the discourse of liberalism stresses the political "truth" of the former and the economic "truth" of the latter, while ignoring the contradiction this involves. In the event that dissatisfaction is felt on account of subjects experiencing the "truth" of economic subjugation (e.g., human degradation in the workplace), the prevailing discourse of liberalism reminds subjects that they may draw upon their competencies as citizens and make their voices heard, and that political channels are available, in the voting booth if not the workplace, for the vocalization of discontent.

For the workers, the contradiction takes the following form. First, they believe the liberal "truth" of their own subjectivity: they are free, self-willed, autonomous agents. But such freedom brings with it its own dissatisfaction. Because the workers buy into this "truth" of their own freedom, they find burdensome the "necessity" of alienating their labor and subjugating themselves under the wage-capital relationship. Moreover, they do not deny that political channels *may* be available in ways that allow them to exercise their capacities as political agents, but they also recognize that such channels are far removed from the everyday humiliations and degradations that they must suffer regularly within the workplace. Against *this* power which subjugates them, they view themselves as having few if any realistic political options.

The workers' recourse is to adopt "nonpolitical" resistance stratagems, one of the more visible of which being the deployment of a vocabulary of politics which consists of words and meanings that exist in opposition to the words and meanings that have currency within the prevailing discourse of liberalism. What is most interesting about the workers' vocabulary of politics is that it is positioned conscientiously against capitalist ownership and control; but that since capitalism itself draws its legitimacy from the prevailing discourse of liberalism (i.e., the right to private ownership), the workers' vocabulary ultimately opposes not *only* capitalist ownership and control but *also* liberal politics. This can be explained in the following terms: because the "truth" of the discourse of liberalism successfully suppresses its contradictory relationship with capitalist economics (i.e., granting the rights of economic ownership but without acknowledging as a problem the relations of domination inherent in capitalism), the workers, feeling the strain as subjects of capitalist economic life, develop words and meanings that oppose capitalist domination *and* liberal politics.

Consider, for example, three basic terms: "politics," "power," and "political voice." Although these terms at times are assigned a negative meaning within the larger political culture—for example, "politics" implying corruption and abuse of authority; "power" implying manipulation and coercion—their meanings as produced by the prevailing discourse of liberalism is for the most part overwhelmingly positive: "politics" is bound up with the idea of free-acting subjects ordering and directing their collective affairs, initiating action by which to overcome externally imposed patterns of control, and setting up ends for society and standards by which to evaluate those ends; "power" signifies subjects acting in concert, expressing their interests, values, and needs; and "political voice" is thought to be a primary means to ensure that the impersonal aspect of politics is made personal, a crucial means by which subjects forge alliances with others so as to engage in conflict in a civil manner.

It is quite noteworthy, however, that these terms carry no positive signification whatsoever within the workers' own discourse. "Politics," that is, functions wholly as a negative signifier, associated with such negative terms as "corruption," "lying," "dishonesty," "backstabbing," and "power tripping." "Power" is linked exclusively with either the "power monger" who uses "power" to maintain or extend his political or economic advantage or the "power tripper" who may not possess "power" but who displays a willingness to violate norms of communal solidarity in order to acquire it. And "political voice" is equated solely with "political bullshit" and "shit talk" such that those who exercise "political voice" are viewed as acting "politically," and, like a "politician," are thought to be obsessed with the accumulation or preservation of "power."

The key notion here is the idea that the discourse of liberalism is founded upon and generates "truths" that account adequately for only one side of the workers' contradictory subjectivity: workers are discursively produced as free (political) subjects, on one side, but then are expected to reconcile this freedom with the (economic) reality of wage slavery, on the other. Against the "truths" which undergird their freedom while simultaneously eclipsing it, an oppositional discourse, specified here as an antilanguage, develops within the workers' camp. While accepting the "truth" of their political freedom, but feeling subjugated within the only political arena of which they have intimate familiarity, namely, the workplace, they resist the "truth" of political action expressed within liberal discourse. Rather, the "truth" of the workers' oppositional discourse points to their own exclusion from the political arena, as indicated by the reality of their everyday workplace experiences. The workers are thus spoken as "otherness within" a relationship with power and its legitimating discourse of liberalism.

The "truth" of the workers' oppositional discourse depicts the workers as moral in contrast to immoral "politicians," "power trippers," and "politicals." This morality, however, at the same time legislates against the workers' engagement in any forms of political action which might be sanctioned as legitimate within the dominant discourse of liberalism. As such, operating on the "truths" of their oppositional discourse effectively eliminates any chances that the workers might act as political subjects as so defined by the dominant discourse. Which is to say that in developing an oppositional discourse in and through which to express dissatisfaction with alienation and subjugation, the workers undermine their potential to act as free political subjects who might effectively alter their condition.

This amounts to the displacement of one contradiction, that is, political subjectivity versus economic subjugation, by another: if the workers are not valued within the larger political culture, if their voice is not heard, it is because their own oppositional discourse, founded on a need to express dissatisfaction by political subjects with their economic situation, positions them beyond the compass of legitimate citizen action. Under the regime of "truth" established in and through the prevailing discourse of liberalism, subjects—one and all, irrespective of position within the sociopolitical power structure—are expected to fulfill their moral obligations as citizens through political participation. To withhold one's voice is shirking one's civic duty. Yet this is precisely the effect of the workers' oppositional discourse: to rationalize what in effect amounts to the workers' forfeiture of their political responsibilities. By what justification, then, according to the prevailing discourse of liberalism, should the workers' voice be heeded within the power-infused domain of legitimate, moral, political action?

Discussion

On one level the above analysis serves as illustration of how a non-foundationalist analysis can be adequately descriptive while also being both critical and potentially transformative. On another level, the analysis may be viewed as having accomplished these tasks while overcoming the objections leveled by those of a foundationalist bias. And on yet another level, its accomplishments may be seen as not being linked to a romanticization of resistance; indeed, the analysis focuses on a form of resistance which has few characteristics that would seem to invite moral commendation from anyone who is not a member of the speech community comprised of lumber industrial workers. Each level is further explicated below.

On a descriptive level, the above analysis characterizes the struggle between power and resistance as follows. First, the workers are produced as knowledgeable agents who, faced with the contradiction between their subjectivity as autonomous political beings and their subjection to a political-economic arrangement that renders them alienated and subjugated, respond to a discursive "truth" that gives more adequate expression to their life experiences. However, the "truths" that are constructed in and through their antilanguage can hardly be thought of as being morally commendable by anyone outside of the workers' own speech community. Their oppositional discourse effectively positions the workers outside the arena of legitimate political action: opposition to subjugation within the sphere of capital effectively amounts to a forfeiture of any potentially viable political options to the workers. And such is not lost upon the workers. They know the dominant discourse of liberalism which must be spoken when the workers interact with power holders; and it is this discourse which they actively oppose in and through the workings of their antilanguage. In this sense, while the workers' oppositional discourse constructs nonpolitical action as "moral," they realize that the dominant discourse constructs this "moral" opposition as immoral shirking of one's civic obligations within a liberal political culture.

The above analysis surely does not hold up the workers' discursively constructed alternative universe as something to be morally commended. Nevertheless, the analysis does offer a critical thrust aimed at power. This by showing how the workers' oppositional discourse, by virtue of its development within a relation with power, exposes the partial and contradictory nature of the "truth" of power and its productions. Partial in that the meanings of the dominant discourse fail to fully penetrate this resistant "other", running up against its own created limits. Contradictory in that the "truth" of resistance informs the "truth" of power what power, in fact, is not; and this, moreover, in the face of what the latter claims itself to be. The "truth" of an avowed liberal society stands to be severely shaken when confronted with its failure to nurture liberal citizens, as indicated by the workers' oppositional discourse.

Beyond its critical operation the analysis also directs itself to the transformative potentiality of resistance. Generally speaking, however, this potentiality may be either positive or negative, depending upon the specific forms of power and resistance that are being amplified by the analyst. Whereas elsewhere I have discussed "positive" potentiality, focusing on values of solidarity, equality, cooperation which may be immanently present in oppositional discourses, in the above analysis amplification of the workers' antilanguage functions to expose the "negative" potentiality that inheres in forms of power that sustain a contradictory alliance between liberal political freedom, on the one hand, and subjugation to the wage-capital relationship, on the other. The analysis surely therefore does not hold up the workers' oppositional discourse as an exemplar of moral life; rather, it exposes the negative underside of power on the presumption that power-as-liberal-society which values free agency and its civic expression will be jarred by the contradictions represented by subjugation and political inaction that are held up before power as its own self-created image.

The analyst of course is sensitive to the morality and truths of liberal society: he or she is not writing up the analysis for the direct benefit of the Kung Bushmen of the Kalahari; nor is the analyst's language that of Athabaskan or Sanskrit. Amplification of oppositional discourse, in other words does not require that the analyst alienate himself or herself from the dominant discourse by means of immersion in exotica. Rather, amplification of oppositional discourse, as "otherness within," requires that the analyst immerse himself or herself more deeply into his or her own culture as a means of locating and understanding the partially suppressed "other" that exists as vehicle of critique and transformation.

Finally, this form of analysis should provide sufficient response to the question concerning the rationale for resistance and the struggle against power. To the nonfoundationalist critical analyst who is at the same time inextricably bound up within a system of linguistic, cultural, and social norms, the rationale for struggle is found not only among those who resist. Resistance to a power that subjugates while at the same time creating conditions for free action is not simply a condition of "otherness," but exists "within" a relationship that in many respects defines all of contemporary liberal society. The analyst, as a member of this liberal society, is also subjugated, perhaps not in ways identical with those that define unskilled workers, but in ways that enable him or her to ascertain the conditions and expressions of resistance nevertheless. Amplification of "otherness within," in this sense, can be regarded as a personal operation, designed to elicit the "truths" of resistance with the intent of exposing the effects of power not only at the social and communicative levels, but at the level of the subject-as-analyst as well.

Finally, it bears repeating that analysis of this type may be performed irrespective of whether the "truths" of resistance appear ultimately to the analyst and readers as morally commendable. In fact, either way, the analysis proves its value as critique and transformative potentiality. This is most obvious when the "truths" of resistance point to alternative ways of life that both analyst and readers find appealing: since such "truths" of the "otherness" of resistance are also "within" the compass of liberal society, their existence is neither empty nor abstract, but rather eminently realizable. But that such "truths" may prove ultimately unappealing to analyst and readers in no way diminishes their value, as the analyst should be no less interested in espousing such "truths," whether they consist of racism, sexism, or, as in the case above, a shirking of the moral perquisites of democratic life. For as these "truths" too exist as "otherness within," so it is in the analyst's interest to uncover the conditions of their existence, and to hold them up also as eminently realizable. The upshot of this operation is to show power—here liberal society that constructs subjects as free agents, on one side, as subjugated within the wage-capital relationship, on the other—that free agency is impeded by its suppressed "other," and that suppression of this contradiction may only exacerbate subjugation and its concomitant ills.

Notes

1. This essay is largely a response to a set of objections to an earlier paper raised by Arthur DiQuattro in a personal correspondence. In that earlier paper I argued that the critical analytical techniques offered by Michel Foucault are superior to those of some of his most influential critics, especially Charles Taylor and Michael Walzer. The earlier paper, "From power/knowledge to truth/resistance: The makings of a Foucauldian dialectic," is available to readers upon request. In this essay I depart from a strict defense of Foucault's theory and attempt instead to defend a version of critical hermeneutics that I have been developing over the past several years (e.g., Huspek 1989, 1991; Huspek and Kendall 1991). Although my version of critical hermeneutics is greatly influenced by Foucault's writings, it departs from Foucault on a number of critical points, most notable of which concerns the role of meaning in critical analysis. Thus, although readers will undoubtedly recognize Foucauldian propositions throughout this essay, I've decided to present the ideas here without explicitly noting their specific relation to the entire corpus of Foucault's work. My rationale is founded on economic considerations: I am not so much concerned with delineating all possible aspects of analyses which are both critical and nonfoundationalist (Foucault's analyses being but one example of many), nor am I concerned here with grounding varied aspects in their respective literatures; I only want to argue the merits of this form of analysis, in its broadest possible form, against the kinds of objections raised by DiQuattro.

2. Here I refer primarily to a critical scholarship conducted in ways that are consistent with Marx's "Contribution to the critique of Hegel's Philosophy of Right" (1964).

3. The works by Poulantzas (1973, 1975, 1978) and Althusser (1971, 1977) are representative of this line of critique.

4. For general commentary, see Smart (1983).

5. The most obvious scholar who comes to mind of course is Foucault (1980). For applications of Foucault's theory to organizational life, see Ferguson (1984) and Clegg (1989).

6. Expanded discussions of power are found in Foucault (1979, 32–69; 1980, 78–145). Discussions of the relatedness of power and discourse are found in Foucault (1972, 79–125, 215–37; 1978, 92–102).

7. This line of thought is more fully elaborated in Huspek and Rincon's (forthcoming) "The necessity of antiscience: Foucault's discourse of Otherness," and Rincon and Huspek's (forthcoming) "The ironies of resistance."

8. The term has been used by William Connolly (1983). See also Michael Shapiro (1988).

9. This idea has received fuller treatment in Huspek (1989/1990).

10. DiQuattro expresses this concern as follows: "You sneak in the normatively-laden concept of subjugation, attach it to power, deny it to resistance, and thereby conceptually distinguish between power and resistance. . . . Are you not covertly taking sides with the 'truth' of resistance? If so, why not be open about it? Oh well, then you would have to provide grounds, arguments, rational discourse, to defend the power of resistance against the power of the powerful."

11. DiQuattro again: "Suppose to take a page from history, that the Nazis constitute the resistance (before they took power) against this 'liberalism'. . . . (All of your examples cleverly put the 'bad guys' in power and the 'good guys' in the resistance, but that's not always the case, in spite of its sophistical and rhetorical use: 'Oh, but is there any other use for language?' reply Foucault and Thrasymachus!) Is there anything in your analytical framework that enables us to critically evaluate and move against fascism on the basis of that critical evaluation? I am not interested in the 'truth' of fascists, because there is so little truth there; critical evaluation presupposes a distinction between 'truth' and truth; to deny this is to forfeit one's justification for critical evaluation of anything, including one's own theory."

See also Habermas's (1990) charge that Foucault's writings on resistance invite the charge of cryptonormativism.

12. This question is raised by Fraser (1981) and Habermas (1990, 284) in their respective treatments of Foucault.

13. This analysis draws upon a three year ethnography of communication study of lumber industrial workers. See for example, Huspek (1986, 1987, 1989, 1993, and 1994) and Huspek and Kendall (1991).

References

Althusser, L. 1971. *Lenin and philosophy*. New York: Monthly Review Press.
———. 1977. *For Marx*. London: Verso.
Clegg, S. 1989. *Frameworks of power*. London: Sage.

Connolly, W. 1983. Discipline, politics and ambiguity. *Political Theory* 11 (3):325–41.

Ferguson, K. 1984. *The feminist case against bureaucracy.* Philadelphia: Temple University Press.

Foucault, M. 1972. *The archaeology of knowledge.* Harper & Row.

———. 1973. *Madness and civilization.* New York: Random House.

———. 1978. *The history of sexuality: An introduction.* Vol. 1. New York: Vintage.

———. 1979. *Discipline and punish.* New York: Vintage.

———. 1980. *Power/knowledge.* New York: Pantheon.

Fraser, N. 1981. Foucault on modern power: Empirical insights and normative confusions. *Praxis International* 1:272–87.

Habermas, J. 1990. *The philosophical discourse of modernity.* Cambridge, MA: MIT Press.

Huspek, M. 1986. Linguistic variation, context and meaning. *Language in Society* 15:149–63.

———. 1987. A language of powerlessness: Class, context and competence in the world of lumber industrial workers. Unpublished doctoral dissertation, University of Washington.

———. 1989. Linguistic variability and power. *Journal of Pragmatics* 13:661–83.

———. 1989/1990. The idea of ethnography and its relation to cultural critique. *Research on Language and Social Interaction* 23:229–312.

———. 1991. Taking aim on Habermas's critical theory: One the road toward a critical hermeneutics. *Communication Monographs* 58:225–33.

———. 1993. Dueling structures: The theory of resistance in discourse. *Communication Theory* 3 (1):1–25.

———. 1994. Oppositional codes and social class relations. *British Journal of Sociology* 45(1): 79–102

Huspek, M. and K. Kendall. 1991. On withholding political voice: An analysis of the political vocabulary of a "nonpolitical" speech community. *Quarterly Journal of Speech* 77 (1):1–19.

Huspek, M. and O. Rincon. Forthcoming. The necessity of antiscience: Foucault's discourse of otherness.

Marx, K. 1964. A contribution to the critique of Hegel's Philosophy of Right. In Karl Marx: Early writings, ed. T. B. Bottomore. New York: McGraw-Hill.

Poulantzas, N. 1973. *Political power and social class.* London: New Left.

———. 1975. *Classes in contemporary capitalism*. London: New Left.

———. 1978. *State, Power, Socialism*. London: New Left.

Rincon, O. and M. Huspek. Forthcoming. The ironies of resistance.

Scott, J. 1990. *Domination and the arts of resistance: Hidden Transcripts*. New Haven: Yale, University Press.

Shapiro, M. 1988. *The politics of representation*. Madison: University of Wisconsin Press.

Smart, B. 1983. *Foucault, Marxism and critique*. London: Routledge and Kegan Paul.

STANLEY A. DEETZ

9 Representational Practices and the Political Analysis of Corporations: Building a Communication Perspective in Organizational Studies

For all of recorded history people have studied and discussed communication processes within their dominant organizations. In many respects these discussions differ little from those present during the past three decades of institutional organizational communication study. They have been concerned with the systematic manners by which communication practices can be used to help coordinate and control the activities of organizational members and relations with external constituencies. With this interest most have conceptualized communication in the relatively linear terms of influence and information transfer. Further, they have defined communication as a particular practice among the many practices involved in organizational life. Certainly from one point of view the study of communication as influence and information transfer within and between organizations continues to be a significant issue. Such a perspective, however, is ultimately limiting. From it communication researchers often become subservient to dominant group goals, they fail to gain the power that the understanding of communication has for the understanding of organizations, and finally they fail even to understand the nature of influence or information as they exist in specific corporate sites.

I propose in contrast to build a communication perspective on organizations. I am interested in what we find, and can do, if we think of organizations as complex communication processes and analyze them using concepts from a communication perspective. Many have thought

211

about organizations in psychological, sociological, historical, and economic terms. When they do so communication processes become reduced to information processes. A concern with information processes has been central in organizational studies since Simon's (1957) work (see Boland 1987). I purpose to sketch here a new research agenda by using communication as a mode of analysis and explanation.[1] The philosophical-conceptual-empirical reconsiderations required by such a position go to the roots of our understanding of organizations and communication. As such allow me to begin with a fundamental description of the relation of person to world, person to person, and language to people and world (much of what follows in this section is worked out in more detail in different forms in Deetz 1992, 1994; Giddens 1984; Bourdieu 1977; Gadamer 1975; Habermas 1984, 1987).

The basic perspective here is fairly straightforward. Human beings are interpretive creatures. They, like other living creatures, live and work in a world that is formed in particular manners given their specific sense equipment and manners of comportment extended in humans by institutionalized practices and linguistic systems of distinction. Such a position is widely held today, for example, including biologists (Maturana and Varela 1980), philosophers (Merleau-Ponty 1964; Rorty 1989), sociologists (Bourdieu 1977; Giddens 1984), anthropologists (Douglas 1986; Geertz 1973), and psychologists (Harré and Secord 1972; Gergen 1991). In fact, few today would hold out for a directly experienced, in-itself, version of the world, though many researchers and practitioners evoke a "methodological" fiction of such for political purposes.

Further, for humans much of their interpretive mode of being is provided socially rather than genetically. In this sense a series of social interactions and social decisional processes stand behind each perception, each feeling, each experienced need. In other words, each psychological state and conception of personal identity arises out of a background of social practices in which such things are constructed as possible, feelable, imaginable (see Harré 1986; Hochschild 1983). Every social structure can be seen as an arbitrary, routine, habitual way that social interactions have come to be played out. As such they have no stature except as reproduced and legitimized in ongoing social interaction. In this sense psychological and sociological theories are attempts at reifying ongoing productive and reproductive interactions usually for the sake of advantaging certain historical practices over others. Their attempts at explanation are merely freezing a process in time establishing arbitrary independent and dependent variables that are then often mistaken as real things. Communication analysis properly attempts to describe and explain the productive and reproductive processes through accounts of specific ongoing representational practices.

Communication as a phenomenon and mode of explanation

Communication, in the view I am suggesting, refers to the social processes by which meanings, identities, psychological states, social structures, and so on are both produced and reproduced (see Deetz 1992, chapters 3–5). In both its constitutive and reproductive modes, communication processes are central to how perceptions, meanings, and routines are held in common. In all interactions, including those in organizations, perception, meaning, and data transmission are all complex, multileveled phenomena produced out of and producing conflicting motives and structures. As Eco (1989) made clear, the issues of meaning and communication are never reducible to conceptions of information and information transfer; they are not just inadequate, they are contrary in intention (see also Lazega's 1992 differentiation of information control and information elaboration). The complexity of the communication process can initially be seen in the way it both produces and reproduces objects and persons.

In the productive or constitutive mode, interest is directed to the conflictual, tension-filled antagonisms out of which objects are differentiated and redifferentiated and preconceptions are given over to new conceptions. Some version of this is clear in Gadamer's (1975) genuine conversation, Habermas's (1984) communication directed toward understanding, or in the various poststructuralist agent responding to "otherness" (for review, see Deetz 1978, 1990; 1992, 113–70). The most basic question here is not how do we come to share independent perceptions, but rather on what basis do independent creatures have the same perception. Intersubjectivity must precede subjectivity "'communication of consciousness' presupposes a community of 'unconsciousness' (that is, of linguistic and cultural competence)" (Bourdieu 1990, 58).

At this constitutive level a communication perspective draws attention to a politics of perception and person formation (for review, see Coward and Ellis 1977; Weedon 1987). To make distinctions, to be able to perceive this rather than that, empowers one to particular forms of action but also precludes other ways of attending to the world and hence precludes other ways of being, of objectifying the self and world. Every formation is a response from a relatively stable set of

practices and linguistic forms that constrain variety, and to an actual
set of events that could have been described and responded to in a variety of fashions (i.e., that potentially demand variety). Thus each moment of production is constrained but relatively autonomous. Power
configurations specify the prejudicial preconditions of the relatively
open, but directional, response to an outside.

Much of life and interaction with others, however, lacks this formative quality and evidences reproductive communicative processes
(see Deetz 1978). Reproduction can be described in both an unobtrusive and obtrusive form. Unobtrusive reproductions arise from what
Bourdieu (1977) calls the "habitus." These are sets of routines, taken
for granted schemes, socially inscribed object-distinctions, and self-
conceptions that are ready at hand. We feel as if the world is already
demarked into this object and act as if socially arbitrary distinctions
between things resides in nature itself (Bourdieu 1990, 58). This is a
kind of natural attitude, lacking doubt of the nature of things and having no interest in the conditions necessary for their construction as they
appear. This is politically laden in that the routines are produced out
of power relations and reproduce the presence of group distinctions
that advantage particular groups in their "innocent" reproduction (Epstein 1988). In examining communicative reproductions, Habermas
(1979, 1984) describes latent strategic action and systemically distorted communication, and others from Gramsci (1971) forward discuss the political organization of common sense. As Bourdieu (1990,
58) would describe the relation.

> One of the fundamental effects of the harmony between practical
> sense and objectified meaning (*sens*) is the production of a common-
> sense world, whose immediate self-evidence is accompanied by the
> objectivity provided by consensus on the meaning of practices and
> the world, in other words the harmonization of the agent's experi-
> ences and the constant reinforcement each of them receives from ex-
> pression—individual or collective (in festivals, for example),
> improvised or programmed (commonplaces, sayings)—of similar or
> identical experiences.

This practical or common sense directs person-world-knowledge
reproduction in particular directions but usually without personal intent or awareness. This conception specifies an awareness that not only
is all rationality bounded, but it is interested and directed. Hence, it is
fundamentally, if not intentionally, political. The presence of common
sense, decisional rules, routines, role identities, and shared practices
each specify a reproduction of an interested way of being in the world

and a means of indirect control of participants. Such indirect control processes are central to the politics of everyday action and lessen the need for persuasion, influence, or other direct control processes in various social settings including organizations (see Etzioni 1961).

In addition, however, important "direct" control processes exist. I will describe them here as obtrusive reproductions. This is what most scholars studying communication study. Their central issues regard influence through the effective presentation and transmission of information. The concern with the transmission of information, however, is directed at information that was already produced and unobtrusively reproduced (Deetz and Mumby 1985; Eco 1989). Common research concerns such as self-presentation, self-disclosure, argumentation, conflict resolution, and integrative problem solving, First Amendment rights, informed publics, explicitly strategic interaction, manipulation, and propaganda direct attention to forms and issues of obtrusive reproduction. Most discussions of politics, control, power, legitimacy of authority, and domination stay at this level even though much of what is interesting in these issues have already taken place in the constitutive or unobtrusive realm. These discourses rarely penetrate into the workings of unobtrusive reproduction and its consequences for these analyses.

Following this multileveled view of communication, this essay will conceptualize modern corporations as important, complex political sites that can be explained in communicational terms. Corporations could be a positive social institution providing a forum for the articulation and resolution of important social conflicts regarding the use of natural resources, the production of meaningful goods and services, and the development of individuals. But this politics is often largely closed owing to a variety of practices which produce and privilege certain interests—principally managerial—in both public decision-making and in the production of the type of person that exists in modern organizations and society (Deetz, in press b).

The politics can be explained by an examination of the organization of representational practices within corporate sites. Later, I will conceptualize specific organizations of representational practices as "orders of simulacra" (see Baudillard 1983a). In this essay I will focus on three dominant simulacra. Each produces and reproduces particular recognitions and construals of both the inner and outer world. Each has liberating and democratic potential, and specific conditions of constraint and domination potential.

Since communication issues go to the heart of what we will become as a species and who will have how much say in that determination, every system of representation and mode of analysis has a moral-political dimension. And since we have no way to speak of an essential world out there or person in here from a communication perspective, no representational practice can be nonarbitrarily privileged. Hence, I see no way to avoid accepting a democracy ideal that no social group or practice should be arbitrarily privileged in organizations or any social product. If we accept this moral/democratic responsibility, studies of organizations must consider control of any sort as potentially illegitimate and focus on decision processes in light of multiple potential and actual goals. Critique of domination and promotion of more open decision-making become the primary reason for doing communicational analyses of organizations. If dominant groups privilege certain codes of representation, a dysfunctional self-referential system can be produced which wastes resources, sustains arbitrary advantages in resource distribution, and constrains practical responsiveness to problems encountered by different social groups. After a brief discussion of the growing importance of the corporation as a site of analysis and the issues of social domination there, the remainder of the chapter explores how each simulacra exists and how specific forms of domination can be critiqued or deconstructed.

The corporation as a significant political site and social domination

The modern commercial corporation is central to public decision-making today. In most modern societies corporations make crucial decisions for the public regarding the use of resources, development of technologies, products made, and working relations among people. While state political processes are significant, the shaping of these central decisions through regulation and incentives is considerably less important than the central decision-making processes within corporations themselves. Corporate practices pervade modern life by providing personal identity, structuring time and experience, influencing education and knowledge production, directing artistic expression, and instituting particular structures of family life. Additionally, the commercial domination of the mass media, the mass dissemination of advertising, the production of information and sponsored news, and control of information networks leaves a virtual corporate monopoly on public information (Bagdikian 1990; Schiller 1989). Increasingly, corporate institutions are "colonizing" other institutions in modern society (see Deetz 1992). Following this there is little surprise that political decision-making in interpersonal, community, and state communication processes is replaced by economic decision-making organized in corporate representational practices. Every contemporary political philosophy or investigation of societal decisions must consider the representational practices involved in market economy and other internal decisional processes in corporations.

While corporations increasingly make decisions for the public, the inequitable distribution of political, economic, and social power supports a narrow and distorted system of interest development and representation within them. Even in democratic state societies, corporations rarely operate with democratic principles in either the traditional sense of interest representation or in the politics of everyday—the politics of meaning, perception, or the personal. In recognizing this condition and its moral and practical consequences, many scholars and social critics have focused on how decisional control happens in the workplace and how the corporation extends its control outside of the workplace (Alvesson 1987a; Deetz 1992).

Following these authors it is clear that control in the workplace today is clearly multifaceted (see also Alvesson 1993; Alvesson and Willmott 1992; Bullis and Tompkins 1989; Mumby 1988). The workplace contains both traditional forms of coercion and authority and ideological meaning formations (Valas 1993; Burawoy 1979; Edwards 1979). But is also includes social processes by which the "subject" is formed with particular identities and interests by what can be called social technologies of control that routinize and normalize the very movements and feelings of the body (Burrell 1988; Clegg 1989, 1990; Foucault 1988). These processes produce an individual who is disciplined and actively engages in self-surveillance and correction on the company's behalf. The development of social technologies of control often replaces the passing authority in the managerial control process (Alvesson 1993; Deetz 1992, 249ff; Kunda 1992). With such a concept, the workplace need not be shown to be well-integrated and hegemonic to demonstrate domination. Many corporations are filled with conflict, but only certain types of conflicts which hide potentially more important ones. People largely know a version of their own interests and act on them, but these interests are produced in standard codes along normalized and one-sided lines. Surveillance is both internal and external to the individual, but understood as for the good or efficiency of all members. The new fear by many corporate employees is not a fear of an authoritarian manager, but often that one's own self will not behave and conform.

In this conception, managerial domination can be seen as taking place through ideological control, economically-based structures, *and* systems of discursive monopoly through which personal identity and group interests are formed, each form of domination is clearer if rendered in communication terms. In most modern corporations, advantages are not so much conceptualized as a right or as legitimate but are unproblematically reproduced in routines and discourses where rights and legitimacy never arise as concerns (Giddens 1984). As such, privilege is treated as natural and neutral and perhaps even necessary since the employee conceives of the self as lacking the information, expertise, or self-control to decide on one's own behalf (employees as children [infantocracy] is a dominant image, see Czarniawska-Joerges and Kunda 1992). This presumed neutrality of the organization makes understanding the political nature of organizations more difficult. If we accept at the outset that these are not neutral, we can focus our energies on seeing how different representational practices advantage and how intervention is possible.

Workplace activities as representational practices

Certainly a worker's labor or an investor's money "exist" in an organization, but it takes nothing away from this commonsense ontological certainty to claim that they only meaningfully exist as produced and presented in representational systems. This is not a claim for the significance of the sign over what the sign stands for as a general principle. The issue is deeper than that. The "worker" only exists as worker as distinguished from management or owner, as distinguished in some system of demarcation specifying who is the same and who is different.

Representational practices both indicate the conditions of formation—the practices producing distinction—and the manner of display. A "worker" is an object of experience. An object requires both an indefinite something that can be described (called here an "element") and a system of representation. The "worker" as signified thus stands in relation to other group members as both constructed out of practices of separation (thus objectified in representation) and in specified relations to others through the relation of distinctions to other distinctions, thereby recursively justifying separation as natural and reproducing it. The same can be said about each element of organizational experience. Each element is "articulated" in the double sense that it is brought to appearance in some manner of expression and jointed or connected to other elements as articulated (Epstein 1988; Laclau and Mouffe 1985). As various types of work, people, psychological states, needs, interests, resources, information, financial statements, and so forth become articulate in various relations, the workplace is a jumble of coordinated and conflicting realities as represented. The workplace is filled with objects and objective relationships, that is filled with stuff—elements—that appear as objects with object relations based on the existence of specific practices.

No attempt here is made to deny the extralinguistic person or any other element but rather to claim that the person *is* in many potential modes of presentation. Neither the "person" nor any other organizational element can be known outside of systems of constitutive representation (Epstein 1988; Weedon 1987). Arguments over what the person really is or what is empirically certain are not about truth but conflicting representations each with their own truth conditions or disinterest in truth (Rorty 1989). Thus agreement on "real," "truth," and "knowledge" rest in the power of one representational practice over another. Every element admits to multiple representations (to many truth claims) as well as to "false" statements that purport to be about it but suppress or stand over and against it. In the attempt to guard against these latter claims, theorists often omit the multiplicity of the former and inadvertently foster the latter through nonresponsive methods and conceptual schemes.

The elements and activities of organizational life are not irrelevant, nor do they simply pass away to symbolism. Losing money or losing one's job is real. But losing money, for example, is not some simple empirical thing knowable as a thing in itself. Profit and loss statements arise out of a set of constitutive social practices such as standard accounting practices. Money is never actually lost. It passes from one place to another and whether the other place is inside or outside the system—the money is "transferred" or "lost"—is itself an arbitrary distinction (consider the problem of internal and external marketing or trying to figure out which goods you should buy to ensure a favorable balance of trade). Money is not an *element* of organizational life. It is an *object*. As an object it is constituted by representational practices and has its play based on relations specified in a constructed system. But it is also a sign, a sign in a representational practice which specifies other elements as objects in a social determination process. As Barthes (1972) showed, every object is a sign which stands for and puts into play the very system of distinction which makes it possible as an object held up as an appearance of an element with many possible articulations. *Power is present in the attempt to hold one sign value or articulation as preferable over others. Domination occurs when one articulation is systematically, but arbitrarily, privileged through practices suppressing alternatives.*

A communicational understanding of how decisions happen—how conflict arise and are resolved—in organizations through constitutive practices or through unobtrusive controls requires insight into operant representational practices. This would provide insight into the practices that provide the context for explicit conflict, persuasion, and strategic control and influence. The dominant practices are different in different sites yet ultimately in interdependent systems fit together in mobile but specifiable ways. One of the easiest ways to show clusters of different representational practices is in looking at the three dominant conceptions of organizations in our century—traditional organizations, rational organizations, and chaotic organizations.[2]

The three orders of the simulacra

The choices available for building a communication analysis by describing representational practices are many. They include structuralist and semiotic accounts such as Barthes (1975) and early Foucault (1970), feminists works such as Weedon (1987) and Epstein (1988), and various works in cultural studies such as Hall (1977, 1989) and Bourdieu (1977, 1984). But here I want to do a bit of a dance with Baudrillard as an illustration of how we might think about certain representational practices. I am not intending to do a Baudrillardian perspective on organizations, but to appropriate a piece of his conceptual frame in *Simulations* (1983a) as a point of departure in a communication perspective on organizations. The conception I am most interested in is his "orders of simulacra."

In Baudrillard's conception, "simulacra" arose with the modern period. At this point the relatively fixed social order in which signs stood in a relatively clear, fixed, and transparent relation to "intrinsic values" weakened and with that signs could have a life of their own and be used instrumentally.[3] For example, if in the feudal period social position could be read directly from signs such as dress, in the modern period one could dress in particular ways to represent social position. Symbolism is thus understood, and the real and the counterfeit take on new meaning. Symbolic negotiation of social order replaces a presumed given, ordained order. The term 'simulacra' refers to a world as reproduction. Reproduction is used here in the unobtrusive constitutive sense described earlier. In such a situation the relation to the world not only is imaginary, but with competing orders different groups are trying (often unwittingly) to portray/create a world in their own image. Such a situation could enable unheard of control of nature and material progress as now only the imagination served as an ultimate limit on what the natural environment could be made as.[4] All worlds are illusions, they are specific recognitions and misrecognitions, construals and reconstruals of the elements. But they are not illusionary in the same way. Nor are they necessarily all totally self-referential or reproductive. For example, while the feudal understandings were rigid, the outer world was fully felt.[5] The restriction of the outside in simulacra undermines the liberating potential of the modern period.

Simulacra in a general way specifies the presence of human values and identities, particular practices, and various accounts of reality. Several concepts other than simulacra have been used to study similar ways of displaying relations. Foucault's (1970) modern *episteme,* Bourdieu's (1977) *habitus,* Therborn's (1980) *subject qualification,* and Althusser's (1971) *interpellation* have been used. Even in a very general sense the concept of culture as it arose in the nineteenth century tried to demonstrate how a particular society thought and acted. But simulacra does not just suggest particular relations of person to the inner and outer world and social community—a social construction of reality. It specifies in addition a particular kind of relation in reality construction—one where the sign rules. With this, the self, other, external world, and social community become reproductions. In this sense modern society is progressive in only a particular fashion, its ability to mass reproduce signs—signs that once represented social values. It has less accomplished these values than it has acquired the signs of these values.[6] As will be clear later, terms like culture, thus, better refer to a particular order of simulacra.

Baudrillard argued that there have been three orders of simulacra—three ways appearances have dominated modern social life. Each of which had as an inherent goal, the production of a flexible and controllable universal system of order and power in a world in which the world did not give order on its own. The domination by the first was clearest in nineteenth-century Europe and the United States. With it arose an awareness of culture and cultural difference and an attempt to ground—and thus justify—one's own signs in nature. Natural rights and natural laws served as the rising middle classes justification for overturning the remnants of the fixed medieval hierarchy. Knowledge based on authority would give way to that grounded in representation. The second order became dominant with the Industrial Revolution. In this, mass reproductions of representations overcome the grounded representation. Natural law is replaced by the probabilistic series and precedent replaces natural rights. In this formation worth cannot be grounded in laws of nature but now in the exchange, the laws of the market. In serial production inherent worth is lost to equivalences. Reproducibility becomes the fundamental logic and code of society, reproducibility the logic of science.

The new, growing domination of the past thirty to forty years is by the pure simulation. Today, Baudrillard claims, "we are in the third-order simulacra; no longer that of the counterfeit of an original as in the first order, nor that of the pure series as in the second" (1983a, 100–101). The third order draws attention to the dominance of the model over any representation. The idea is reminiscent of Boorstin's famous quip, "if you like the baby, just wait until you see the pictures." The picture does not represent the baby even in a positive light, but produces the baby in the model of what a baby could be. The model works in what Baudrillard (following Eco) called the "hyper-real" world—it is not unreal nor a picture of the real, it is more than real. Disneyworld is the America Americans imagine as their real home—a hometown that never was and always was "real" (see Eco 1986). It is not an imitation of a dream vacation spot or a nostalgia for a past, it is a model community, a model science. But the model is not just somewhere models are everywhere. People buy the model house which is needed only since it exists to be needed, rather than a home. The comfort of home itself is a model rather than a feeling. The model job, the model career, the model home, each are needed not to fulfill aspirations and meet needs, but define what a better person than I in a better world would have as real aspirations. They define what the model "I" would be.

The value of these general social descriptions come in beginning to specify how organizations exist in the simulacra, or more to the point, what they are. Baudrillard's conceptions are handy because they both parallel and yet provide a different look at the three dominant conceptions of organizations—the traditional, rational, and chaotic organization. The terms can be combined as: first-order/early modern/traditional; second-order/late modern/rational; and third-order/post modern/chaotic.

Like with the three orders of simulacra, when organizational descriptions like traditional, rational, and chaos are applied, it is very easy to think in terms of historical succession of types partly because dominance is more easily seen at different points in time. But organizations as constructed in our world today are composed in all three principal representational forms and dominance by a form is only momentarily held. The organization is a mixed site of the traditional/early modernity, rational/late modernity, and chaotic/postmodernity. The various representational practices intersect, overlap, and compete. One of the reasons the actual workplace is so hard to critique is that critique in one code is co-opted in the enactment of contrary codes which use the critique to support another power-laden agenda. For example, a discussion of workers' rights can only be had in the context of the competing rights of management, capital providers, and the general society. But when one advocates worker rights and the reply is in the terms of economic costs or the open giving away of such rights in signing the work contract, the notion of "rights" in traditional discourse has already been transposed into the rational one. Rights are suddenly like other personal desires like owning a second car. And, the choice is made between them based on costs. Democracy itself becomes merely one of many potential costs or resources. Critiques of the limits of rational planning, float into the assertion of cultural management in the traditional mode. There is no solid ground for critique. It is constantly displaced.

In such a context we can hope for no communicational metacode to transcend these discourses. Rather, I think we need to move in and out of them, displaying the language of each. Such a multilingual communication approach allows the attempt to voice in each, yet without trying to ground one's stand simply in one or another. To accomplish this I wish to briefly (1) lay out the dominant practices in these three modes, (2) suggest in each the forms of domination characteristic of it, and (3) show how the critique of domination operates in each. I will be brief in regard to each but will point to other work for details and pose possible research issues.

The symbolic/political simulacra and cultural critique

The first-order simulacra will be called here the symbolic/political in that its forms of order and domination rest in representational practices that attempt a symbolic reproduction of natural value and the political struggle over preferred symbolic reproductions. Implicitly the political focused on whose central values would serve to integrate a society when sovereignty, and hence old political power, is spread across the general public. The "public" defined the site where competing value premises are worked out in free and open discussion and the hope of a new agreed-upon world order. In such a conception, the resolution of conflicting interpretations is a political problem, not one left to science. If is not a question of which is correct, but which is right. Community morality and practices grounded the traditional organization.

As Weber recognized clearly in describing the rise of bureaucracy, the prebureaucratic integration was organically produced around community values and extra-organizational social structures. Authority was legitimized through appeals to extra-organizational natural rights and the social contract. The primary forms of knowledge and reasoning were practical in Habermas's (1971) sense, they relied on wisdom more than knowledge. Job skills were primarily acquired through apprenticeship. The natural language of the host community served as the primary mode of expression and cognition. In this sense the workplace was well integrated into other aspects of everyday life. Explicitly value-laden communal representational practices extended into the workplace fostering concepts of honor, social responsibility, and rights organized around dominant social values. Here capital could be seen as the possession of things of intrinsic worth, including land and such things as skills and objects produced by skill.

Despite industrialization and bureaucratization, the workplace never escaped symbolic/political practices nor the world as produced thereby. The first-order simulacra does not pass away with emergence of the second. Most would agree that the emerging "rational" workplace always counted on extrarational values and practices to offset the weaknesses of pure instrumental reasoning and to supplement the means of control (see Habermas 1975). The rise of organizational culture studies in the past twenty years clearly supports this position. The "rational" organization relied on extrarational values (principally honesty and a work ethic) for its operation since rationalization itself can not produce these necessary values. And, as the external culture failed to provide legitimacy and motivation in the workplace, the attempt was first to find host cultures which would, and finally to engage in massive efforts at cultural management (Alvesson 1987a, 1993; Deetz 1992). This management move, and the studies that support it, attempts to produce a solidarity through representational coordination that would reduce the reliance on supervision and direct motivation devices. The hoped for outcome would be loyalty and commitment not possible in the rational representation alone. The recent preoccupation with a corporate vision to integrate cultural perception and priorities is an attempt to reenact traditional communal representational practices.

Symbolic/political representations are not just property of non-managerial employees. While scientific management appeared to try to drive extrarational considerations out of the workplace, the symbolic/political continued to exist along side the emerging rational code. Management was never as rational as their self-presentation suggested, even if a narrow culturally based conception of rationality is used

(Clegg 1990, 154ff.). Management has long preferred intuitive over "rational" judgments as best seen in their preference for the lesson of the good story and the tradition-based decision rule, over data-based judgments. Greater size, too much information technology, and greater control over the workers, each appear valued for themselves and continued to be pursued even after considerable evidence suggested negative effects on productivity (Skillman 1991).

The various forms of cultural studies in organizations have been an explicit attempt to describe the symbolic/political representational practices. It is little surprise that most of these studies have modeled themselves after the study of nonindustrial societies. Their focus is nearly always on organic forms of integration in, for example, the way stories and rituals are used to reproduce dominate worldviews and community values (see Martin 1993 as an exception). In many ways they have preferenced the politics of the community over that embedded in the rational. But in most cases they have left power and the political as invisible as the various nineteenth-century attempts to ground one's preferred worldview in representations of the natural order. Culture is rarely a critical concept but rather is seen as leading to positive social integration (Kunda 1992; Smircich and Calás 1987). Rarely have cultural researchers taken an interest in displaying cultural management as a strategic action intended to enact systematically distorted communication through implicit control of means of speaking and thinking in the workplace (see Alvesson 1987b; Deetz 1992, 173ff.).

The critique of domination in symbolic/political representational practices is best represented as ideological critique.[7] Clearly traditional as well as contemporary cultural representational practices are ideological in the sense that they recognize and reconstrue along lines arbitrarily favoring certain people. Systems of distinctions and relations carried by language use, both literal and metaphorical, produce and reproduce a particular world with specific objects, types of subjects, and manners of thinking and valuing (Bourdieu 1984; Deetz and Mumby 1985). Within specific representational practices certain people have more symbolic capital and they tend to produce systems in which their presumed intrinsic qualities count for more (Bourdieu 1984). The feminists have been especially active in showing how gender itself is produced and reproduced in the workplace along with a string of implicated advantaging and disadvantaging practices (see especially Epstein 1988).

Using ideological critique, critical theorists have shown that workers and the general society often have interests in work that are only partially and indirectly represented in corporate goals as implemented by management groups. These include the quality of the work experience and work environment, mental health and safety, the skill and intellectual development of the worker, the carryover of thinking patterns and modes of action to social and political life, and the production of personal and social identity (Alvesson 1987a). Such critiques attempt to change the workplace to an explicit site of political struggle where different groups try to realize their own interests and overcome the systematic distortions or dominant representations. Much of this work is well known and need not be summarized here (see special issue of *International Studies of Management and Organizations* 1987; Alvesson and Willmott 1992; Deetz and Mumby 1990; Mumby 1987, 1988).

The rational/instrumental simulacra and the money code

The second simulacra can be presented as the rational/instrumental organization conception that is most often contrasted with the traditional—symbolic/political. Marx was partially right in what he saw in the rise of capitalism and industrialization. Rationality, specified through commodification and exchange value while always present to some extent, would come to dominate value-laden practical representational practices. In some respects he can be seen as more conservative than many of his industrial contemporaries. Unlike most of them he held out for a traditional concept of intrinsic worth (a labor theory of value) against the emerging "rational system." His analysis remained limited and reductionistic since he, because of a basic essentialism, saw the economic as a causal driving force rather than as the emerging dominant representational practice of the time.

The industrialists' emphasis on the "rational" over traditional or cultural values in the workplace was and is often still conceptualized in liberal terms. The freedom from traditional-bound authority relations, older social divisions, and handed-down work skills was assumed to allow freedom from arbitrary constrains on personal advancement and to enhance the application of science to work processes. The assumption of the cumulative and progressive nature of science was seen as assuring freedom from superstition, ending fighting over irresolvable ideological positions, and enabling material wellbeing through greater efficiency and effectiveness. Even ordinary language was seen as problematic. The solution was to try to produce a "neutral" descriptive "scientific" language without implicit values and ideology (the development and popularity of "general semantics" in communication and management studies literature is one example). Language was thus transformed into a "code"—as if conventional words could stand in an isomorphic relation to preexisting objects. This misrecognition was decisively political in that it would advantage certain groups, but it would do so without an integrative worldview or set of values. A process or procedure for making the elements of the world into objects became privileged, thereby enabling the appearance of a presumed objective, value-free science. This science was so completely dominated by its subjective manner of object production that it would proclaim its objects as natural, self-evident, and real—*its* world became *the* world. Not only would such a science study an objectified, commodified world but its results became increasingly codified and the possession of "knowledge" increasingly replaced "insight" into processes as the preferred form of knowing. The presence of a point of view in all information is forgotten as all information is treated as data (Boland 1987). Management groups came to justify their decision-making processes in an appropriation of this historically situated concept of science.

Within such a context, information transfer in the rational representational practice works in opposition to symbolic communication (see Eco 1989; Lazega 1992). Or as Baudrillard (1983b, 96) demonstrated: "information is directly destructive of meaning and significant, or neutralizes it. The loss of meaning is directly linked to the dissolving and dissuasive action of information." Information technologies in filing, coding, and retrieval would arise with the rational but reach their most advanced state as the world in which they have relevance begins to disappear partly owing to their own effect of killing the symbolic integration and extrarational values from which they arose and on the basis of which they survived.

The rational world, however, still needs integration and a form of valuing to enable consensus. With the objectification and stripping of values the communication process requires that these now isolated independent objects be representationally reconnected. While the reclaiming of the symbolic/political accomplishes this in some areas, this is accomplished directly in the rational/instrumental representation by using exchange value presented in the monetary code. From a rational stance if everything can be valued in the same code we truly can compare apples and oranges. Collective decision-making is no longer a political discussion debating relative values but only a calculus. The primary way to represent interests is in the money code and decisions arise from the exchanging of commodities. Everyone and everything is represented and the calculation is not messed up by private, irrational agendas. Few communication researchers have grasped well the way money is primarily information in this system. Some have seen how money buys air time to influence political decision making in the traditional value-laden code, but fewer have seen money flows themselves as a representational practice in making political decisions. The conception of consumer "dollar-voting" demonstrate a general public awareness of the conceptual shift. This is central to understanding communication in organizational decision-making and the corporate role in general social choices.

The development of industrialization created a physical and representational split between the declining community and the ascending workplace. Taylor's scientific management, Weber's bureaucracy, and Marx's theory of value represented (both favorably and negatively) and fostered (either through advancement or negation) a different set of practices and a different way of thinking and talking about the workplace. Organizational science was inscribed and a "new" form of rationality was given central importance. In place of a set of representations based on intrinsic values came a system of exchange values. Specification, measurement, and commodification became alternative expressions of new objects constituted in new practices and increasingly represented by money. In this set of representations disciplinary power in Foucault's (1977, 1980) sense has already replaced sovereign power. Power is dispersed in the motion of the assembly line and work processes, new concepts of the individual, work tools and technologies, and ubiquitous surveillance. Management becomes less visible as management itself is inscribed in processes, guidelines, and procedures and internalized by employees (e.g., Edward's [1979] concept of *technical* control or Etzioni's [1961] concept of *normative* control). Capital could be articulated in terms of money and ownership of the means of production. Workers, managers, and owners of the means of production together provided a representational practice where labor became articulated as a "cost" to the organization. In many cases of publicly "owned" firms, even "capital" investors can be calculated as a "cost" in the payment of dividends. In this context management came to be articulated as *the* organization since they were the medium of coordinating all the various claims of other produced groups which were each reproduced in this logic as a "cost" (Deetz 1992, 221ff.). Ownership (whether based in labor, capital, or social purpose) as having rights is rearticulated in such a system as the coordination of an organization which is relatively autonomous. The completion of this process would exist if an organization purchased all its own stock. In even a less extreme version, instrumental reasoning institutionalized through system steering media as described by Habermas (1987) dominates over practical reasoning in life-world terms (Fischer 1990). Since everything in such an organization's environment is a potential resource/cost, it is apparent why it extends out to colonize all outside institutions and the life world itself. An organization's autonomous self-defining movement requires control of anything that might effect it. The attempt is to calculate and rationalize everything. Knowledge is codified, self-reflexive. Both discipline and the information age are "discovered" as the logic they model reaches the outer limit, perhaps the only condition under which they could be discussed (Baudrillard 1987).

In the monetary code, the life-world emphasis on practical reasoning is translated into instrumental system terms. The modern corporation as it enacts this order of simulacra would hardly be recognizable or thinkable without this primary mode of representation. Certainly for many in modern corporations, the reason for working is to make money. Alternative motives of enjoying production, producing a quality product, having a good time, or helping people may be considered but often only in regard to their effects on commitment, productivity, and sales usually translated into monetary terms (see Kunda 1992, chapter 4 for a good example of this process in motion). The implications of the privilege of the monetary code is seen in two areas—the production of a managerial prerogative and in the change of political to economic questions.

The use of the monetary code as a representational practice has a decisive effect on workplace control. This is largely through a produced "managerial prerogative." Today the managerial prerogative is no longer justified as a natural (but debatable) right, it is ground in management's socially produced conceptual and legal fiduciary responsibility (see Storey 1983). Since the prerogative rests in fiduciary responsibilities, the translation into monetary terms is not simply the evoking of an arbitrary medium of exchange, it is a shifting of responsibility and control. Articulating life-world issues in terms of corporate costs shifts the decisional responsibility from other corporate members to the manager. Management becomes responsible for anything which has a potential financial implication. And of course control shifts with the responsibility. The fiduciary responsibility lays a ground for a managerial prerogative in all matters of the workplace (and elsewhere if they have financial implications).

Further, the reduction of political battles to economic ones appears as a necessary and rational consequence of pluralistic, separate but equal, value systems in rational/instrumental representations. The rationality of economic determinations appears to be a positive replacement of the arbitrary, irrational determination by symbolic/political power relations. With such a practice in place, democracy is rewritten as dollar voting, where the public has representation through its decisions of what it is willing to pay for. But the invisible hand is better described as *quiet* (and often distorted) *communication* than *market rationality*. But there are a number of catches which give rise to important critiques of this as a representational practice (see Narveson 1992). Since such a practice does more to situate and extend control than represent diverse interest, it becomes systematically distorted. The monetary representation essentially presents us with a heavily value-laden but presumably rational and neutral system of conflict resolution that distorts the expression of values and suppresses awareness of important conflicts (see Gortz 1987; Simonds 1989; Power 1992; Schmooker 1992). The political advantage and self-interests extended in place of consenual foundations leads to more sophisticated systems of power as the arbitrator.

Despite these obvious difficulties, the critique of rational/instrumental simulacra is somewhat harder than trying to reclaim rationality or support alternative values in the symbolic/political. But its costs to a democratic society and moral choice are clear. The representative practices of market-driven managerial societies privilege instrumental reasoning and behaviors and consequently suppress diversity of interests (Ramos 1981). The concern is both with the managerial prerogative in decision-making and the presumed rationality of market-driven decisions. The managerial prerogative often undermines what exists of democracy in a market-driven system. And the dysfunctions of representational equality can only be overcome by recovering alternative claimants and modes of representation. The reclaiming of the tension among multiple logics and human interests in corporations is of central importance to democracy. The question is can we have adequate alternative representative political processes to compete with those in the monetary code? Perhaps people without money should get two votes in elections to have equal effect on social policy as those who can or chose to represent their interests in the economic code? Unfortunately the problem is greater than this. The economic code often colonizes the mind, leading the individual to realize only economic interests or believe that all potential interest can be accomplished with enough money.

Successful critique must go to the commodification process itself since this is central to the serial reproduction which drives the practice. Here we are concerned with the ways elements become articulated into reproducible objects. For example, the development of personality theory and personality testing are central to the corporate object/person (Hollway 1984). Forms and reporting categories commodify work along arbitrary, advantaging lines. Issues of what is and is not reported and what becomes part of the record and history are significant (see Sless 1988). Monetary representational practices could be reformed and made more representative (Power 1992; Schomooker 1992). Many working with "green" and "social" accounting have made progress in this regard. Accounting practices have recently become of great interest in their communication function (see Hopwood 1987; Laughlin 1987). Works like these must be taken more seriously if communication studies are to engage with this representational practice.

The simulation simulacra: Hyper-reality and control

The story of chaos is familiar in both organizations and the recent literatures on postmodernity (see Cooper and Burrell 1988; Burrell 1988; Peters 1987). As traditional integrative values lose force and interdependence exceeds the ability to build rational models, the system "jerks" about. "Traditional" social-linguistic distinctions seen in social group and object differentiations give way to situated distinctions leading to rapid de- and re-differentiation based in momentary (but often strategically organized) power arrangements (Clegg 1990, 1991). The strategic steering system in the rational mode overloads without a stable traditional integrative background (Habermas 1984). This gives both a sense of profound liberation and capacity to negotiated self-identity and reality as well as different operations of power and forms of domination (Gergen 1991). Such a condition is most extreme for U.S. corporations since the traditional values basis is weakest here and interdependence the greatest. In the chaos, organizations have the capacity to mobilize incredible resources toward largely chance and unpredictable ends in which their own mobilization factors as both a determinant and effect. The market environment is fragmented and unstable, the organization struggles to produce the environment to which it must adjust. As it does so it moves rapidly into the future and colonizes it (Giddens 1991) but without any guiding principle save its own survival in the increasingly chaotic future it creates. In such a world the rational and irrational coincide since the governing systems cannot escape the system as produced. Any faith in evolution or system correction disappears as the environment is no longer outside the system. The organization survives on the basis of environment enactment rather than adaptation. The discovery of a market is too late, the product must create the market and a new product must be in production as the market will be saturated at the same time that it is created. "High-speed management" (Cushman 1991) is often merely an attempt to rationalize irrational practices in an irrational world. Organizations become, in Baudrillard's sense, pure *simulations* in a *hyper-reality.* In such a world, signs are disconnected from representation, the "model" replaces responsive action.

If signs in the traditional mode were assumed to represent intrinsic properties defined and integrated along dominant values, and signs in the rational mode objectified and commodified in exchange systems, in the chaos mode signs reach the structural limit of representation self-referencing only themselves having little relation to the elements at all. In Baudrillard's (1975) early work he makes a first stab at this relation as follows:

> The form-sign describes an entirely different organization: the signified and the referent are now abolished to the sole profit of the play of signifiers, of a generalized formalization in which the code no longer refers back to any subjective or objective "reality," but to its own logic. . . . The sign no longer designates anything at all. It approaches its true structural limit which is to refer back only to other signs. All reality then becomes the place of semi-urgical manipulation, of a structural simulation.

As value codes and commodifying codes are each seen as arbitrary and temporary, the imaginary and imagistic properly become more real and lasting than the realities that they "misconstrue." The check on the free-for-all of such representational systems thus can not be referenced to an inner or outer world, though such systems may proclaim such a reference in their own moves.

A statement is no longer right or wrong, correct or incorrect, but operant or inoperant. Integration is neither by hierarchical value positions nor by translation into a universal code, rather integration disappears and fragmentation is everywhere and embraced. In such a context the fiction, the lie is not just the hidden side of every integration nor a strategic move for gain. The fiction rules because it has no opposite. Baudrillard (1983a, 5) used the example of the difference between feigning and simulating an illness to show the character of this postmodern representation: "feigning or dissimulation leaves the reality principle intact; the different is always clear, it is only masked; whereas simulation threatens the difference between 'true' and 'false,' between 'real' and 'imaginary.' Since the simulator produces 'true' symptoms, is he ill or not? He cannot be treated objectively either as ill, or not ill."

This concept became most clear to me in a project observing a corporate group whose primary function was the development and delivery of information system hardware.[8] Particularly noteworthy was the observation that they frequently "lied" in business transactions. When asked about it they could talk in the terms of "truth" and "falsity" in symbolic/political terms. For example, one employee, Jim, said explicitly that he knew that he had fewer parts in stock than he had just promised to send out immediately, but that when they didn't get them he would blame it on someone else who would give them a story and so on. By the time they sorted it out he would either have the parts or they would have forgotten who said what—lying keeps it ambiguous and no one is held responsible, if everyone lies everyone gains. But while it was clear that Jim could talk this way, it is equally clear that this is not the way he thought in the system (see Kunda 1992 for similar examples of engineers falsifying bids). Questions of honesty arose but neither as a moral problem nor for simple expedience. More to the point there were *models* of talk and persons which superseded the truth context of the statement (see Jackell 1988 for a similar analysis). The person asking for the parts probably did not need as many as soon as requested (demanded) either. Jim didn't really know how many parts he had or what others had promised. The most important thing to him was to sound confident, to sound like the situation wasn't confused or complex, that he was in control. All things he *genuinely* simulated (not feigned) and could only simulate as detached from any "real." He wasn't just "trained" to disregard relevant complexity, he lives in a remarkably simple world—one where he is master. And the person ordering the parts did not primarily want to get the parts from someone who had them, but from a doer, someone who takes charge, who knows what's going on, who will get them delivered. In Jim's situated world-order the statement was not true or false, but something which was now part of the environment, something that had to be considered in making the next choice. "Lies," "truth," "existence," "nonexistence"—it all depends on who asks what question when. There were serious penalties for any falsification in the science culture of which these technical personnel were also a part. The context must be indexed to know which reality is now in play. Science is differentiated from business, and yet the commercial context makes the differentiation increasingly tenuous (as Clegg 1990 showed the modern/postmodern interface rides on the mutual modernist move of differentiation and postmodern dedifferentiation). No description is stable, a story is needed for each story. The analysis of these stories, however, has to be far different from the cultural analysis of stories. They do not simply reenact legitimacy or integrated values, they divert, they mix metaphors, they keep the world-order unstable and confused as well, they are fast and ride a surface. As Argyris (1986) showed a similar phenomenon in his defense routine as part of his description of the skilled production of chaos.

Trust conceivably could have been lost due to the "false" information as would be expected in a symbolic/political or even rational order. Here trust seemed to be enhanced by it—"He'll get the job done," "He's like me," "He knows the game and is good at it." But this is not building toward a stronger business relationship based on similarity nor does it intend to be. One or both employees may be gone by the next transaction and an equally anonymous game player will take part giving a different set of stories. Neither the having or getting or the parts nor the social relation is either real or not real in any lasting sense. The signs interplay and produce the reality they presumably represent but not for the sake of that. Data is gone because always too much and not enough exists. Actual surveillance is gone, because no one knows what the job is, what doing it well is.

Both rationality and integrated values are too simple and too slow in this context. Conflict is everywhere but yet since no one wants to appear to be in genuine conflict, conflict is suppressed or fragmented. Everything is too complex for a reality or calculus to sort out stable differences. Data-based reports present seemingly contradictory findings. And users of these reports pick and choose based on convenience rather than rationally trying to find out how different ones could be produced or used to produce an integrated theory. Facts are convenient reports, operant and then inoperant. Journalists exceed the social scientist as commentators on social events. All become spectators since observers are too slow and see too much complexity. It is a world filled with complexity and well educated people and yet oversimplified ("Everything I Really Needed to Know I Learned in Kindergarten"). Management talk especially around important complex issues is filled with superficial slogans and reiterated pop-science jargon. This is a world filled with what could be called "mirror-tower" thinking, a highly subsidized, rapidly reproduced imaginary world, self-proclaimed as real and hard-nosed.

In this context, the workplace's representational practice is one of signs in the simulation. Social status is no longer conferred in symbolic/political or the rational realm. For example, the manager/secretary separation is represented in the symbolic/political as natural differences based on gender or social class recognizing a rightful difference. In the rational/instrumental representation the division of labor is based on commodity values of different activities and the secretary-provided task support so that the manager can do more highly priced activities. In the simulation, the secretary is not needed for the activities but as a sign to separate the manager out from others, to show that the managerial he or she is different, that he or she does valued work. The office size, the car, the expense accounts, the manner of dressing may appear to enact a symbolic realm or be needed to make sales in the rational one, but in many cases only have sign value in the simulation, the play of an enacted reality. The vanity, the conspicuous, rather than social structure or monetary value, rules. Arrogance (even if warm and friendly) rather than efficiency or pleasure appear to rule. The production of signs rather than the production of products and services operates in the workplace both in relation to the external as well an internal environment.

As the assessment of work and its qualities in the monetary code becomes more difficult in particular contexts, the simulation is more dominant. These work in the workplace much as the battle over designer labels work in a consumer market of indistinguishable products. The employee has to produce the self as differentiated, as distinguished, as a designer label, but can only use other signs, or products as signs, rather than products as products to do it. In such a context we might well expect to see conflicts amongst those with sign value, those with product value, and those with moral value since each is attempting to enact a representational practice in which not only are they and their group dominant but in which the world makes sense and is real. The intensity of these conflicts arises because the sensible world and the person's place in it is at stake, but the intensity can not be focused, since its expression is lost in the representational practice of the other. The individual is left anxious rather than angry. There is neither a proper political realm nor a calculus to resolve the difference. The violence of this anxiety is either directed inward as stress or outward in disorganized violence. But the hyper-real in some sense always wins, for the inability to reach resolution reproduces its fragmented context and its peculiar openness to diversity.

The difficulty of deconstructing or intervening in the simulation is great. A political agenda is increasingly difficult to hold in a fast-changing interdependent world. And, since the simulation resides alongside a rational discourse and a symbolic/political one, the representations float. The employees at the computer system company can immediately turn and talk about quality, excellence, good science, and the "bottom line" and "mean it." The mixing of the symbolic, the real, and the hyper-real simultaneously protect each from scrutiny and pursuit. Not only is the simulation self-referential, but it cannot be held in place long enough to develop a position in regard to it. Since critique would seem to be impossible, some type of deconstructive strategy seems essential if our descriptions are to move along a political democratic agenda (see Knights and Morgan 1991; Martin 1990). This would entail breaking the simulation's self-referential quality. The elements would have to be rearticulated in such a way that the system becomes responsive to an outside, a possibility that it has not yet made its own. I think such a notion resonates well with Gadamer's pull of otherness (1975). Rorty's edifying discourse (1989), and Gergen's (1978) generative theory.

From an applied perspective this would entail both an enrichment of the existing language of the organization to open a view onto a world which cannot be denied and the development of systems that foster the maintenance of difference. Because of the need for constant negotiation of identities, knowledge, social order, and policies in chaotic organizations, members are left with a choice between increasing control and attempting to simplify, or increasing coordination activities and complexifying. Many diversity programs, participation plans, and "partnering" arrangements have potential for increased coordination and complexification, but are often hampered by control systems and strategic enactments. If organizations are to increase productivity and meet the needs of people, they must work in the other direction. Thinking through the organization in communication terms helps considerably with this. If as much time and energy were put into negotiation, collaboration, and coordination programs as have been put into information technologies, much progress would be possible.

Summary

This essay has been by necessity a gloss of a complex set of positions that together suggest a new perspective on organizational communication studies. At root is both a more fundamental sense of what corporate organizations are and do and a richer exploration of communication than have traditionally been considered. Corporate organizations are central institutions in contemporary life making important developmental decisions for individuals and society as a whole. While they are in this sense political to the core, we have not done enough to understand how this politics works or to explore its relation to democracy. Using a communicational mode of analysis focusing on representational practices enables a sensitive analysis of the multiple forms of power and domination as they exist in corporate sites. While only the broadest outline of issues is present here, such an understanding can lead researchers to engage in projects that foster corporate practices that lead to decisions that are less wasteful of resources and more fully accomplish the goals of the variety of stakeholders.

Notes

1. This does not suggest that everything is communication, hence nothing can be meaningfully said about it. Simply, among other ways, everything can be seen in an interesting fashion if asked how does it function in a representational practice.

2. Traditional is used here in the same restricted sense that it is used in most organizational research literatures. It references the general assumed patterns of work processes in the period immediately preceding industrialization in Europe and the United States. Chaos refers to a variety of current management science literatures. Most of which were made popular in Peters' (1987) treatment of chaos. It has only a weak but symbolically important family resemblance to chaos theory proper.

3. For me the historical issue is not of special relevance, though is does parallel Foucault's (1970) much more detailed account. The idea of "simulacra" is heuristic whether it arose at a particular point, has always existed, or is a useful conceptual fiction.

4. We may now question this based on nature's nasty reintrusion as in the effects of global warming, depleted ozone, and so forth. But the faith in the various orders of simulacra is that enough control, enough domination of these now "unnatural" intrusions can lead to a world reproduced in one's image. That is the kind of Disneyworld—a hyper-reality—the world better than nature could have been that is dominant throughout the modern into the postmodern period (Eco 1986).

5. Practical consciousness was critical to nonindustrial work processes. While the integration provided through dominant values, routine practices, and common sense supported a variety of institutional authorities and a sense of order, life itself was filled with tragedies, hardships, and shifts of fortune. Work itself generally resulted in a direct and knowable product, a product of one's own activity. Since language and other practices related to an immediate world which appeared directly before people as self-evident, reflective recon-

sideration of these practices was minimal. While in retrospect we would see these representations as constitutive and value-laden, few had any reason to doubt that which was practical and at hand. Enlightenment science would of course shatter this basic faith and essentially lead to a public reconsideration of each seemingly personal and universal perception. The social structure and work processes to follow would further challenge the organic unity of traditional life.

6. Baudrillard's work has been criticized in that he appears to destroy the difference between the sign and what the sign represents. Clark (1988), for example, claimed that Baudrillard is unable to distinguish the food from the menu, the materiality of objects as signs from the materiality of language texts as signs. More properly, Baudrillard would claim that he is drawing attention to the way modern people confuse the two. Modern society does not so much have better food in its great restaurants, but has mastered the ability to mass reproduce the symbols and appearance of great restaurants' presentation of food.

7. Ideological critique has been much criticized (see Deetz in press a). The following are some of the more common objections. Many studies are elitist to the extent that they appear to imply that the intellectual can better know the "objective" needs or interests of people than those who have more direct experiences. Equally problematic, other studies suggest that acting individuals under the proper conditions can know their own interest. Such a position proclaims a return of the centered, humanist subject that has been shown as an illusion and is a central component of most systems of domination by consent. Other analyses appear to advance a conspiratorial theory in suggesting a dominant group uses intentional strategies to maintain control (Abercrombie et al. 1980). And most analyses give a negative account of power and privilege a particular Western form of reason. Underlying all of these objections is the rejection of the faith in a potentially knowable world, a set of real conditions, or utopian society to which to compare the present circumstances. Unfortunately, the various French authors who are often the source of such objections have rarely considered the workplace. And, only a handful of organizational researchers have borrowed on these to produce a deconstruction or postmodern account of corporate practices (see Bergquist 1993; Cooper and Burrell 1988; Knights and Morgan 1991; Martin 1990; Smircick and Calás 1987). Drawing on various French theorists such as Baudrillard, Bourdieu, and Foucault can help in constructing a communication perspective which can consider and engage in the politics of the workplace without the limitations often associated with ideological critique and the values implied therein.

8. It is not my intent here to report on my ongoing study of this high-tech organization. The point of this essay is to describe a theoretical perspective for analysis rather than to conduct an analysis. Certainly some of my experiences

at this site have influenced my theoretical choices. But at this point I only wish to use a few casual illustrations from this site to aid understanding.

References

Abercrombie, N., S. Hill, and B. Turner. 1980. *The dominant ideology thesis.* London: Allen and Unwin.

Althusser, L. 1971. Ideology and ideological state apparatuses. In *Lenin and philosophy and other essays,* trans. Ben Brewster. London: New Left Books.

Alvesson, M. 1987a. *Organizational theory and technocratic consciousness: Rationality, ideology, and quality of work.* New York: de Gruyter.

———. 1987b. Organizations, culture and ideology. *International Studies of Management and Organizations* 17:4–18.

———. 1993. Cultural-ideological modes of management control. In *Communication Yearbook 16,* ed. S. Deetz. Newbury Park, CA: Sage.

Alvesson, M., and H. Willmott. (eds.). 1992. *Critical management studies.* London: Sage.

Argyris, C. 1986. Skilled incompetence. *Harvard Business Review,* September-October, 74–79.

Bagdikian, B. 1990. *The media monopoly.* 3rd ed. Boston: Beacon Press.

Barthes, R. 1972. *Mythologies.* New York: Hill & Wang.

Baudrillard, J. 1975. *The mirror of production,* trans. M. Poster. St. Louis: Telos Press.

———. 1983a. *Simulations.* New York: Semiotext(e).

———. 1983b. *In the shadow of the silent majorities.* New York: Semiotext(e).

———. 1987. *Forget Foucault.* New York: Semiotext(e).

Bergquist, C. 1983. *Postmodern organization.* San Francisco: Jossey-Bass.

Boland, R. 1987. The in-formation of information systems. In *Critical issues in information systems,* ed. R. Boland and R. Hirscheim. New York: Wiley.

Bourdieu, P. 1977. *Outline of a theory of practice.* Cambridge: Cambridge University Press.

———. 1984. *Distinction: A social critique of the judgment of taste,* trans. R. Nice. Cambridge, MA: Harvard University Press.

———. 1990. *The logic of practice,* trans. R. Nice. Stanford, CA: Stanford University Press.

Bullis, C., and P. Tomkins. 1989. The forest ranger revisited: A study in control practices and identification. *Communication Monographs* 56:287–306.

Burawoy, M. 1979. *Manufacturing consent.* Berkeley: University of California Press.

Burrell, G. 1988. Modernism, post modernism and organizational analysis 2: The contribution of Michel Foucault. *Organization Studies* 9:221–35.

Clark, J. 1988. Enter the cybernauts: Problems in post-modernism. *Communication* 10:383–401.

Clegg, S. 1989. *Frameworks of power.* Newbury Park, CA: Sage.

———. 1990. *Modern organizations.* London: Sage.

Cooper, R., and G. Burrell. 1988. Modernism, postmodernism and organizational analysis. *Organization Studies* 9:91–112.

Coward, R., and J. Ellis. 1977. *Language and materialism.* London: Routledge & Kegan Paul.

Cushman, D. 1991. *High speed management.* Albany: SUNY Press.

Czarniawska-Joeges, B., and G. Kunda. 1992. Socialization into modernity: On organizational acculturation in infantocracies. Lund, Sweden: Institute of Economic Research.

Deetz, S. 1978. Conceptualizing human understanding: Gadamer's hermeneutics and American communication research. *Communication Quarterly* 26:12–23.

———. 1990. Reclaiming the subject matter as a guide to mutual understanding: Effectiveness and ethics in interpersonal interaction. *Communication Quarterly* 38:226–43.

———. 1992. *Democracy in an age of corporate colonization: Developments in communication and the politics of everyday life.* Albany: SUNY Press.

———. 1994. The future of the discipline: The challenges, the research, and the social contribution. In *Communication Yearbook 17,* ed. S. Deetz. Newbury Park, CA: Sage.

———. In press a. The new politics of the workplace: Unobtrusive control and the construction of identity. In *Ideological critique and beyond: Cultural studies in a postmodern age.* ed. H. Simon and M. Billig. Newbury Park, CA: Sage.

———. In press b. The micro-politics of identity formation in the workplace: The case of a knowledge intensive firm. *Human Studies.*

Deetz, S., and D. Mumby. 1985. Metaphors, information, and power. *Information and Behavior* 1:369–86.

————. 1990. Power, discourse and the workplace: Reclaiming the critical tradition. In *Communication Yearbook 13,* ed. J. Anderson. Newbury Park, CA: Sage.

Douglas, M. 1986. *How institutions think.* Syracuse, NY: Syracuse University Press.

Eco, U. 1986. *Travels in hyper-reality.* New York: Harcourt Brace Jovanovich.

————. 1989. *The open work.* Cambridge, MA: Harvard University Press.

Edwards, R. 1979. *Contested terrain: The transformation of the workplace in the twentieth century.* New York: Basic Books.

Epstein, C. 1988. *Deceptive distinctions.* New Haven: Yale University Press.

Etzioni, A. 1961. *A comparative analysis of complex organizations.* New York: Free Press.

Fischer, F. 1990. *Technology and the politics of expertise.* Newbury Park, CA: Sage.

Foucault, M. 1970. *The order of things.* New York: Random House.

————. 1977. *Discipline and punishment,* trans. A. Sheridan. New York: Random House.

————. 1988. *Technologies of the self,* ed. L. Martin, H. Gutman, and P. Hutton. Amherst: University of Massachusetts Press.

Gadamer, H. G. 1975. *Truth and method,* ed. and trans. G. Barden and J. Cumming. New York: Seabury Press.

Geertz, C. 1973. *The interpretation of culture.* New York: Basic Books.

Gergen, K. 1978. Toward generative theory. *Journal of Personality and Social Psychology* 31:1344–60.

————. 1991. *The saturated self.* New York: Basic Books.

Giddens, A. 1984. *The constitution of society.* Cambridge: Polity Press.

————. 1991. *Modernity and self-identity: Self and society in the late modern age.* Stanford: Stanford University Press.

Gortz, A. 1987. *Critique of economic reason,* trans. G. Handyside and C. Turner. London: Verso.

Gramsci, A. 1971. *Selections from the prison notebooks,* trans. Q. Hoare and G. Nowell Smith. New York: International.

Habermas, J. 1971. *Knowledge and human interests,* trans. J. Shapiro. Boston: Beacon Press.

————. 1975. *Legitimation crises,* trans. T. McCarthy. Boston: Beacon Press.

————. 1979. *Communication and the evolution of society,* trans. T. McCarthy. Boston: Beacon.

———. 1984. *The theory of communicative action.* Vol. 1: *Reason and the rationalization of society,* trans. T. McCarthy. Boston: Beacon Press.

———. 1987. *The theory of communicative action.* Vol. 2: *Lifeworld and system,* trans. T. McCarthy. Boston: Beacon Press.

Hall, S. 1977. Culture, media, and the "ideological effect." In *Mass communication and society,* ed. J. Curran et al. London: Edward Arnold.

———. 1989. Ideology and communication theory. In *Rethinking communication I: Paradigm dialogues,* ed. B. Dervin, L. Grossberg, B. O'Keefe, and E. Wartella. Newbury Park, CA: Sage.

Harré, R. ed. 1986. *The social construction of emotions.* Cambridge, MA: Blackwell.

Harré, R. and P. Secord. 1972. *The explanation of social behavior.* Totow, NJ: Rowman & Littlefield.

Hochschild, A. 1983. The managed heart: Commercialization of human feelings. Berkeley: University of California Press.

Hollway, W. 1984. Fitting work: Psychological assessment in organizations. In *Changing the subject,* eds. J. Henriques, W. Hollway, C. Urwin, C. Venn, and V. Walkerdine. New York: Methuen.

Hopwood, A. 1987. The archaeology of accounting systems. *Accounting, Organizations and Society* 12:207–34.

Jackell, R. 1988. *Moral mazes: The world of corporate managers.* Oxford: Oxford University Press.

Knights, D., and G. Morgan. 1991. Corporate strategy, organizations, and subjectivity: A critique. *Organization Studies* 12:251–73.

Kunda, G. 1992. *Engineering culture: Control and commitment in a high-tech corporation.* Philadelphia: Temple University Press.

Laclau, E., and C. Mouffe. 1985. *Hegemony and socialist strategy,* trans. W. Moore and P. Cammack. London: Verso.

Laughlin, R. C. 1987. Accounting systems in organizational contexts: A case for critical theory. *Accounting, Organizations, and Society* 12:479–502.

Lazega, E. 1992. *Micropolitics of knowledge: Communication and indirect control in workgroups.* New York: de Gruyter.

Martin, J. 1990. Deconstructing organizational taboos: The suppression of gender conflict in organizations. *Organization Science* 1:339–59.

Martin, J. 1993. *Culture in organizations: Three perspectives.* Oxford: Oxford University Press.

Maturana, H., and F. Varela. 1980. *Autopoiesis and cognition: The realization of living.* London: Reidl.

Merleau-Ponty, M. 1962. *Phenomenology of perception*, trans. C. Smith. London: Routledge & Kegan Paul.

Mumby, D. K. 1987. The political function of narratives in organizations. *Communication Monographs* 54:113–27.

———. 1988. *Communication and power in organizations: Discourse, ideology, and domination.* Norwood, NJ: Ablex.

Narveson, J. 1992. Democracy and economic rights. *Social Philosophy and Policy* 9:29–61.

Peters, T. 1989. *Thriving on chaos: Handbook for a managerial revolution.* New York: Knopf.

Power, M. 1992. *After calculation? Reflections on Critique of Economic Reason by André Gor.*

Ramos, A. G. 1981. *The new science of organizations.* Toronto: University of Toronto Press.

Rorty, R. 1989. *Contingency, irony and solidarity.* Cambridge: Cambridge University Press.

Schiller, H. 1989. *Culture, Inc.: The corporate takeover of public expression.* Oxford: Oxford University Press.

Schmookler, A. 1992. *Illusion of choice: How the market economy shapes our destiny.* Albany: SUNY Press.

Simon, H. 1957. *Administrative behavior.* New York: Free Press.

Simonds, A. 1989. Ideological domination and the political information market. *Theory and Society* 18:181–211.

Skillman, G. 1991. Efficiency vs. control: A strategic bargaining analysis of capitalist production. *Review of Radical Political Economics* 23:12–21.

Sless, D. 1988. Forms of control. *Australian Journal of Communication* 14:57–69.

Smircich, L., and M. Calás. 1987. Organizational culture: A critical assessment. In *Handbook of organizational communication*, ed. F. Jablin, L. Putnam, K. Roberts, and L. Porter. Newbury Park, CA: Sage.

Storey, J. 1983. *Managerial prerogative and the question of control.* London: Routledge & Kegan Paul.

Therborn, G. 1980. *The power of ideology and the ideology of power.* London: Verso.

Valas, P. 1993. *Power in the workplace: The politics of production at AT&T.* Albany: SUNY Press.

Weedon, C. 1987. *Feminist practice and poststructuralist theory.* Oxford: Blackwell.

ELIZABETH J. NATALLE
MICHAEL J. PAPA
ELIZABETH E. GRAHAM

10 Feminist Philosophy and the Transformation of Organizational Communication

The purpose of this chapter is to examine how women are changing organizations through communication strategies embedded in feminist philosophy. Specifically, we will analyze the contributions offered by liberal, radical, and materialist feminisms for the transformation of organizations. The uniqueness of the present approach is not simply to determine the individual contributions of each feminist perspective, but rather to suggest how these feminisms, working in concert, can change the manner in which men and women work together.

The current status of women in organizations

During the last three decades there has been a remarkable transformation in the numbers and roles of women in the workplace. Indeed, whereas in 1960 only 28 percent of the U.S. labor force was comprised of women, today women comprise 45 percent of all U.S. workers (U.S. Department of Labor 1991). Furthermore, women have successfully torn down many of the barriers that once limited their entrance into a broad range of occupations. For example, women now work at positions that were once exclusively male domains such as financial management, computer programming, labor relations, construction, automobile manufacturing, and government office (Salzman 1991). Finally, not only do women occupy CEO positions in large corporations, but over 3 million women started their own businesses in 1990 (Salzman 1991).

Despite the significant gains that have been made during the last thirty years, the political environment of the American workplace is still unresponsive to women in many respects. First, although women have successfully entered a broad range of occupational specialties, over 60 percent of women are mired in low-paying clerical, sales, or service positions (U.S. Department of Labor 1991). Unfortunately, many men justify closing certain positions to women. In fact, when one male service supervisor was recently asked why no women worked in his department as an automobile service technician, he responded, "I've never interviewed a competent women applicant. Those I've interviewed are not capable for the job. They are not strong physically" (Fleming 1991, 32). Second, while many women own their own companies as well as occupy the position of president or CEO in some organizations, in 1989 only three women were in the position of CEO of a Fortune 500 company (Baker 1991).

The advancement barriers women still face in U.S. organizations have not gone unnoticed by the federal government. In 1991, Labor Secretary Lynn Martin issued a report dubbed "the glass ceiling initiative" that addressed gender discrimination at executive levels in U.S. companies (Salzman 1991). As a concept, the "glass ceiling" is a metaphor for the unseen barriers that keep women from rising any further than general management positions in corporations. Morrison, White, and Van Velsnor (1987) contend that the glass ceiling applies to women as a group and that the barriers to advancement have nothing to do with lack of skill and everything to do with the fact that the candidate is a woman. Statistics support the glass ceiling effect. According to the U.S. Bureau of the Census (1980), 31 percent of the managers in U.S. organizations were female. However, most of these women are trapped in low-level or dead-end middle management positions (Baker 1991). Indeed, recent estimates indicate that only 3 percent of top executive positions at the largest U.S. companies are held by women (Salzman 1991).

Not only are women restricted from top management positions, when they work alongside men, they are often paid less for performing the same job. Overall, the most recent estimates from the U.S. Department of Labor indicate that women earn 72 cents for every dollar a man takes home (U.S. Department of Labor 1991). Furthermore, consider the average weekly earnings reported for men and women in specific positions: (a) computer programmers—men $691, women $573; (b) financial managers—men $837, women $558; (c) lawyers and judges—men $1,184, women $834, (d) managers (marketing, advertising, public relations)—men $902, women $616, (e) sales jobs—men $505, women $292, and (f) teachers (college and university)—men $808, women $620 (U.S. Department of Labor 1991). Although career advancement and pay equity are critical issues facing women today, there are also other important concerns about the work environment that need to be addressed. In 1990, 58.2 percent of mothers with children under the age of six were in the labor force (Veum and Gleason 1991). However, these working women face two major obstacles. First, a recent survey by the Bureau of Labor Statistics indicates that only 11 percent of workers had the choice of flexible work schedules to accommodate parents who must care for sick children, attend school functions, and transport children to and from after school activities (Hyland 1990). Second, as of 1989 only 5 percent of medium and large establishments offered childcare assistance (Hyland 1990). When parents attempt to seek out private childcare centers, problems also occur. The House of Representatives Committee on Education and Labor observed in 1988 that "unless a major effort is launched, the demand for childcare will continue to increase more rapidly than the supply" (House of Representatives Committee on Education and Labor 1988, 4). As evidence of the problem facing many parents, New York City officials reported that there are 250,000 children in the city under age five who are competing for 44,000 licensed day care slots (House of Representatives Committee on Education and Labor 1988).

With fertility rates up by 10.5 percent between 1985 and 1990, not only are childcare issues important, so is the issue of parental leave (Bernstein 1991; Salzman 1991). Parental leave refers to "time off, either paid or unpaid, for employees to care for newborn or newly adopted children" (Hyland 1990). However, in 1989 unpaid maternity leave was available to only 37 percent of full-time workers in medium and large private establishments, while unpaid paternity leave was available to only 18 percent of full-time workers. Even the family leave bill signed by President Clinton, which went into effect in August of 1993, only covers people who are employed by companies with 50 or more employees, which is about 40 percent of the American work force (Greensboro News & Record 1993). Paid leave will still be difficult to obtain since there is no provision for compensation in the family leave bill. Compare the situation facing U.S. parents to families in Sweden. The Child Care Act of 1978 permits Swedish workers to take up to twelve months of leave to care for their children. According to the plan, parental leave can be divided between both parents "and can be taken in full days or in partial-day increments until the child reaches age 8. While on paternal leave, employees are paid 90% of pay for nine months and a flat rate for the remaining three months" (Meisenheimer 1989, 23).

The final major problem that women face in U.S. corporations is viewed by many as the most disturbing, namely, sexual harassment. The harassment women experience ranges from sexually oriented activities that create a hostile or offensive working environment (e.g., comments about a woman's physical appearance that are sexually oriented) to demands for sexual favors in exchange for economic considerations such as promotions, raises, or continued employment with a firm. The extensiveness of the harassment problem was substantiated in a recent survey by the National Association for Female Executives that found that 53 percent of the 1,300 respondents were sexually harassed or knew someone that was (cited in Galen 1991). Furthermore, in the 1992 *Working Woman* Sexual Harassment Survey, 60 percent of 9,000 respondents reported being personally harassed, and over one-third knew a co-worker who had been harassed (Sandroff 1992).

The preceding examination of the working environment within U.S. corporations suggests that substantial changes are needed for women to achieve their fullest potential. Women must be given access to any position for which they are qualified and they should receive the same pay as their male counterparts. Organizations must also become more responsive to family-oriented issues such as child care and parental leave. Finally, sexual harassment must be attacked with a combination of federal and state statutes as well as corporate initiatives that protect women in the workplace.

The women's movement in the United States, in large part, has been responsible since the mid-1960s for providing women with the impetus to confront the issues that face them in organizations. Over the years a variety of strategies emanating from a wide range of feminist philosophies has assisted in the process of transforming organizations to become more responsive to the needs of women. Now let us examine how women are changing organizations through communication strategies embedded in feminist philosophy.

Feminism

Feminism as a theoretical perspective is a multiple rather than a singular concept. *Feminisms* is a more accurate approach and requires the delineation of the concept on a philosophical continuum. While there are many feminist perspectives that can be appropriately applied to the analysis of organizational process (Mills and Tancred 1992), we have selected three types of feminism, liberal, radical, and materialist, as *exemplars* of how organizations are changed when practical implementation follows each of the three philosophies. We recognize that feminist standpoint theory (Bullis 1993) and feminist deconstruction (Mumby 1993) are fruitful theoretical frameworks that enjoy current popularity among organizational theorists; however, our choice here is to take longstanding and familiar branches of feminist philosophy to demonstrate how theory has concrete, practical consequences in everyday life. To begin, we acquaint the reader with basic definitions.

Liberal feminism

The modern women's movement is premised on the philosophy of liberal feminism. This perspective argues that people are categorized on the basis of sex, and the balance of power rests with men. A patriarchal social structure emerges where women are the oppressed group. To shift the balance of power, liberal feminism argues for equal opportunity within the existing social structure.

In line with the democratic underpinnings of liberal feminism, the National Organization for Women (NOW) put forward an 8-point Bill of Rights in 1968 that served as a platform for equality in employment under constitutional law (Hole and Levine 1971). A central component of NOW's initial agenda was the passage of an Equal Rights Amendment (ERA), something that had not passed Congress since its first introduction in 1923. ERA was a response, from the beginning, to the discrimination faced by women workers in American organizations. Working within the legal system for equal rights is at the core of liberal feminism. The goal of such a strategy is equal valuation of the contributions of both women and men.

Radical feminism

While liberal feminism works within the established political system, radical feminism advocates the separation of women and men as a means of removing the oppressive power relationship. Women are viewed as autonomous beings with the right to self-regulation (e.g., reproductive rights). The inherent biological and constructed social differences between the sexes are emphasized, and radical feminism draws the conclusion that women are superior to men. Power is transferred to women and the understanding is that women can exist separate from the status quo. Radical lesbian feminism would be the extreme perspective here since the "woman-identified woman" (Radicalesbians 1972) would derive her economic, social, and physical actualization from a matriarchal kinship network. From an organizational perspective, all-women owned and operated businesses would exemplify a radical feminist approach.

Materialist feminism

This philosophical position derives its assumptions from Marxist and socialist theory. Whereas Marxism exclusively points to capitalism as the source of women's oppression, socialism takes a broader explanatory approach and includes the integration of race, class, and gender as equal agents in oppression. Materialist feminists believe that human nature is a product of social construction, thus gender is a complex composite that requires complete redefinition in order to eradicate oppression. The groups in power (e.g., wealthy Caucasian men) will ultimately have to be removed from power so that a redistribution of resources and power can be made to guarantee that all citizens will benefit from the economy. Interestingly, but ironically, materialist feminism pits democracy and capitalism against each other in an ideological debate that eludes easy resolution. We will address this debate again in the conclusion of the essay.

An important inference that can be drawn from the preceding discussion is that feminism recognizes the inequality of power in cross-sex communication relationships. This has a direct bearing on the relationship of gender and organizational process since power is a core variable in the study of organizations (Daniels and Spiker 1991; Dobos, Bahniuk, and Hill 1991; French and Raven 1959; Frost 1987; Kanter 1977; Mumby 1988; Pfeffer 1981; Richmond Davis, Saylor, and McCroskey 1984). If the organization of the twenty-first century must accommodate a demographically different workplace from the past 25–30 years, then feminism asks the heuristic question about how power will shift in the organization.

In the remainder of the essay, we want to address several intertwined issues that will help to answer the larger power question. First, how will transformation itself occur in organizations as a result of feminism? Second, how will communication processes implement change? Third, how will those changes assist in the shift of power? And finally, how must the deep structure (Mumby 1987) of the American organization change to accommodate the larger social transformation that will also occur?

Add women and transform: Liberal feminism

While the ERA has failed to pass in Congress, women have made significant inroads in their quest to become an equal partner in the corporation. Demographics alone show that women have enrolled in higher education in substantial numbers since the 1950s. Professional schools—law, medicine, business—have matriculated women in higher numbers than ever before in this country. Management and professional positions are filled with women because women are appropriately qualified to be hired (Schwartz 1989). Where equal opportunity failed, women took discrimination cases to the courts. Affirmative Action and Comparable Worth laws guarantee women both a place and a salary that puts women in square competition with male colleagues.

Liberal feminists have worked inordinately hard to protect the value of women workers, but as Borisoff and Merrill (1992) point out, the transformation of the organization has been impeded by conventional attitudes toward women's capabilities. Most women are employed in the 60 percent, a term used by the Labor Department to denote low-paying, dead-end jobs such as clerical and secretarial positions. Borisoff and Merrill would argue that women find themselves in the 60 percent in large part because *"women's conventional communication strengths have been used against them,* as an excuse for hiring women, and keeping them in positions where they are expected to smile, greet and serve others" (p. 91).

Women in management, who thought careers could be actualized at the highest levels of the corporation, are "hitting the wall" even after "breaking the glass ceiling" (Morrison et al. 1987, 139). While the United States was without a national family policy until President Clinton's signing of the 1993 family leave bill, Skrzycki (1990) reports that barriers to promotion do not revolve around daycare, dual careers, or family problems. Instead, climbing the corporate ladder is hampered by sex-role stereotyping, lack of career planning assistance, and corporations' unwillingness to put women in line positions.

The visibility of women in organizations has not resulted in the easy "add women and transform" formula that liberal feminism believed would work. The persuasion campaign to hire women has been fought out through the legal system in this country, and some of the fallout of government-mandated change has increased resentment from male

colleagues toward women. The amount of research on gender and conflict in organizational settings may have as much to do with the fact that
gender-related conflict is *there* as well as the realization that there may
be communication differences between women and men.

The concept of communication differences became apparent when
women entered management positions and conducted themselves in a
manner that did not always correspond to male behavior. Virginia
Schein's (1973, 1975) groundbreaking research found that middle-line
managers, both male and female, paired management traits with masculine traits significantly more than with feminine traits. The research
results suggested that men were more likely to be selected for management positions because they held the requisite management characteristics. Questions arose concerning whether women were capable of
exercising effective leadership if the stereotyped differences discovered
by Schein were true. Deux (1979) supported the different and inferior
mentality found by Schein in a study that examined self-evaluations
where men rated themselves more positively than women in performance, ability, intelligence, and job difficulty.

Much of the "gender-differences" research is framed by socialization theory. The differences are attributed to gender-typed life experiences where women are not socialized in the same way as men,
therefore women lack leadership skills. Maxine Dalton (1991), a consultant at the Center for Creative Leadership, argues that managers are
faced with three options given the implications of socialization research: (a) women managers should learn to communicate more like
men, (b) all managers should learn androgynous communication behaviors, or (c) women should continue to communicate as themselves
while increasing their participation in the management ranks. In our
estimation, none of these options is entirely satisfactory.

Women who tried the "dress for success" strategy (Molloy 1977)
and who followed the advice to "break the glass ceiling" by being
women but dressing and acting like men have not found success in the
organization. Not only do men resent women acting like men, women
themselves are often uncomfortable pretending to be someone they are
not. For those women who did adopt male behaviors, they now find
themselves characterized by male peers as "too hard-edged," "too aggressive," and "too shrill" (Mize 1992).

The option to learn how to be more androgynous has not fared
particularly well either. Androgyny, which Bem reintroduced in 1974
as the psychological internalization of both feminine and masculine
characteristics, has been a generally misunderstood concept by the lay
public. People associate androgyny with sexual preference, homosex-

uality, and androids. Unfortunately, this conceptual confusion has not assisted in the broadening of managers' communication repertoires.

Dalton's (1991) option for women to behave like themselves while increasing their participation in the management ranks has been embraced by liberal feminists because this strategy is perceived as the ideal way to work within the system yet still increase the value of women's contributions. This option is based on the perception that any differences in male and female communication behavior has no detrimental effect on management effectiveness. This perception, however, has not been borne out by real life circumstances.

Staley (1988) outlines a wide range of research showing mixed results concerning similarities and differences in male and female managers' communication. Staley concluded that women managers do have doubts about their own communicative power because of "cultural attitudes which lag behind current realities" (p. 42). When differences are confirmed, Staley finds evidence that the perception of difference contributes to the assessment of management *ineffectiveness*. Such a result is in direct opposition to what liberal feminists intend.

There are several problems with a liberal feminist approach to transforming organizations. Increasing the sheer numbers of women in the workplace has not solved problems of inequity, nor has the organizational climate for women become more supportive. Indeed, U.S. Department of Labor statistics (1991) cited earlier in this essay have shown a steady concentration of women in low-paying, dead-end jobs and very few in upper management or CEO positions. The balance of power in the American organization is still in the hands of Caucasian men, and Baker's (1991) report that in 1989 only three women held the rank of CEO in Fortune 500 companies is a depressing indicator of how few women hold the economic power that runs this country.

The communication climate for the average female employee is still "chilly" at best. Women's presence in the workplace has been greeted by an increasing amount of reported sexual harassment at all levels of the organization (Sandroff 1992). The shocking revelations of women (Fraser 1991; Fugh-Berman 1992) since the Clarence Thomas confirmation hearings have indicated that women who work alongside men do not receive the same valuation from either their co-workers or the organization. The "backlash" that Susan Falludi (1991) explicates in her book by the same name, is all about the ways in which liberal feminism's attempt to participate fully and equally in society has resulted in a negative reaction by most social institutions in the United States. The result is an attempt to put women in their place and to diffuse the progress of the women's movement.

A controversial, but realistic, criticism of women in management careers was Felice Schwartz's startling 1989 article in the *Harvard Business Review* which argued that it costs more to employ women because of maternity. The argument ran along these lines: The enduring difference (reproductive capability) is biological, but the socialization of people's attitudes toward maternity is what causes business problems and career derailment for women. In criticizing the glass ceiling concept, Schwartz makes a cogent, alternative case for why organizations keep women from advancing along with women's concomitant dropping out of the organization altogether: "The barriers to women's leadership occur when potentially counterproductive layers of influence on women—maternity, tradition, socialization—meet management strata pervaded by the largely unconscious preconceptions, stereotypes, and expectations of men. Such interfaces do not exist for men and tend to be impermeable for women" (p. 68). The result of these gender differences leads to the recognition of two types of career women: career-primary and career-and-family (the latter is also referred to as the "mommy-track"). Schwartz argues that in order to be productive these two types of women need different considerations from the organization. For Schwartz, the recognition of a changed demographic profile of the labor pool is a given, so in order to take advantage of women workers, *corporations* must respond by changing policies and employee attitudes.

Schwartz's thinking is in line with others who have not found the glass ceiling a satisfactory explanation for women's problems with career advancement. Mize (1992) argues that shattering the glass ceiling requires individual organizations to assess their own employees to find out what stereotypes operate as barriers to women's advancement. Through conducting research in her own company, Mize was able to debunk some of the old myths about women and men as leaders. She found that both women and men needed to work together on specific interpersonal communication competencies such as approval-seeking behavior and affiliation skills. Mize's conclusion: "Any plan for helping women to get promoted should include a developmental plan for men. And whatever the plan, make sure you base it on specific research" (p. 62).

Rosabeth Moss Kanter's research has consistently centered on the concept that opportunities for women's career advancement are created by the inherent quality of the organizational structure. In an early article, Kanter (1976) stated that the manner in which power was distributed in an organization had substantial influence on who received the rewards of organizational decision-making. Obviously, "sex is a very important determinant of who gets what in and out of organizations" (p. 34). Kanter illuminated some of the problems women face in organizations that are still relevant today. Using a structuralist model, Kanter discusses how women are a class without power who perform routine service while the men in viable leadership positions constitute the real power to reward themselves and shape the system as a whole. These separate organizational classes are marked not only by sex and power, but "each class may have its own internal hierarchy, political grouping and allegiances, interactional rules, ways of coming into contact with other classes, promotion rules, culture, and style, including demeanor and dress" (1976, 50). It is no wonder, then, that Kanter points toward conflict and tension in mixed-sex management groups. When a woman is the token in a group of men, both her formal and informal role behavior may be mistakenly attributed; uncertainty in communication may abound; isolation and invisibility could be imposed; and exercising real leadership over reluctant peers and subordinates may be extremely difficult.

Liberal feminists would argue that sixteen years after Kanter's observations, little has changed for women at any level of the organization. Communication channels are not open and neither female nor male employees are necessarily satisfied (Allen, Seibert, and Rush 1990). Radical feminism provides an alternative perspective for women to achieve success. In the next portion of the chapter, we will examine ways in which women have worked outside the status quo to transform organizational structure and communication networks to gain power for themselves.

Separate and superior transformation: Radical feminism

In 1990, over three million women started their own businesses (Salzman 1991). This astounding figure is evidence that women are no longer confined to traditional modes for employment and/or career advancement. The "self-made woman" is now just as realistic as the "self-made man," and more women are choosing independent avenues for success by creating their own organizations. Moore, Buttner, and Rosen (1992) report that entrepreneurship is a career alternative that has been initiated by women at three times the rate of men. In many ways, the radical feminist approach is a response to the failure of liberal feminism's strategy to infiltrate organizations with large numbers of women at the middle and upper levels of management. The motto of the independent business women could easily be, "If you can't join 'em, beat 'em!" Many women business owners are not only beating 'em, they are finding an economic and political autonomy that would not have been possible thirty years ago.

Women who own corporations do pay a certain price because they are outside the established power structure and communication networks that are traditionally associated with Fortune 500 companies. To compensate, women have established their own networks. DeWine (1983) defines professional networking as "a process of *linking people to each other as career resources;* and assisting, supporting, and helping others to find the resources they need" (p. 86). Inter-organizational networks often function like professional associations and provide a formal communication network for the membership. Intra-organizational networks are usually more informal and provide support for women at most levels of the organization. Additionally, there are media to support these networks such as magazines like *Working Woman* and *Women Entrepreneurs.*

Formal networks are numerous and accessible on local as well as national levels. For example, the Women's Caucus of the Speech Communication Association (SCA) provides its membership with a variety of benefits: research information through a newsletter and programs at the SCA annual convention; a political voice in SCA; names of other women in affiliated research areas; mentoring; and job information. In addition, within many metropolitan areas women's networks are available. The Women's Professional Forum (WPF) in Greensboro, North Carolina is one example of such a network. The WPF is a highly select group of women who may own their businesses, hold management positions in local corporations, practice law or medicine, or hold office in city, county, or state government. Membership is by sponsorship and the dues are moderately expensive. Meetings are held monthly with diverse program topics and speakers (e.g., Justice Sandra Day O'Connor and founding editor of *Working Woman* magazine, Kate Rand Lloyd, have been speakers). Business is done at the cocktail hour or over meals, and political power is bargained. When Harvey Gantt ran for the U.S. Senate in a highly publicized campaign against incumbent Jesse Helms in 1990, much of the money and political clout in support of Gantt came from women with ties to the Forum. The National Women's Political Caucus, in fact, often has a relationship with the same women who are active in business networks. Business women want political as well as economic power and are willing to contribute to the campaigns of political candidates who will make policy decisions in the interest of women.

Intra-organizational networks often function with less clout, but nevertheless, serve important communication purposes. At the University of North Carolina at Greensboro, for example, coauthor Natalle is a member of the twelve-year-old Association of Women Faculty and Administrative Staff (AWFAS). Even though AWFAS functions outside the political structure of the university, the organization has had a substantial influence on the quality of life for women in the university community. Concerns about the hiring of women, salary inequities, curriculum, student affairs, professional development, and promotion and tenure have all been discussed on the floor, and proposals are often communicated to the highest levels of the university. Informally, group cohesion is built through contacts made in other departments across the campus. A telephone call to another member of AWFAS for information or services results in an immediate response. Such a network assists in the smooth implementation of responsibility and substitutes as well or better than the old boy network.

These networks are numerous and operate all over the United States. DeWine (1983) documents the fact that hundreds of networks are operational, some more well known than others (e.g., 9 to 5, WICI, Business and Professional Women). The obvious common denominator in all these groups is the gender-exclusive membership profile. Men are not part of the group, nor is their participation intended. The separatist philosophy that undergirds these associations is linked to a goal to reverse the flow of power and resources (primarily information) in the organization. Women view these networks as necessary and effective. Men are often unaware of the existence of such networks, or they fear the possibilities of what such networks can accomplish.

Separatism in communication networks is only one aspect of a radical feminist approach to transforming organizations. Another area of great concern to radical feminists is leadership style. If liberal feminists recognized and celebrated differences in the management styles of women and men, then radical feminists are apt to argue that the differences that separate the genders place women in a superior position in the organization. Brenner, Tomkiewicz, and Schein (1989) replicated Schein's trait research done in 1973 and 1975. The results indicated that male managers still rate masculine and management traits together, while female managers showed no significant differences in their pairing of masculine, feminine, and management traits. The research team concluded that women do not sex-type and that "unlike her male counterpart, today's female manager would be expected to treat men and women equally in selection, promotion, and placement decisions" (p. 668).

Where does the notion come from that women are superior in their leadership communication behavior? While there is no direct evidence of a superior position, Carol Gilligan's (1982) research on women's moral development set the stage for feminists to claim female superiority in decision-making. Mary Belenky's (1986) subsequent research on women's epistemology added evidence to the separate and superior argument. While Gilligan and Belenky initially aimed to complement the research of Kohlberg (1984) and Perry (1970) with female samples, the results of the studies have been used to validate and argue for female leadership. Gilligan's (1982) feminine ethic of care describes women's moral decision-making as a result of one's responsibility to self and others where connections between people require communication in order to solve problems. The ethic of care has been pitted against the masculine ethic of justice where the protection of individual rights is considered within a hierarchy of moral values. Belenky (1986) and her research team concluded that women need not always construct knowledge in order to actualize the self. Subjective (intuitive) knowledge emerged as a legitimate and useful epistemology. Other researchers have used the idea of male and female models of behavior to describe management styles in particular, placing positive value on the feminine style and negative value on the masculine style.

Marilyn Loden (1985) has developed models of feminine and masculine leadership which she grounds in both sociocultural and biological explanation. Each of Loden's models contains five dimensions: operating style, organizational structure, basic objective, problem-solving style, and key characteristics. The masculine style is based on competition and uses hierarchy to organize people. The basic objective is to win and problems are solved rationally. Key characteristics of the masculine style include high control, strategic moves, less emotional interaction, and an analytical approach to business. Compare that to the feminine style where the bottom line is cooperation and people are organized in teams. The basic objective is quality output and problems are solved with a combination of intuitive and rational approaches. Key characteristics of the feminine style include lower control, empathy for employees, collaborative interaction, and an emphasis on high performance standards. While both styles get the job done, the communication involved is very different, and Loden argues for the feminine model.

A more recent example of the models approach is Sally Helgesen's *The Female Advantage* (1990). Like Gilligan and Belenky, Helgesen used prior research as the basis for asking her own questions, and in fact, Helgesen's subtitle, *Women's Ways of Leadership*, is a purposeful choice taken from Belenky's *Women's Ways of Knowing*. Using a case-study approach, Helgesen delineated characteristics of women's leadership to compare to Mintzberg's *The Nature of Managerial Work* (1973). Of the eight characteristics that describe management/leadership, only one—maintains outside networks—is comparable in both models. The differences in style are almost diametrically opposed. Men prefer an unrelenting pace with no breaks while women work at a steady pace with small scheduled breaks. Men view interruptions as a source of discontinuity and fragmentation while women do not see interruptions as a problem. Men's outside activities are work-related and part of the male view of identifying self through the job. Women see their identity as complex and multifaceted and engage in activities away from work that may or may not be related to the job. Men prefer interpersonal encounters and avoid the mail. While women also prefer interpersonal encounters, they schedule time to look at the mail. Men typically do not take time to reflect and plan long-term, but women focus on the ecology of leadership. Finally, men have difficulty sharing information while women schedule time to share information with employees. Helgesen concludes that women's qualities and approach to leadership will ultimately assist the workplace in creating a communication climate that is functional for *all* employees.

In a similar vein, Judy Rosener's recent article in the *Harvard Business Review* entitled "Ways Women Lead" (1990) chains onto the idea that there are gender-based models of leadership. Using results from a survey sponsored by the International Women's Forum, Rosener characterizes male leadership as "transactional," where the job is viewed as a series of transactions with subordinates performing in a command-and-control style. Female leadership is "interactive" because women "encourage participation, share power and information, enhance other people's self-worth, and get excited about their work" (p. 120). In contrast to Loden and Helgesen, Rosener clearly delineates the advantages and disadvantages of each style and concludes that the best style depends on the context of the organization. In addition, Rosener cautions organizations to expand their ideas of what effective leadership means in order to give women more opportunity to develop careers in management. This diversity argument is a softening of the radical view held by other writers, like Loden and Helgesen, who have widely influenced women through the popular press.

The superior position has also been questioned by social scientists. Eagly and Johnson (1990) conducted a meta-analysis of 162 studies in relation to four types of leadership style and gender. They concluded that our views of how women and men lead need revision. In actual organizational settings, women were more democratic, but not more interpersonal than men. Men were found to be more autocratic, but not more task oriented than women. Such findings challenge both the stereotypes we have formed and the conclusions we have drawn about management behavior. The radical feminist position itself is challenged by such compelling conclusions and the realization on the part of many people, including women in management positions, that a superiority argument is simply a tradeoff in hegemony. What radical feminists want is to shift the balance of power into the hands of women rather than sharing power. This is unrealistic to a certain extent because men and women need to function together in most organizations. Learning to coexist rather than dominate one another is a solution that most people would find reasonable.

What about the steady rise of women entrepreneurs? This is an area where the United States is likely to see substantial changes in the economic outlook for the future. As Moore, Buttner, and Rosen (1992) argue, it is an equal right for women to seek self-employment. These women, called New Moderns, will use the corporate environment as incubators for their own entrepreneurial development. If corporations will not allow women to advance, then women who want to develop a career will use resources in established settings to learn how to do it on their own. Even given the barriers facing women entrepreneurs, such as restrictive credit laws and limited access to start-up capital, networks are providing the New Moderns with the information and resources necessary to be successful. In this sense, the radical feminist position to work outside the status quo not only can be implemented, as the statistics indicate, but these women may influence the nature of the typical organization in dramatic and powerful ways.

Redefinition and transformation: Materialist feminism

We come now to the implementation of materialist feminism in the workplace. With its integration of race, class, and gender as a framework for inquiry, materialist feminism is considered by many to be on the cutting edge of feminist philosophy. There are interesting and contradictory applications that can be made to organizational theory and practice. In reality, very little actual research in organizational communication is being done from a materialist feminist perspective, however this philosophy has the potential to guide and transform the organization in the face of a multicultural world.

One of the most important corporate buzzwords for the 1990s is "managing diversity." Business schools and business periodicals are training management in how to incorporate employees with very different demographic profiles than the all-male, largely Caucasian work force of previous decades. Materialist feminists applaud the attention to diversity while recognizing that the demographic changes in the employee profile are not easy for companies to accommodate. Nevertheless, the absorption of women and racial minorities will have profound effects on the culture of the organization and, ultimately, the structure of the organization.

Fortune magazine author Joel Dreyfuss focuses on the essence of managing diversity: "To survive population shifts and to prosper amid them, companies are training workers to be more tolerant of language and cultural differences, to identify and reject any racial and sexual prejudices, and to be more accommodating to the handicapped" (1990, 165, 168). Companies like Xerox, Avon, Hewlett-Packard, and AT&T are serving as models for how to put together a successful plan. Included in their programs are hiring guidelines to attract a variety of qualified workers, training and development of employees, and retention benefits including childcare and access to professional networks. From the perspective of the popular press this all sounds well and good. The corporation of the twenty-first century will reflect the melting pot that this country has always claimed to be, but from a materialist feminist perspective the integration of race, class, and gender needs to be more than a sophisticated Affirmative Action program. If Dreyfuss (1990) is taken at his word, then the transformation of language, the rejection of prejudice, and cultural tolerance are absolutely necessary to the success of the work environment.

In the organizational literature, radical humanism and radical structuralism articulate a materialist feminist voice. Radical humanists argue that the organization oppresses women and minorities because of the language and meaning inherent in the system (Burrell and Morgan 1979). Sexual harassment or racial prejudice would be a result of language that dehumanizes people. Language subsequently influences our attitudes and perpetuates oppression that can be attributed to power differentials and other inequalities inherent in the organization's structure. Segregation of jobs by sex or race denies employees access to information and subsequent career advancement. This is the argument made earlier by Rosabeth Moss Kanter (1976) in regard to gender, but is now being expanded in the 1990s to include other minorities, thus a multicultural framework emerges to study communication process in the organization.

Marlene Fine (1990, 1991) is studying the impact of cultural diversity on organizational communication processes. She is particularly interested in how employees from diverse backgrounds "can create organizations in which each of their voices is heard and respected and all of their voices work together productively" (1991, 260). Since current organizational theory provides no means for creating multicultural communication, Fine (1991) proposes a two part framework, based in feminist theory, which includes two processes: (a) resisting privileged discourse, and (b) creating harmonic discourses. To create harmonic discourse is to first recognize language differences and then to integrate those differences together for the good of the group.

Fine's conceptualization of harmonic discourse is in line with the socialist underpinnings of materialist feminism and radical humanism. Not all researchers would agree, however, that decentralizing power and group participation are the wave of the future. McCallister and Gaymon (1989) found that subjects responding to a questionnaire assessing goals and values of young workers/managers were not interested in becoming part of the American corporation. Over a third of the female subjects desired to become a CEO of their *own* company rather than work within someone else's company. The study concluded that the managers of the next century are not necessarily interested in the general goal model of organizations, rather they are looking for a construct model to account for individual interests. In the face of multiculturalism, the findings of studies such as this one could play out in two ways. Workers who are not committed to the organization may see cultural diversity as a burden to individual success and may choose to leave the organization as soon as possible. On the other hand, organizations that attend to the needs of individuals may produce harmony and a work environment that challenges the employee in regard to variety and diversity in the job—something that the males in the McCallister and Gaymon (1989) study reported was lacking in their jobs. Either way, the organization of the next century may be compelled to transform its structure to retain *any* employees.

If materialist feminism, through cultural diversity, is implemented in the organization, then we may see the solution to many problems faced by women. Pay inequity, barriers to career advancement, sexual harassment, daycare needs, and parental leave problems should all be addressed. A completely transformed organization could result in the sharing of power and tangible resources that materialist feminism desires. If cultural diversity, however, is nothing more than 1990s jargon for Affirmative Action, then progress will continue at the current pace, and feminists will be disappointed.

Discussion

A meaningful transformation in organizational structure and communication is only possible through the integrated efforts of liberal, radical, and materialist feminists. The reason we are taking this stance is that each feminist perspective contains weaknesses that limit its ability to contribute to substantive changes in the way organizations operate. However, *collectively*, the three feminist perspectives build upon one another in ways that can transform corporations from male-dominated enclaves to institutions in which women and men have an equal stake in directing organizational processes and controlling outcomes. First, let us briefly consider the weaknesses associated with each feminist perspective.

Although liberal feminists have been largely responsible for many of the advances made by women in U.S. corporations, there are limits to this approach to organizational transformation. In working through the established political system, liberal feminists face the insurmountable hurdle of persuading wealthy Caucasian men to surrender some of their power in the name of equality. Certainly Affirmative Action programs have been somewhat successful in eroding the "white-male power base," but men have only been willing to cede some of their power. Thus, women continue to confront the glass ceiling since men will only allow a certain number of women to advance in the corporation, and their progress will be halted at the middle management rank. Unfortunately, the liberal feminist approach has allowed men to drag their heels when it comes to meaningful change with respect to women. Quick, substantive change is rare and when it does occur it is usually linked to the threat of a law suit.

Radical feminism attempts to more directly confront the white-male power structure. By establishing all-women owned and operated businesses, radical feminists give women the opportunity to work outside the male-dominated power structure that exists in most U.S. corporations. However, the radical nature of this approach is also its greatest weakness. Most Americans would be unwilling to consider the separation of men and women in organizational life in order to promote equality. In addition, although corporate leaders have perpetuated a system of male domination in this country, it is not likely that radical feminists will be able to replace that system with one that argues for women's superiority over men. Ultimately, any philosophical system that promotes the dominance of one group over the other is doomed to failure.

The materialist feminist approach is limited by the fact that its ultimate success is based on the transformation of capitalist society. Capitalism is based on the premise of market competition. Those people and institutions that are the most powerful and operate with the greatest efficiency are those that succeed. Consistent with Darwin's principle of the survival of the fittest, the strongest always rise to the top. However, for the materialist perspective to work at transforming organizations, the principles of capitalism must be abandoned or at least radically altered.

As mentioned earlier in the essay, materialist feminism pits capitalism against democracy. Whereas a capitalist society is based on competition and domination, democracy is based on the principles of equality and opportunity. In the United States we have lived with the contradictions between capitalism and democracy for over two hundred years. Indeed, when this country was founded capitalist concerns for profit allowed landowners to possess and trade slaves. Today, capitalists allow women to be dominated in organizations under the guise of maintaining profits.

The contradictions that exist between capitalism and democracy are not easily resolved. However, the sort of societal transformation that would be required to implement materialist feminist philosophy in U.S. organizations is unlikely to happen. Radical societal change is neither easy nor quick, and too many Caucasian men, whose jobs place them in the highest government and corporate positions, have a vested interest in allowing business to proceed as usual.

Although each feminist perspective is limited with respect to producing organizational transformation, collectively the three feminist perspectives offer significant opportunities for change. First, liberal feminists will continue to appeal to those who believe that the American system ultimately supports equality. Flawed as it is, the U.S. capitalist democracy is supported by the majority of the American people. Thus, there will always be a place for a feminist movement that attempts to work within the system to bring about societal and organizational change.

Despite the appeal of the liberal feminist philosophy, it is limited. Women are growing increasingly frustrated by barriers that can only be removed by men in top corporate positions. This is where radical feminism offers some opportunities. As the radical feminist movement continues to grow, all-women organizations will begin to penetrate markets that have been traditionally captured by male-dominated organizations. When male corporate leaders begin to suffer a decline in profits, they may be willing to listen to the feminists' demands for equal treatment and advancement opportunities in American organizations. Additionally, as women's communication networks continue to take information away from the old boy network, corporate power brokers will realize that women are serious about gaining access to communication channels and partaking in decision-making processes.

The arguments advanced by materialist feminists are also needed to promote organizational transformation. Materialist feminists need to point to the inherent contradictions that exist between capitalism and democracy. If only those in power (mostly Caucasian men) can create substantive change, what is their motivation to do so? Capitalism sustains a system of race, class, and gender oppression that cannot be tolerated in a democratic society. Thus, one goal of materialist feminism is to force capitalism to come to terms with the rights and freedoms Americans are supposed to have in a democratic society.

On an organizational level, corporate leaders need to be held accountable for their oppressive actions, and materialist feminism has been successful in pointing out the factors of oppression. Sexual discrimination, racial prejudice, segregation of jobs by race and gender, harassing language, and pro-male bias in the structure of the organization are all items on the agenda of materialist feminists that continue to be addressed. If Fine (1991) is correct in her assessment that multicultural (harmonious) discourse is the wave of the future, then language will have a powerful influence on the reconstruction of gender roles in society as a whole.

Exactly how would materialist feminists go about accomplishing organizational transformation? First, the materialist feminist does not focus solely on the oppression of women but on the oppression of all groups. Second, advocates of this perspective wish to create organizational "environments in which respect and caring undergird all relationships" (Bandarage 1991, 348). One way to create such an environment is to eliminate the language of oppression that dominates organizations and restricts any access to power by women, people of color, the disabled, and the poor. In addition, it will be necessary to eliminate the structural barriers that keep oppressed groups from exerting power in organizational settings.

The materialist feminist holds that mechanisms are needed to enable workers to organize across countries. As Bandarage (1991, 351) observed: "A specific global agenda on women's rights needs to be developed, focusing on economic and reproductive issues common to women across cultures. Property rights, training and education, equal wages, and worker's rights have to be included in an expanded definition of women's human right."

As committed as materialist feminists are to radical societal change, they are equally committed to nonviolence as a means of accomplishing their goals. Indeed, Bandarage (1991) explains that commitment to nonviolent methods of confrontation is one of the strengths of the women's movement. This does not solely imply passive resistance in the face of oppressors but rather an active power that requires creative confrontation. Unfortunately, if women continue to face violence and backlash in their attempts to assert power, they may eventually be driven to take up violence themselves.

More generally, feminists need to consider the "deep structure process through which certain organizational realities come to hold sway over competing world views" (Mumby 1987, 113). In most U.S. organizations these deep structure processes legitimate and sustain a system of white-male dominance. The only way to effectively alter a system that has historically oppressed women is to engage in a multipronged attack that attempts to alter the way men and women perceive one another in organizational roles. The combination of all three feminist perspectives constitutes just such an offensive.

Mumby (1987) explains that power is a double-edged phenomenon to the extent that "it serves not only as a means for domination, but also as the vehicle through which social actors can potentially liberate themselves from domination" (p. 117). As Mumby concludes, simply to be a human agent implies having power. Thus, all women possess some power in all organizations.

As women begin to gain and use their power, the deep structure rule system of the organization will change and with that social behavior will evolve. For example, corporations that hire women and subsequently groom women for upper management positions send the message that women are capable and effective as leaders. Women who hold those leadership positions take part in changing the rules as the feminization of the workplace occurs. The culture of the organization changes as women's interests are assimilated into the everyday social interaction of the group. Ultimately, what was once an organization based on male ideology will transform into an organization based on a male-female ideology. The stories will include women; the communication practices will represent women's language and style; and the interpersonal interaction will reflect equality of participation. As cultural diversity continues to be a concern, then the race, class, and gender of communicators will be agents to help destroy oppression rather than maintain it.

Women can transform organizational life, but only through the diverse efforts of each feminist perspective. Men have dominated women in organizational settings for centuries, so no single strategy can be effective at producing substantive change. The transformative capacity of the feminist movement is linked to the execution of integrated strategies that: (a) change the way women and men think, talk, and act toward one another; and (b) promote true equality between men and women in the workplace.

References

Allen, M. W., J. H. Seibert, and R. R. Rush. 1990. Gender differences in perceptions of work limited access to decision-making power and supervisory support. *Women's Studies in Communication* 13(2): 1–20.

Baker, M. A. 1991. Reciprocal accommodation: A model for reducing gender bias in managerial communication. *Journal of Business Communication* 28:113–30.

Bandarage, A. 1991. In search of a new world order. *Women's Studies International Forum* 14:345–55.

Belenky, M. F., B. M. Clinchy, N. R. Goldberger, and J. M. Tarule. 1986. *Women's ways of knowing: The development of self, voice, and mind.* New York: Basic Books.

Bem, S. 1974. The measurement of psychological androgyny. *Journal of Consulting and Clinical Psychology* 42:155–62.

Bernstein, A. 1991. Do more babies mean fewer working women? *Business Week,* 5 August, 49–50.

Borisoff, D., and L. Merrill. 1992. *The power to communicate: Gender differences as barriers.* 2nd ed. Prospect Heights, IL: Waveland.

Brenner, O. C., J. Tomkiewicz, and V. E. Schein. 1989. The relationship between sex role stereotypes and requisite management characteristics revisited. *Academy of Management Journal* 32:662–69.

Bullis, C. 1993. Organizational socialization research: Enabling, constraining, and shifting perspectives. *Communication Monographs* 60:10–17.

Burrell, G., and G. Morgan. 1979. *Sociological paradigms and organizational analysis.* London: Heinemann Educational Books.

Dalton, M. 1991. *Gender differences in management style: What difference does it make?* Paper presented at Greensboro College, Greensboro, NC, October 1991.

Daniels, T. D., and B. K. Spiker. 1991. *Perspectives on organizational communication.* 2nd ed. Dubuque, IA: Wm. C. Brown.

DeWine, S. 1983. Breakthrough: Making it happen with women's networks. In *Women in organizations: Barriers and breakthroughs,* ed. J. J. Pilotta. Prospect Heights, IL: Waveland.

Dobos, J., M. H. Bahniuk, and S. E. K. Hill. 1991. Power-gaining communication strategies and career success. *The Southern Communication Journal* 57:35–58.

Dreyfuss, J. 1990. Get ready for the new work force. *Fortune*, 23 April, 165–81.

Eagly, A. H., and B. T. Johnson. 1990. Gender and leadership style: A meta analysis. *Psychological Bulletin* 108:233–56.

Falludi, S. 1991. *Backlash*. New York: Crown.

Fine, M. G. 1991. New voices in the workplace: Research directions in multicultural communication. *The Journal of Business Communication* 23:259–75.

Fine, M. G., F. L. Johnson, and M. S. Ryan. 1990. Cultural diversity in the workplace. *Public Personnel Management* 19:305–19.

Fleming, A. 1991. Back shop bias: Why aren't more women making a living tuning engines. *Automotive News*, 8 July, 32.

Fraser, L. 1991. The doctor's dilemma. *Vogue*, October, 306–11.

French, J. R. P., and B. Raven. 1959. The bases of social power. In *Studies in social power,* ed. D. Cartwright. Ann Arbor, MI: Institute for Social Research.

Fugh-Berman, A. 1992. Tales out of medical school. *The Nation,* 20 January, 1, 54–56.

Frost, P. J. 1987. Power, politics, and influence. In *Handbook of organizational communication: An interdisciplinary perspective,* ed. F. M. Jablin, L. L. Putnam, K. H. Roberts, and L. W. Porter. Newbury Park, CA: Sage

Galen, M. 1991. Sexual harassment: Out of the shadows. *Business Week,* 28 October, 30–31.

Gilligan, C. 1982. *In a different voice: Psychological theory and women's development.* Cambridge, MA: Harvard University Press.

Greensboro News & Record. 1993. Some questions and answers about the family leave bill. Feb. 6, 1993, A1.

Helgesen, S. 1990. *The female advantage: Women's ways of leadership.* New York: Doubleday.

Hole, J., and E. Levine. 1971. *Rebirth of feminism.* New York: Quadrangle.

House of Representatives Committee on Education and Labor. 1988. *Report on the Act for Better Child Care Services of 1988.* 100th Congress, 2nd Session, Report 100–985, Part I. Washington, DC: U.S. Government Printing Office.

Hyland, S. L. 1990. Helping employees with family care. *Monthly Labor Review,* September 22–26.

Kanter, R. M. 1976. Women and the structure of organizations: Explorations in theory and behavior. In *Another voice: Feminist perspectives on social life and social science,* ed. M. Millman and R. M. Kanter. New York: Octagon.

———. 1977. *Men and women of the corporation.* New York: Basic Books.

Kohlberg, L. 1984. *The psychology of moral development.* San Francisco: Harper & Row.

Loden, M. 1985. *Feminine leadership, or how to succeed in business without being one of the boys.* New York: Times Books.

McCallister, L., and D. L. Gaymon. 1989. Male and female managers in the 21st century: Will there be a difference? In *Beyond boundaries: Sex and gender diversity in communication,* ed. C. M. Lont and C. A. Friedley. Fairfax, VA: George Mason University Press.

Meisenheimer, J. R. 1989. Employer provisions for parental leave. *Monthly Labor Review,* October, 20–24.

Mills, A. J., and P. Tancred (eds.). 1992. *Gendering organizational analysis.* Newbury Park, CA: Sage.

Mintzberg, H. 1973. *The nature of managerial work.* New York: Harper & Row.

Mize, S. 1992. Shattering the glass ceiling. *Training & Development,* January, 60–62.

Molloy, J. T. 1977. *The women's dress for success book.* New York: Warner.

Moore, D. P., E. H. Buttner, and B. Rosen. 1992. Stepping off the corporate track: The entrepreneurial alternative. In. *Womanpower: Managing in times of demographic turbulence,* ed. U. Sekaran and F. T. L. Leong. Newbury Park, CA: Sage.

Morrison, A. M., R. P. White, and E. Van Velsnor. 1987. *Breaking the glass ceiling: Can women reach the top of America's largest corporations?* Reading, MA: Addision-Wesley.

Mumby, D. K. 1987. The political function of narrative in organizations. *Communication Monographs* 54:113–27.

———. 1988. *Communication and power in organizations: Discourse, ideology, and domination.* Norwood, NJ: Ablex.

———. 1993. Critical organizational communication studies: The next 10 years. *Communication Monographs* 60:18–25.

Perry, W. G. 1970. *Forms of intellectual and ethical development in the college years.* New York: Holt, Rinehart, & Winston.

Pfeffer, J. 1981. *Power in organizations.* Marshfield, MA: Pittman.

Radicalesbians. 1972. The woman-identified woman. In *Out of the closets: Voices of gay liberation,* ed. K. Jay and A. Young. New York: Douglas Books.

Richmond, V. P., L. M. Davis, K. Saylor, and J. McCroskey. 1984. Power strategies in organizations. *Human Communication Research* 11:85–108.

Rosener, J. B. 1990. Ways women lead. *Harvard Business Review* 68(6): 119–25.

Salzman, A. 1991. Trouble at the top. *U.S. News & World Report,* 17 June, 42–48.

Sandroff, R. 1992. Sexual harassment: The inside story. *Working Woman,* June, 47–51, 78.

Schein, V. E. 1973. The relationship between sex role stereotypes and requisite management characteristics. *Journal of Applied Psychology* 57:95–100.

———. 1975. Relationships between sex role stereotypes and requisite management characteristics among female managers. *Journal of Applied Psychology* 60:340–44.

Schwartz, F. N. 1989. Management women and the new facts of life. *Harvard Business Review* 67(1): 65–76.

Skrzycki, C. 1990. Female execs still hitting the 'glass ceiling.' *Greensboro News & Record,* 25 February, D1, D3.

Staley, C. C. 1988. The communicative power of women managers: Doubts, dilemmas, and management development programs. In *Women and communicative power: Theory, research, and practice,* ed. C. A. Valentine and N. Hoar. Annandale, VA: Speech Communication Association.

U.S. Bureau of the Census. 1980. Part 1, chapter D, section A, table 276.

U.S. Department of Labor. 1991. *Employment and Earnings* 38 (11). Washington, DC: U.S. Government Printing Office.

Veum, J. R., and P. M. Gleason. 1991. Child care: Arrangements and costs. *Monthly Labor Review,* October, 10–17.

MARSHALL SCOTT POOLE

11 *Afterword*

The early 1990s witness a new agenda for organizational communication research. While the late sixties ushered in a focus on pure rather than applied research and the early eighties a turn toward interpretive approaches, the early nineties seem to mark a shift in the fundamental questions facing organizational communication research. The contributions to this volume illustrate the diverse concerns and intellectual movements underlying this new agenda.

One set of forces driving this shift arises from global changes attending the dawn of the postindustrial era. The emerging global economy, rapid and accelerating growth in technology and knowledge, and major political upheavals are changing the nature of organizations and organizational communication. Most previous organizational communication research has been conducted in the relatively sheltered environment of stable industrial and governmental settings. However, such stability is no longer the norm, and a key problem for organizational communication theory and research is how to factor in change. This cannot be done simply by focusing on organizational change and innovation or by studying "process" (however defined), because we must deal with several different types of change. On one level, it is true that organizations must change to cope with the increased turbulence of their environments; innovation and the ability to adjust to shifting conditions have become imperatives in most organizational sectors. But at a more fundamental level, there is continuing change in the grounds of organizations—the technologies, structural configurations, and human resources which constitute organizations are evolving rapidly and new organizational forms are emerging. In addition, technological advances and environmental demands have also stimulated rapid change in the communication media. The nature of communication itself may be undergoing fundamental alterations due to the capacities of new communication media.

A second set of forces are the intellectual currents set up by two movements, one in the social theory and one in the natural sciences. For about twenty-five years social theory has been engaged in a prolonged self-critique centering on the problems of the postmodern era. Such enlightenment concepts as the individual, the possibility of truth, and scientific method have been challenged, and new critical perspectives have developed. The resulting positions offer a radically different conception of what organizational communication is and what it should be. On a different front, increasing attention is focused on powerful new systems theories from the natural and biological sciences, such as chaos theory, dissipative structures, and self-organizing systems theory (see the chapter by Contractor). These approaches promise to help address knotty problems facing quantitative research, such as the apparently unpredictable and chaotic nature of human behavior and sudden qualitative changes in behavior and social structure. To add to this ferment, the new social theories and the new systems theories are potentially at odds. To the present neithe r position has paid much attention to the other, but a dialogue between them is in the offing.

These economic, social, technological, and intellectual currents pose at least three critical questions for organizational communication research:

First, how can organizations accommodate different cultures and interests? This is a pressing problem due to the increasing integration of the global economy, the need to draw on the resources of increasingly diverse work forces to promote innovation and quality, and the growing demand for participation and self-determination by workers and the public. Numerous critical arguments developed in the literature of postmodernism argue that no one viewpoint is correct or complete. On this view, the only way to overcome arbitrary privileging of one position is by dialogue among multiple voices representing different interests and communities (Deetz 1992). The problem confronting organizational communication research is how to surface repressed voices and how to enable them to express themselves in the face of dominant groups embedded in current power structures.

For the most part, traditional organizational communication research has adopted a "culture-free" standpoint. That is, it has tended to ignore the issues surrounding encounters between diverse cultures in the workplace and to regard international organizational communication as a subspecialty. This results in de facto valorization of white, U.S.-style capitalist organizational practices, because these organizations are the setting of almost all organizational communication studies. It also hides the operation of power structures which maintain these practices as the norm and muffle other voices which might express different or opposing positions.

Rather than using this assumed standard as a reference point, several chapters in this volume wrestle with the issue of how to encompass a multiplicity of viewpoints in organizations. The chapters by Deetz, by Huspek, and by Finet consider a number of theoretical issues involved in critique of dominant positions and the development of discourses which include unspoken and repressed positions. Natalle, Papa, and Graham explore how one previously unheard voice has changed the nature of organizational communication. Ju discusses human relationships in Japanese enterprises, portraying an alternative to U.S. practices. These chapters do not adequately resolve all the issues they raise, but they help to set an agenda for future research.

Second, how will burgeoning technologies change organizational communication and, hence, organizations? It may well be the case that communication in organizations twenty years hence will be as different from today as today's practices are from those at the beginning of the century. The growth of networked computing, advances in telecommunications, and miniaturization of technology have given birth to a new generation of communication media, and change seems to be just picking up speed. It is crucial for organizational communication research to investigate the nature of these new technologies and explain how they affect communication. Already it is evident that new communication technologies are changing organizational structures and how work is organized. New forms, such as the dynamic network and the modular organization, are currently being described and studied. Telecommuting, team-based management, and globally dispersed organizations are just some of the new ways of organizing work. Several contributions to this volume center on technological impacts. King and Cushman describe a new management form, high-speed management, which utilizes new technologies and tight coordination of information gathering, product development, and marketing to respond to environmental turbulence. Horvath and Fulk review the evidence on changes in organizations wrought by information technologies and speculate on the directions in which these technologies will lead future organizations. Seibold, Heller, and Contractor summarize an array of studies on group decision support systems and suggest an integrative taxonomy of GDSS impacts. These chapters reflect the burgeoning interest in this question by researchers in communication, information systems, sociology, and psychology.

Third, what is the place of communication studies in organizational inquiry? Deetz's (1992) book and his chapter in this volume throw this question into stark relief. Deetz argues that communication studies has emerged as a central discipline due to the prominence given communication by recent developments in fields including biology, philosophy, sociology, anthropology, psychology, and critical theory. The centrality of communication processes in the definition of self, the mediation of perspectives and the construction of psychological and social worlds places communication studies at the nexus of intellectual discourse. Hence, Deetz argues, we should not look to other fields for the definition of what organizational communication is, but we should develop communication theories of organizations.

The beginnings of such theories can be discerned in several chapters. In his chapter Deetz explicates what he means by a communication theory of organizations. He elaborates several models (simulacra) of communication common in organizations and their role in the construction. Huspek's chapter attempts to develop a communication-based answer to a knotty problem in critical theory. On the surface, most other chapters in the volume fit the old mold: they take theories and concepts from outside the field of communication and apply them to organizational communication. However, we can see the outlines of communication-related perspectives in several chapters. Horvath and Fulk's chapter on information technologies and Seibold, Heller, and Contractor's chapter on group decision support systems raise the issue of the social construction of technologies. Rather than regarding technologies as material entities which exert deterministic control over behavior, it is important to see how technology impacts are produced and mediated by the human interaction systems which incorporate them. A communication theory of organizational technologies would focus on the realization of technology through communication processes. In their discussion of the several feminisms and their impact on organizations, Natalle, Papa, and Graham note that one way in which they are transforming organizations is to fundamentally change the nature of organizational communication. Here may lie the way to a feminist communication theory of organizations. As Deetz argues, this is a propitious time for the communication field to step forward and inform inquiry on the key issues of the day. Several chapters in this book illustrate how this might be done.

As organizational communication addresses these and other questions, it is also important to acknowledge some problems and issues facing these efforts. One is connected with the emphasis on power as discourse characteristic of postmodern critical theory. A very strong case has been made that power operates in a hidden fashion through discourse and that discourses distribute power unevenly among groups. In view of such a strong case, there is sometimes a temptation to equate power and discourse uncritically. In a trivial sense it is true that any difference created in language is connected to a difference in power. But what differences makes a difference? Which discourses are really effective in tipping the scales and privileging certain groups? It seems incumbent on researchers to go beyond the simple statement that power is discursive and to analyze degrees of power, countervailing powers, the relationship among competing discourses, processes by which power is exerted and articulated, and related issues. This research must be grounded in careful investigation of individual cases and it must go beyond the generalistic statements found in many critical pieces. This approach would move investigation beyond what could become a tautology—if every discourse distributes power, then whenever we find a discourse there must power operate—and promises to elucidate how power works through discourse and how it could be counteracted. Chapters such as Huspek's and Natalle, Papa, and Graham's give some indications of how this might be done.

A second problem associated with the recent surge of interest in critical approaches is the possibility of broad rejection of quantitative methodologies. Several contributions to this volume seem to regard quantitative approaches as inappropriate because they see them as reductionistic and oriented toward control of others rather than understanding. I believe this is a short-sighted position. There is nothing inherent in quantitative methods that makes them inapplicable to critically oriented research, as many articles in the sociology journals demonstrate. Quantitative analyses do not take the holistic and broad-brush approach of qualitative or historical critical studies, and for this reason they may be dissatisfying to some critical researchers. But quantitative studies can achieve an unprecedented degree of precision, handle large bodies of data, and allow rigorous comparison of competing models—all valuable qualities for some questions in critical research. It would be a serious mistake to reject them outright.

Studies of new communication technologies also face challenges. They are attempting to project a future which is not yet here, to anticipate changes in communication practices as yet unimagined. One mistake which is only too easy to make is to take the current ideal—dyadic interpersonal communication in the face-to-face mode—as the implicit referent for theories of new communication technology and for design of communication systems. Unquestionably, the "natural attitude" toward communication, which we all experience in face-to-face conversation, is eminently satisfying. However, it is only one of many satisfactory communicative possibilities. Anyone who has had a fulfilling telephone conversation is aware that other media, with their own norms and models of expression, can promote effective and valid communication. Some of the newer technologies, such as group decision support systems, voice mail, and personal communication devices, provide users with novel capabilities for connecting with others, with novel channels, and with novel computational power. It is hard to know what norms will evolve concerning these systems, but to compare them to or model them after an idealized face-to-face norm is likely to retard realization of their impact and potential. Novel communication patterns are hard to recognize. We have no standards or models, and hence it is possible that we will misapprehend them or overlook them altogether. Moreover, as Ong has noted, new technologies typically are adapted to old modes of communication when first employed. Hence, they are likely to assimilate older patterns and norms, and the unique impacts and changes in interaction which they create emerge only later, when users grow accustomed to them. It is important not to limit our research on new communication technologies to what we can currently imagine, because our imaginations are trapped in the present.

Another danger is unintentional valorization of the future. There is a tendency to overestimate either the benefits or the dangers of technology, and most research on new communication technologies leans toward optimism. For example, the King and Cushman chapter focuses mostly on the benefits of high-speed management, and leaves off considerations of possible problems for communities or employees in which these organizations operate. Likewise, there is a tendency to assume that technologies such as group decision support systems can be designed to enhance group decision-making and that other problems will not arise (or can be handled). While it would be a mistake to focus only on the negatives, it is equally a mistake to assume the future will be smooth.

These issues and problems are not raised as indictments of the various contributions, but as challenges whose resolution will lead to still further advances. The intriguing new directions staked out in this book clearly illustrate the intellectual ferment of recent years. A few years ago, a general volume on organizational communication would have had chapters on superior-subordinate communication, communication climate, communication networks, leadership, feedback, and similar topics. The chapters of this book show how much the field has changed in a short time. They offer a novel, refreshing, and provocative view of organizational communication in transition.

Havelock Ellis wrote, "We cannot remain consistent with the world save by growing inconsistent with our past selves." This is equally true of scholarship. It is important to frame new questions and to advance new positions to keep our discipline lively and growing. This book makes more than its measure of contribution to this process.

ABOUT THE AUTHORS

Noshir Contractor is Associate Professor of Communication at the University of Illinois at Urbana-Champaign, where he teaches courses and doctoral seminars on organizational communication processes, communication network analysis, computer and collaboration technologies, and quantitative research methods. His research interests include applications of systems theory to communication, the role of emergent communication networks in organizations, and information technologies in the workplace. His current research focuses on the role of computer-based tools to augment collaboration and group decision making processes. His articles have appeared in *Decision Science, Organization Science, Social Psychology Quarterly, Human Communication Research and Management Communication Quarterly*. He currently serves on the editorial board of *Human Communication Research* and *Management Communication Quarterly*.

Donald P. Cushman (Ph.D., University of Wisconsin) is Professor of Communication at the State University of New York at Albany. He is author of over eighty journal articles and book chapters. He is also author or coauthor of nine books, including *Message-Attitude-Behavior Relationships*, with R. McPhee (Academic Press, 1980); *Communication in Interpersonal Relationships*, with D. Cahn (Albany: SUNY Press, 1985); and *High-Speed Management: Organizational Communication in the 1990's*, with S. King, forthcoming. In 1982 he received the Speech Communication Association's Charles Woolbert Award "for research of exceptional originality and influence which has stood the test of time."

Stanley A. Deetz (Ph.D. Ohio University) is Professor of Communications at Rutgers University, New Brunswick, where he teaches organizational theory, interpersonal relations, and communication theory. He is author of *Managing Interpersonal Communication* (Harper & Row, 1986), *Democracy in an Age of Corporate Colonization: Developments in Communication and the Politics of Everyday Life* (SUNY Press, 1992), and editor or author of five other books. He has published numerous essays in scholarly journals and books regarding decision-making, human relations, and communication in corporate organizations and has lectured widely in the United States and Europe. He is editor of the *Communication Yearbook* series and is completing a book entitled *The Negotiative Organization: Building Responsive and Responsible Workplaces.* His current research focuses on international dimensions of communication and culture in knowledge-intensive businesses sponsored by a Fulbright Senior Award and a significant grant from the Rickart Maimsten Foundation (Sweden).

Dayna Finet is Assistant Professor of Speech Communication, University of Texas at Austin. She received a M.S. in journalism from the Medill School of Journalism, Northwestern University, and a Ph.D. in communication theory and research from the Annenberg School of Communication, University of Southern California. Professor Finet's teaching and research interests focus on organizational interaction with sociopolitical environments, communication ethics in organizations, communication and organizational civil rights, and social justice processes in organizational communication.

Janet Fulk (M.B.A. and Ph.D., Ohio State University) is Associate Professor at the University of Southern California in the Annenberg School for Communication. Her research interests include the processes and effects of implementing new communication technologies in organizations, social systems in organizations, and the management of professional and technical expertise in organizations. She has served on the faculties of the School of Business at USC and Kent State University, and the Management Centre at University of Ashton. Her publications include *Organizations and Communication Technology,* as well as articles in such journals as *Journal of Applied Psychology, Communication Research,* and *Information and Management.*

Elizabeth E. Graham (Ph.D., Kent State University) is Associate Professor at Ohio University in the School of Interpersonal Communication. Her research interests include communication skills development in instructional and organizational settings, measurement of communication behavior, and the use of humor in interpersonal relationships. She has published recently in *Communication Education, Western Journal of Communication,* and *Communication Quarterly.*

Mark Heller earned a M.A. in organizational communication in 1992 from the University of California, Santa Barbara. He currently works with entertainment software developers integrating film and video productions into interactive software programs.

August T. Horvath (Ph.D. Annenberg, School for Communication at the University of Southern California is a student at Harvard Law School). His research interests include communication technology in organizations, the social history of personal computing, and other topics in the sociology of technology.

Michael Huspek (Ph.D., University of Washington) is Assistant Professor in the Communication Department at SUNY–Albany. He has published articles in such journals as *Quarterly Journal of Speech, Communication Theory, Semiotica, Journal of Pragmatics, Language in Society, Communication Monographs, British Journal of Sociology,* and *Human Studies.*

Yanan Ju is Professor of Communication at Central Connecticut State University. He received his Ph.D. in political science from the University of Belgrade, Yugoslavia. He has written five books in Chinese and one in English, dozens of book chapters, and is the author of over fifty articles. Ju's most recent books include *The Handbook of Public Relations,* coedited (Shanghai Culture Publishing House, 1990); and *The Great Wall in Ruins: Communication and Cultural Change in China* with Godwin C. Chu (East-West Center, Honolulu, Hawaii 1992).

Sarah Sanderson King is Professor and former Chair of the Division of Communication Arts at Marist College, the Department of Communication at Central Connecticut State University, and the Department of Communication at the University of Hawaii. She has served as a fellow or research associate at the University of Chicago, Ohio State University, Harvard University, and the East-West Center in Honolulu. She was a Fulbright Scholar to Yugoslavia. She has written in the areas of communication management and change, communication ethics, stress in the workplace, technology transfer, and high-speed management. She has edited a book *Human Communication as a Field of Study* (also published in Chinese), written a manual *Effective Communication Skills: An Interfactual Approach,* and edited a reader to accompany the manual, *Effective Communication: Theory into Practice.*

Branislav Kovačić (Ph.D., State University of New York at Albany) is Assistant Professor of Communication at the University of Hartford in Connecticut. His interests and publications center on communication theory, organizational communication, and relationships between interpersonal networks/communication and mental health. He is currently working with Donald P. Cushman on a book on communication theory to be published by the SUNY Press.

Elizabeth J. Natalle (Ph.D., Florida State University) is Assistant Professor of Communication Studies at the University of North Carolina at Greensboro. Dr. Natalle's research interests include feminist criticism, interpersonal process, and gender and communication theory. She has published in *Western Journal of Communication, Communication Education,* and *Women's Studies in Communication.*

Michael J. Papa (Ph.D., Temple University) is an Associate Professor at Ohio University in the School of Interpersonal Communication. His research interests center on the study of conflict management, technology diffusion in organizations, and management development. He has published recently in *Communication Research, Communication Education,* and *Management Communication Quarterly.*

Marshall Scott Poole (Ph.D., University of Wisconsin) is Professor of Speech Communication at the University of Minnesota and Adjunct Professor in the Hubert H. Humphrey Institute for Public Policy. He has conducted research and published extensively on the topics of group communication, computer-mediated communication systems, conflict management, and organizational innovation. Scott is a principal co-investigator with the Minnesota Group Decision Support Systems Project. He is co-developer of the Software Aided Meeting Management (SAMM) system.

David R. Seibold (Ph.D., Michigan State University), Professor in the Department of Communication, University of California at Santa Barbara, has published more than fifty books, chapters, and articles. His current research interests include computer-augmented group decision making, influence strategies in the workplace, and organizational innovation processes (a recent article appeared in *Academy of Management Review*). He also is on the editorial board of *Management Communication Quarterly,* and reviews regularly for *Administrative Science Quarterly* and numerous communication journals.

INDEX

Printed in Great Britain
by Amazon.co.uk, Ltd.,
Marston Gate.